331+ Essential Tips and Tricks

FOR THE

GUN COLLECTOR

by
Stuart C. Mowbray

editor of
Man at Arms for the Gun Collector
magazine

MOWBRAY PUBLISHING, 54 E. SCHOOL ST., WOONSOCKET, RI 02895

LIBRARY OF CONGRESS
CONTROL NUMBER: 2005933672

    Stuart C. Mowbray
    331+ Essential Tips & Tricks for the Gun Collector
    54 East School St., Woonsocket, R.I. 02895:
    ANDREW MOWBRAY INC. — PUBLISHERS
    272 pp.

ISBN: 1-931464-22-7

© 2006 Stuart C. Mowbray

All rights reserved. No part of this book may be reproduced in any form or by any means without permission in writing from the publisher and the author, except for short excerpts used in book reviews.

To order more copies of this book, or to receive a free catalog of other fine antique arms publications, call 1-800-999-4697.

Email at orders@manatarmsbooks.com or visit www.manatarmsbooks.com

Printed in China.   9 8 7 6 5 4 3 2 1

Acknowledgements
No book this detailed can be written without a lot of help. The author wishes to thank the following people for their assistance: Jim Supica, Herb Glass, Jr., Norm Flayderman, Herb Houze, the curatorial staff of the Metropolitan Museum of Art, Bill Ahearn, Erik Goldstein, the Higgins Armory Museum, Phil Schrier, Robert S. Anderson, Lee Taylor, Ron Romanella, Joe Puleo, Sotheby's, the National Firearms Museum, Wallace Beinfeld, the Wadsworth Atheneum, Christie's, Jay Hansen, The Colonial Williamsburg Foundation, Bill Guthman, Russ Malcolm, Dennis Kroh, the Smithsonian Institution, Doug Adams, Walter Karcheski, the Frazier Arms Museum, Amoskeag Auction House, David H. Arnold, the Springfield Armory National Historic Park, Frank Graves, Roy Marcot, Jack Richardson and the staff of *Man at Arms for the Gun Collector* magazine.

Important Notice: Although every reasonable effort has been made to ensure the accuracy and reliability of this guide, the possibility of error in a book of this scope always exists. Many of the recommendations herein are based upon the unique experiences of the author, including conditions and circumstances that are not reported. The experiences of the reader may be different. The author and publisher will not be held responsible for any losses, damages or injuries that occur to readers or their possessions. Any readers who feel that information in this book is incorrect are encouraged to contact the publisher in writing so that the error can be corrected in future editions. Readers are reminded that firearms and ammunition, by their very nature, can cause injury or death. This is not a book about firearms safety, handling or repair. These are separate topics, and readers should seek out reputable sources of information on these subjects before purchasing or handling firearms. No used firearm should be loaded or fired without consulting a competent gunsmith.

Table of Contents

Getting Started	5
Better Safe Than Sorry	7
Buying the Smart Way	17
Warnings and Suggestions	71
Examining a Gun	105
Rust and Other Evils	169
Storage and Display	205
Shooting Guns with a Camera	235
Tools, Gadgets and Tricks	255
It's a Hobby: It's OK to Have Fun	270
Suppliers and Contacts	272

Getting Started

Gun collecting has changed a lot over the last couple of decades. In fact, "old timers" are often stunned at how little today's hobby resembles collecting as they knew it back when they got started.

In past generations, there were only a few places where you could buy antique guns. There weren't even very many gun shows. Most collectors made their purchases from a dealer's printed list, or perhaps visited his store in person. These antique gun shops of the past were amazing, colorful establishments where "gun nuts" would spend half the day gossiping, digging through huge piles of muskets and cutting pieces of meat off of salamis that hung from the rafters. Dealers generally had huge inventories by today's standards, including vast quantities of parts from which they would make repairs or assemble guns from pieces. There were barrels of Colt grips, which were used to upgrade pistols without a second thought to keeping the gun in factory original condition. That just wasn't a consideration in those days.

Aside from these specialist antique gun dealers, there were also a number of very active military surplus houses, mostly located in New York City. The granddaddy of them all was Bannerman's, whose famous catalog was the bible of arms collecting and the source for almost every collector's first purchases.

Where I live, in the Northeast, it was common for collectors and dealers to prowl rural neighborhoods during work days. They would pull up at an old-looking farm, hoping to catch the wife at home and her husband in the fields. A quick offer of cash money pried loose many a Kentucky Rifle and Brown Bess that had been sitting in an attic or barn, sometimes for centuries.

Those days are gone, but today we have surplus military rifles imported from Russia, Martini-Henrys coming out of storage in Nepal, the Internet, gunshows nearly every weekend and rapid communication. It is much

A Revolutionary War Charleville musket with American provenance. (Bill Ahearn collection)

harder to find a true bargain, but it is also much easier to get what you want — as long as you are willing to pay for it. And that's the problem. Collectible guns have become valuable. Really valuable. As a result, we can make fewer purchases and have to take better care of what we've got.

This tends to happen to every collecting hobby. More knowledge and better books make the items more valuable and, in turn, attract the attention of fakers and fraud artists who are lured by the big money being spent. There probably aren't more challenges than previous generations experienced…just different ones. Before, you couldn't find what you wanted. Now you can probably find it, but you can't afford it and it might not be real.

So gun collecting has matured. And with this brave new world comes new ways of doing things that are in line with a more sophisticated and professional collecting public. That's what this book is all about — the tools and techniques that you will need to succeed in today's collecting climate. Are all of the tips offered in this book perfect or absolute rules that have to be followed with no exceptions? Of course not! They are just some ideas that have worked for me and my friends. Every situation is different and you will have to decide on your own which way is best for you. That's why I have tried to include lots of alternatives.

So be careful out there. But don't forget what made people start collecting guns in the first place — it really is a lot of fun. Despite all the science, research and risks, try to keep it that way. A hobby is only worthwhile if you enjoy it. I hope that this book helps you to achieve that goal.

Better Safe Than Sorry

Let's imagine a scenario. You have a collection of firearms and someone breaks into your house and steals them. Pretty upsetting, huh? Well, take that scenario one step further and imagine the thief using one of your guns to hurt someone.

There is just no way that you would ever recover from a disaster like the one just described, so be sure to do everything you can to prevent it from happening in the first place.

1. Alarms

Alarm systems are a lot like guns...they should only go off when we want them to. Not only are repeated false alarms annoying, but let's face it, if the police get called to your house four or five times every month, they are eventually going to stop paying attention. On the other hand, we certainly want our alarm systems to interrupt or discourage burglaries, which is why they are there in the first place. So what should we do?

I guess that the first point I need to make here is, "Yes, you do need an alarm." At least if you have valuable guns that you don't want to lose or modern guns that could be dangerous in the hands of a criminal. Insurance is great, but it only buffers you financially. We all end up loving our collections and the goal is not to lose them in the first place. So what kind of alarm system should you buy?

Actually, the choices available today are all pretty good and generally effective. The most important part is that the equipment be installed intelligently, so that we don't end up "Crying Wolf" with the local constabulary, or even worse, have the darned thing fail to go off when the wolf is real. Most systems involve a combination of "entry" detection and "motion" detection. Entry detectors catch the thief on his or her way in, and are installed on doors and windows. "Motion" detection catches the thief once he or she is inside, and can actually involve any combination of devices that measure movement, temperature, weight shifts, etc.

For the most part, at least in my opinion, "entry" detection is highly over rated. Yes, it does offer the earliest alarm, but this method tends to be costly (especially in older homes) and only provides an advantage of a few seconds. Remember, these units have to be installed in every window and door, which can add up pretty fast. A carefully installed group of motion detectors inside the house gives you much more bang for your buck. In the old days, these motion detectors used to be a problem for pet owners, because cats and dogs would repeatedly trigger the alarms. However, today that isn't a real problem because modern units have sensitivity and angle adjustments that can accommodate all but the largest pets when installed properly.

A typical motion sensor as used in home alarm systems. They often work best when placed high on the wall so they can "see" the largest area. An intelligently placed array of these devices will detect the most common types of break-ins and can show purposeful movement through your house. They work by measuring temperature shifts.

If you decide to use motion detectors, it is best to think about what you want before talking to a salesman. Many alarm system companies will suggest one or more detectors in every room, when it is much more important to set traps between where a burglar can enter and where you do not want him to go. Remember, most thieves are neither Spiderman nor James Bond. They are probably going to kick in a cellar window and crawl in rather than drop onto your third-story roof from a helicopter and shimmy upside-down through your skylight. Good places to focus on are stairs, major hallways and basements — *not* a master bathroom, which can only be reached through a six-inch, third floor window. Make sure that any intruder will have to pass by a number of detectors before reaching your valuables or the place where the alarm's master unit is located. This does two things: it gives you a better chance of an alarm, and can also tell the alarm company that a series of alarms are going off, showing purposeful motion from room to room and indicating to the police that there is actually a real person moving around inside of your house.

And that brings us to the police. Yes, you do need a service that reports your alarm to the police. A loud siren is almost no good at all. If you think that your grubby neighbor who looks like he is off the porch in the movie *Deliverance* is going to call the police when your

Tips for Choosing an Alarm Co.

- The very best advice is to talk to a policeman. They are the ones who respond to alarms and will probably have an opinion about who does the best job.

- Make sure that the equipment carried by the supplier is from a well-regarded national company and not some no-name brand. If you need repairs or replacements down the road, things will go much easier if you are dealing with a popular, established product.

- Ask about their monitoring set-up. Are they equipped to deal with heavy flow (if a number of alarms go off at once) or would they be swamped?

- The cost of installation and equipment is important, but don't forget that all-important monthly monitoring fee, which repeats over and over again for years and will end up being the most costly part of your purchase over the long haul.

alarm goes off, then think again. Even the best neighbors tend to ignore them. Heck, car alarms go off in my neighborhood all of the time and I have *never* seen the police respond to a single one of them.

Alarm Transmission

Generally, alarms are transmitted to your alarm service by a telephone signal, and it is the service who calls the cops. (By the way, you aren't usually stuck forever with the company who installed your system…most services can monitor many alarm systems, so shop around.) If your alarm is going to be defeated by a thief, it may very well be done right here at the phone connection.

Good Point!

When there is no phone signal, then the alarm company cannot report an intrusion, which means any bozo with a pair of cheap wire clippers can walk right into your house (and gun room) free and clear. For this reason, some people choose a cell phone that can operate on a battery and isn't totally dependent on power and phone lines. You might worry that cell phone transmissions can be jammed electronically, but I am told by alarm professionals that these systems transmit on a sideband, not the actual voice frequency, which is a very secure method. Ask your installer for advice. The phone itself should be located someplace that is far from a point of entry, so the thief will be unable to reach it before a call is made.

Battery Backup

Another thing to remember is that your alarm is useless if it does not have power. What good is a sophisticated alarm system if a thief or thunder storm can shut off the power and disable the alarm completely? For this reason, it might pay to consider units with battery backup.

Low Budget Alternatives

What if your collection isn't large or fancy enough to justify the expense of an alarm system? You don't have a room full of guns, or even a place to display them, but you still want to protect yourself, right? The first place to start, and it will hardly cost you any money at all, is deceptive storage. Some antique pistol collectors I know have gone down to the local Salvation Army store and purchased ratty old suitcases. They put their pistols in the suitcases, which are then put away with the other luggage. Thieves are very unlikely to search your "empty" luggage. Longarms are another problem, because they just won't fit. One collector I know keeps his guns in a closet, but blocks the door with old lumber so that, on initial inspection, it seems like the closet is full of old construction junk. Another idea would be to hang a mop or two from the inside lip of the door, so it looks like a cleaning closet. Use your imagination and make the bad guys look elsewhere, but please remember any applicable laws about firearms or ammunition storage and include them in your plans. You may learn that a gun safe is in your immediate future.

Alarms are Great, But They Can Be Defeated

In the end, however, the brutal truth is that your alarm will only catch random intruders, drunks, idiots and "smash and grab" artists. For this alone it might be worth it — heck, even the sticker on your window advertising an alarm system will probably scare away a few would-be thugs. But a truly professional thief will probably get past your alarm. It is, after all, his job. This brings us to our next point: keeping your mouth shut.

Keeping Your Mouth Shut

If no one knows that you have a room full of valuable guns, they are highly unlikely to steal them. This doesn't mean that you should hide your hobby in shame or fear,

just that you should be careful and prudent. So don't brag to everyone down at the barber shop about the valuable rod bayonet '03 that you just picked up for a song. They probably don't know what one is, anyway.

And if you belong to a collector club, have the mail sent to your work address or a post office box. This is a simple but important precaution. Make the bad guys work to find the address where you keep your collection. I know some people who go so far as to store their guns in a rented vault or safe deposit box. But honestly, if you cannot enjoy your collection and see it every day, then why own it?

A little discretion can go a long way.

7 Safes, Vaults & Strongrooms

Depending on a number of factors (how big your collection is, how modern it is, how valuable it is, whether you live in a rural or urban setting, local laws and how often you travel) you may end up considering a gun safe, vault or strongroom. I have seen many excellent systems, some hidden behind bookshelves or with other deceptive entrances. The options, however, vary so very much with the situation of your home and lifestyle that specific suggestions will be avoided, except for safes, which will be covered later. All I will say for now is that if you do go this route, watch out for climate control, because enclosed, perhaps damp, spaces can be a real invitation to rust.

8 Deceptive Display Tactics

Within your collection itself, you might want to "hide" your most valuable pieces. If you have one or two great guns, then don't set them apart as obvious showpieces. Most casual thieves can't tell the difference between a cheap shotgun and a high-grade Parker, so don't help them out by providing hints. Most robbers will just grab the closest few guns or the ones at the center of your display.

Truly expert gun thieves, however, will enter your house knowing what you have and where you have it. At that point, you might as well call *Man at Arms for the Gun Collector* magazine (1-800-999-4697), which offers free "stolen arms" alerts to tell dealers and collectors what is missing. Most of us never have anything stolen, but just in case, there is insurance. And just like an alarm system, if you have a decent-sized collection, it is an expense that you are going to have to pay.

Insurance

Insurance, like that State Trooper who gives us a speeding ticket, is one of those things that we resent until we need it. The big thing about insurance is not to resent it *after* you need it. There are lots of policies out there, and if you aren't careful, you can end up paying premiums for years only to learn that you were protecting yourself against nothing. Policies added to your pre-existing home owner's insurance should be looked at with special care. Often, there are so many rules and exceptions that you are only covered under ideal (some would say nonexistent) circumstances. For instance, many, and perhaps most, antique gun thefts actually take place *away* from the home. Does your insurance cover you if your gun is stolen while on a trip, when being worked on by a gunsmith, during shipment to a new buyer or from under your table at a gun show? If your flintlock rifle is stolen from the trunk of your car while you are eating lunch on the way to a gun club meeting, will you be OK? What if it falls off of the wall rack and shatters?

Many collectors have answered these questions by contacting specialist insurance agents who regularly cover gun collections. You can usually find advertisements for these agents in gun collecting magazines,

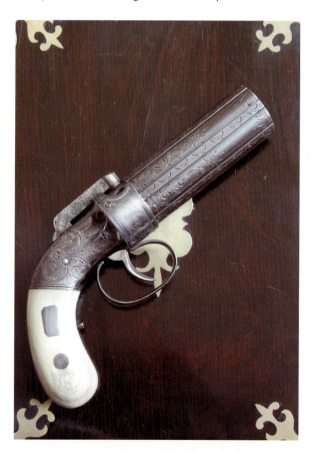

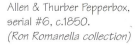

Allen & Thurber Pepperbox, serial #6, c.1850.
(Ron Romanella collection)

like *Man at Arms for the Gun Collector* and *Shotgun News*. Often collectors themselves, these agents can offer policies that cover you during all typical collecting activities. And because our collections can change continually, there are policies that accommodate the needs of your particular gun room, often without a requirement for burdensome record-keeping and appraisals.

Advice From a Gun Insurance Expert

One of the best known insurers of gun collections is Jack Richardson, who was kind enough to answer some of our questions during the research for this book. He made some excellent points.

The first thing Jack pointed out was that theft in your home or office is only about 1% of the risk. The whopping majority of claims made on gun collection insurance policies result from theft or damage during shipment. Next in line are guns stolen while away from home at gun shows and collector club meetings. Also, it is worth noting that many claims are for damage from a mishap or accident rather than a robbery.

Jack warned against trusting alarms alone without the backup protection of insurance. In many rural areas, for instance, it can take police

JACK'S TOP QUESTIONS TO ASK YOUR INSURANCE AGENT

- What is the actual language of the validation clause? This is very important because it gets right to the guts of the protection you are buying.
- Exactly what will you have to go through to get paid? How long will it take before you get a check?
- What do you need to do to prove loss? Will you have to have records, movies or photos, and if so, what kind?
- If your collection increases in value, how will this be handled? Will you be covered automatically or will it be a hassle? What will you need to do to include new purchases and account for guns that you sell?
- Will you be covered if you ship the gun, send it out to a gunsmith for repair, put it on display or store it away from your home in a safe deposit box?
- Can you talk to people who have had claims with that company in the past? What have their experiences been?
- Are you covered for non-theft incidents like devaluation and repair after accidents or storage mishaps?

A Unique semiautomatic pistol made by the Manufacture D'Armes Des Pyrenees in occupied France for the Nazis during World War II.

hours to respond to an alarm report...if they respond at all. Given that many collectors travel frequently or have seasonal vacation homes, this is a huge concern. He also confirms that if a professional thief knows your schedule and where you keep your guns, there is little you can do to stop him. They know how to beat the alarms and can get inside your safe. These precautions are great for the majority of casual burglaries, but they will only go so far towards stopping a truly organized and determined robbery attempt.

Jack's last piece of advice is that we should remember that one of the benefits of insurance is that it lets you enjoy your collection free from worries of financial loss. Also, many people assume that having an alarm system will give you a big discount on your insurance, but this is not the case. The discount is often only in the range of 2%–3%.

One final thought. If your insurance requires you to keep records, videos or photographs of your collection, please keep a copy at a relative or friend's house. If your collection is burning in a fire, then your computer or filing cabinet is probably going up in flames, too.

11 Professional Insurance

While we are on the subject of insurance, if you are an officer or board member for your gun or collector club, you might want to consider adding a Professional Insurance rider to your home owner's insurance. This is fairly inexpensive, but protects you from damages in case the gun club gets sued for any reason.

For instance, suppose you are on the board of directors of a collector club that sponsors a gun show, and someone gets shot by accident at the show. You could be liable for damages. It is definitely something to think about.

> ### Beginner's Hint!
> Some beginners are stumped about how to check whether a muzzleloading firearm is loaded. My Uncle Phil, who taught me to shoot blackpowder muskets when I was about eight (I think I still have the bruises!), told me to put my mouth over the muzzle and blow. If air comes out of the vent down at the breech, the gun isn't loaded. Well, you can just imagine the reaction if I endorsed that method! So I suggest you do just what Civil War soldiers did when they weren't sure if their piece was loaded. While keeping yourself and others clear of any potential discharge, gently slip a ramrod (or dowel) down the barrel. Experienced collectors will be able to tell immediately from the noise it makes at the bottom, but it is always safer to then compare the length of the rod that went down the barrel. Is it enough length to reach the breech face, or is it less? If your rod isn't making it all the way to the bottom, you may have a loaded gun.

12 Not Blowing Your Head Off

Back when we were in Boy Scouts or an NRA youth program, a lot of us had it drilled into our head that we should "Always Treat a Gun as if it's Loaded." Now that we are adults, this is still a great rule to live by. Collectible guns may be collectible, but they are still guns. They can kill you just as dead as a working gun can, even if they are antiques. I know people who have discovered live loads in their flintlocks that dated back over two hundred years. The first thing you should always do with a new acquisition is check if it is loaded. I know that this sounds silly and simple, but it is an easy thing to forget in the excitement of a new purchase. So drop a ramrod down the barrel of that muzzleloader or pull open that bolt action. You might just end up saving yourself a world of trouble.

If you have any questions about general gun safety, which is really beyond the scope of this

(left) Be sure it isn't loaded!

book, many shooting clubs run programs on firearms education. If you don't know how to find one of these courses, ask the owner of your local gun shop or contact the National Rifle Association's Education and Training Division.

Knowledge is the key to success in collecting.

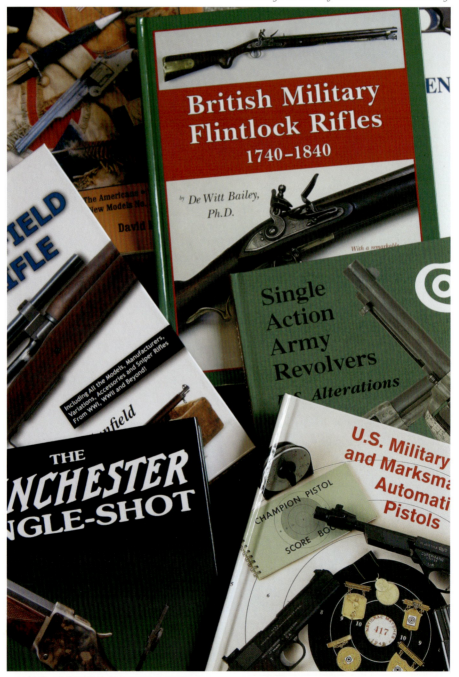

Better Safe Than Sorry

Buying the Smart Way

13

Build a Library

Years ago, a friend of mine visited the office of famed dealer and author Norm Flayderman. And what struck my friend was the huge library Norm had. There were books everywhere. So my friend asked, "Why do you have so many books?" Norm's answer was, "Because they are the very heart and soul for me as a collector and my life blood as a dealer."

Information is the key to success in any field of collecting. A book might cost a few dollars — but mistakes can cost thousands. If you can just get one useful fact out of an entire book, believe me it was worth it.

Here's another Norm Flayderman story for you. One day I asked Norm where he got the guns to sell in his famous, huge catalogs. I had expected him to say that he bought directly from retiring collectors or estates. But the answer

Before you buy everything you can carry home at the local gun show, it might be a better idea to spend your money on some books first.

A lithograph of the U.S. Dragoons cutting their way through an ambush during the Mexican War. It is unlikely that any of the weapons used here would have survived in perfect condition.

was that he bought lots of items from fellow collectors and dealers at gun shows. He was constantly taken aback by what is apparently an all-too-common phenomenon. Many sellers don't recognize the true value of what they are offering...and it's strictly because they have not studied the nitty-gritty details that might make their firearm more desirable. Learning about these features from a reference book (or even Norm's own *Guide to Antique Firearms*) can have significant monetary impact for folks selling guns...or in Norm's case, the fellow about to acquire it.

Are You Buying for Condition or History?

A few decades ago, condition was important, but it was perhaps more crucial that a gun actually "saw history." This is no longer always the case. Much like in stamp or coin collecting, condition has become king for many of today's gun collectors.

Most collectors of Single Action Colts buy them because of their special association with the American West. But these same collectors will spend much more for a perfect gun that stayed in an Eastern banker's desk than for a revolver that exhibits the type of wear that is more typical of Western usage. In many ways this is sad, but it is nonetheless the truth. Condition almost always trumps history, unless the specific historical details (like the name of the original owner) have survived.

This can, however, provide a nice buying opportunity for history-minded collectors who don't demand perfect guns. The firearm with a few blemishes was the gun that was really used, and some very historical guns can be had at good prices, providing hours of enjoyment and opportunities for further research.

15 The Paradox

A model or type of gun that is known to have been issued to the military during wartime will often have a much higher value than an almost identical model issued during peacetime or sold for civilian use.

Sometimes, condition isn't relevant, as on this India Pattern lock found at a War of 1812 site in Connecticut.

The paradox comes in when a mint specimen of one of these wartime guns shows up — a gun that was obviously never issued and may even be unfired. If military use ads value, then why does the one that never left the storeroom often sell for considerably more than another identical example showing some slight evidence of military service?

16 Top Condition

As discussed above, condition is the surest indicator of value. Guns at the very top of the condition scale are worth more than lesser-condition guns and have increased in value disproportionately over all other types.

Cased and engraved Colt Thuer New Model Holster Pistol serial number 185326 made for Louis Laurena Sanz — the Marquis de San Juan and Governor General of Puerto Rico.
(Photograph courtesy of the San Francisco auction house Bonhams & Butterfields)

The differences between a top condition gun and a very good gun may seem slight but they mean a lot. Just one or two small differences in condition can mean a doubling in value — or more. Get picky. Learn to see the differences between an 85% gun and a 95% gun, because as our hobby matures this is where a lot of attention is being spent, and values are following accordingly.

Personally, I don't like this because I think that it leads to overenthusiastic restoration and refinishing and could eventually lead to collectors distrusting any gun in mint condition. But my not liking it doesn't make it any less true.

17 Top Condition — A Rash Prediction

Since we are talking about overenthusiastic restoration and refinishing, I'm going to make a prediction. I think that gun collecting is going to follow the pattern of American automobile collecting.

Back in the 1970s and '80s, car collectors wanted their cars to be perfect. Not a dent or a scratch on the body. The upholstery had to be unblemished. As you can imagine, it is pretty much impossible to find an 80-year-old car that is in mechanically functional yet otherwise brand-new shape. So collectors stripped off the original paint and painted over it, tore out all the seat coverings and replaced them with copies, and generally replaced anything that wasn't perfect with a modern-made substitute. Any cars that were not all shiny and new were looked down

Springfield Arms Company pocket revolver — early type. Serial number 15, it has the exceptionally rare flat-sided frame.

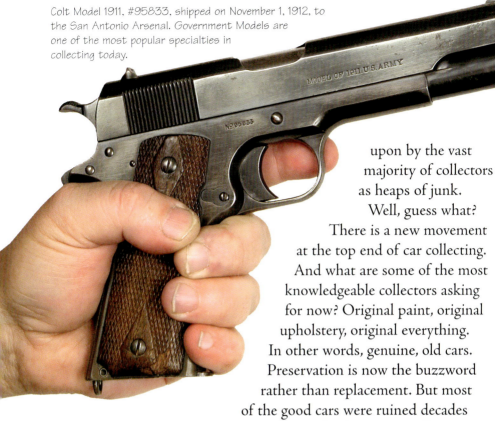

Colt Model 1911, #95833, shipped on November 1, 1912, to the San Antonio Arsenal. Government Models are one of the most popular specialties in collecting today.

upon by the vast majority of collectors as heaps of junk.

Well, guess what? There is a new movement at the top end of car collecting. And what are some of the most knowledgeable collectors asking for now? Original paint, original upholstery, original everything. In other words, genuine, old cars. Preservation is now the buzzword rather than replacement. But most of the good cars were ruined decades ago, so some car restorers of today are actually trying to add a tiny, calculated amount of wear and damage to the replaced parts in order to make them look more authentic and less fake. It would be funny if it wasn't so pathetic.

I'm willing to bet that's the way we are heading. The restoration beast will eventually eat itself. Eventually. But for now, condition is king and probably will be for some time to come.

18 Generalist or Specialist?

It used to be almost "standard advice" that all collectors should specialize. I don't really believe this any more. Specialization can get boring after a while and leaves you with a very narrow view of the gun world. Exploring different fields of collecting can be more fun, introduces you to more people and gives you a wider perspective. Personally, I stopped being a specialist when I realized that many of my purchases weren't exciting me any more; they were just filling empty spots in my collection. Being a generalist allows me to pursue the guns that really get my heart pounding — regardless of what

In order to study and understand specialized topics within gun collecting, it is necessary to handle hundreds, if not thousands, of examples.

they are.

However, the old "specialize" advice is still a great plan for beginners. If you try to buy too many different types of guns as an inexperienced collector, you can quickly become confused and never learn all of the little differences that make one gun better or more interesting than another. Specialization almost forces you to learn — by comparison.

 Mass Quantities

Here's a theory for those who do choose to be specialist collectors — owning mass quantities matters a lot. You need to have hundreds of something pass through your hands before you can start to see the tiny, yet perhaps important, differences that set certain examples apart. If that means buying guns just to study them and then sell later, so be it.

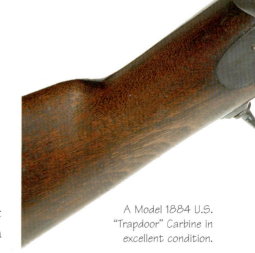

A Model 1884 U.S. "Trapdoor" Carbine in excellent condition.

Buying the Smart Way

20 Guns as Investments

There is a small class of collectors who are in it just for the investment. They don't know or care about the guns themselves and view them purely as a commodity. Most of the guns they buy go directly into a safe deposit box and never see the light of day until they are sold. We tend to see these folks when the stock market is doing very poorly and during periods of historically low prime interest rates.

This book isn't written for this class of collector, but even those of us who buy guns because we love them need to consider the investment value of the things we purchase. To do otherwise would be irresponsible to ourselves and our families. Even the least expensive gun collection represents a serious expenditure for the collector and should be treated as an asset. It should be part

Model 1884 carbines like this one are less popular than earlier types and have lower values. However, they are often found in nearly brand new condition and could represent a shrewd purchase.

of your estate planning and perhaps your retirement plan. With this in mind, it probably is worth directing our collecting efforts towards themes that offer some promise of appreciation.

21 Get in on the Ground Level

Unless you are rich, it can be pretty difficult to build a world-class collection in a popular collecting field. But we all know folks with ordinary incomes who have wonderful collections.

How did they do it? Well, usually they started in their collecting field *before it became popular*. This is a huge concept. For instance, a midwest auction house recently sold a collection that was mostly made up

Johnson M1941 semiautomatic military rifle.

These competitors to the M1 Garand used to be quite inexpensive because sporterized versions were sold at bargain prices by surplus dealers after the war. However, original configuration examples of these rifles have recently tripled in value as collectors have come to accept them as an important U.S. weapon of WWII.

of World War II military weapons — and it took numerous huge catalogs to list everything. What struck the auction-going public was that nearly every weapon was either in perfect condition or could be attributed to an individual soldier. How did that collector do it? He bought these guns before anyone considered them collectible. Today, of course, they sell for a king's ransom.

How do you guess what might become popular and valuable in the future? My own opinion (and it's only an opinion) is that quality and broad historical interest win out over the long haul. If something is well made and was used in a major war or during a romantic period in history, chances are that it will eventually catch on as a collectible.

Prices are Still Local

The now-deceased Speaker of the House, Tip O'Neal, was famous for saying that all politics are local. The same thing goes for gun values. Despite the Internet and other forces making the world smaller, prices are still affected by locality. Western items like Winchesters are worth more money in the West, Confederate items are worth more in the South, English flintlocks are worth more in the Northeast.

So get out there and dig for things where you don't expect to find them. A Kentucky rifle might be a great deal…if you find it in France.

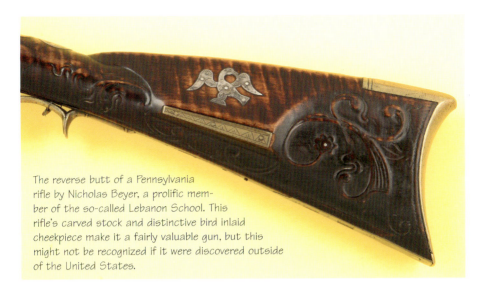

The reverse butt of a Pennsylvania rifle by Nicholas Beyer, a prolific member of the so-called Lebanon School. This rifle's carved stock and distinctive bird inlaid cheekpiece make it a fairly valuable gun, but this might not be recognized if it were discovered outside of the United States.

Passed-Down Wisdom

Here's a tip from my dad, who turned me into a collector by giving me old guns in my stocking every year at Christmas.

He said that the key to collecting success was never buying a common item at its full value and never passing up a truly special item at

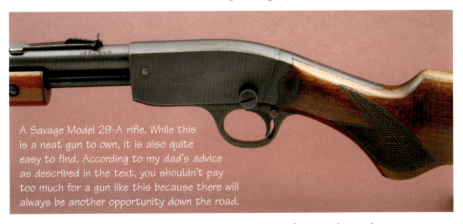

A Savage Model 29-A rifle. While this is a neat gun to own, it is also quite easy to find. According to my dad's advice as described in the text, you shouldn't pay too much for a gun like this because there will always be another opportunity down the road.

any price. In other words, if there are plenty of something, be patient until you can get a great deal, and then apply those savings to the instances when you just have to pull out your money and pay, regardless of what the guy is asking.

The Rarity Myth

Many collectors assume that if a gun is rare, then it is automatically valuable. Nothing could be further from the truth. Many rare guns are poorly made and the reason for their rarity is that they were unsuccessful.

In fact, rarity and value are entirely different concepts that have nothing to do with each other. I'll give you an example. Darling Pepperboxes, which are one of the very the rarest factory-produced guns in American history, are selling today for just about the same amount that they went for in the 1960s. On the other hand, M1911 pistols and Colt S.A.A. revolvers, which are extremely common firearms, have doubled in value time and time again during the same period.

In general, the situations when rarity can really add to value is when it is a rare example within a large group of common and popular items. Rather than trying to sell something no

(right) Darling Pepperbox, serial number 211. Darlings are perhaps the rarest factory-made firearms in America, yet they have never attracted the prices regularly expected for Colts and other more common percussion arms. (Courtesy of the Howard Miller collection)

(below) Bacon Mfg. Co. Pocket Model Revolver, serial number 181. A Second Model (note the fluted cylinder without a roll-engraved scene), this example is in excellent condition, which is quite unusual for these Bacons. This pistol is a great example of how rarity doesn't always effect value. This type was made in considerably lower quantities than some other percussion revolvers, yet it is relatively inexpensive on today's collector market. (Courtesy of the late James U. Blanchard, III)

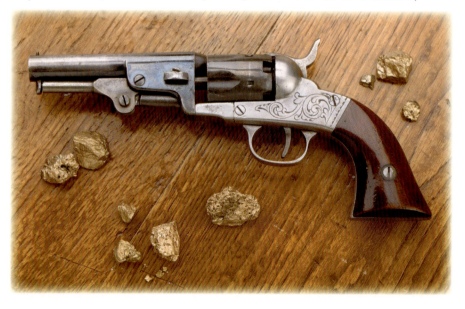

Buying the Smart Way

one has ever heard of, wouldn't you have better luck selling something that is the "Holy Grail" for thousands of like-minded collectors?

Aside from situations when the weapon is of unique historical importance (like the sidearm of a famous war hero, for instance), it is the rare or deluxe variation of a popular gun that was produced in large quantities that is really going to command a high value on the collector market. The amusing irony is that this expensive gun may have almost indiscernible physical differences from the garden-variety examples that you see every day. This is where an observant shopper can sometimes find a needle in the haystack and walk away with a collector's prize.

Prototypes and Experimentals

Sometimes, when a collector encounters a one-of-a-kind gun, it is either made up from parts or is a relatively modern gunsmithing project — often of dubious quality. However, we are all fascinated by things that we cannot identify, and in the backs of our minds we all hope that what we have actually discovered is a rare inventor's prototype or factory experimental model instead of a butchered piece of junk.

In actuality, when you see a firearm being advertised or sold as a possible prototype or an experimental, it sometimes isn't, or at least can't be proven as such. This is almost never dishonesty on the part of the seller, but is more a form of wishful thinking and selective observation. If you really want something to be true, that's often how your brain chooses to see it. And collectors buying these guns regularly fall into the same trap.

So, when you see a gun like that for sale, you have to ask yourself some questions. Do the parts all appear to have been made by

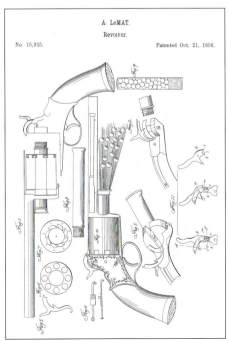

(right) The U.S. Patent drawing for the famous Confederate LeMat revolver. Prototypes for important inventions like this one are extremely valuable, which can lead to a form of wishful thinking by owners of unusual or highly modified firearms.

the same maker? Is the gun marked? Are there any other known prototypes by that same maker marked and constructed in a similar way? Does the piece depict an actual patented invention? What evidence is being offered that the gun is, indeed, what it is being described as? Is the only evidence of its special status the fact that it is strangely constructed and doesn't seem to work? Has the gun been studied by experts who were able to determine what it is, or is this a gun that was discovered by the seller himself, and all you are buying is a wish and a prayer?

There are many genuine prototypes and experimentals out there, of course. And many legitimate examples surely fall into the "real but can't be proven category." Heck, even the ones that fall into the "maybe" category can be a lot of fun and make an intriguing research project. Just try to keep all of this in mind when you are thinking about what a collectible of this type might actually be worth if you had to sell it tomorrow.

26 Condition Rating Systems

Gun condition descriptions like "Fine" and "Good" are regularly used by dealers, collectors and auction houses to help accurately convey information about their firearms. These categories can be useful but should not be confused with the more dependable and exact condition rating standards used in coin or stamp collecting. The problem isn't just that guns are more difficult to grade than coins, it is that different people have different ideas of what makes a gun "Excellent," for instance.

Some finishes offer special challenges to those trying to grade them. Nickel plating, like on this Colt S.A.A. revolver, has a similar color to the underlaying metal. Deciding what percentage of the plating remains on a pistol like this might be difficult, especially in poor light.

Buying the Smart Way

This little Smith & Wesson top break presents another kind of challenge to condition grading systems. It has three different kinds of finish: nickel plating, case colors on the trigger, and a deep, black bluing on the triggerguard. All of these finishes degrade at different rates. To the naked eye, this gun appears to be in perfect condition, however under photographic lighting as shown here, we can see minor flaws like spots of corrosion in the barrel rib hollow.

Most of the time, when collectors use these terms, they are referring to the official NRA Condition Standards. This can be confusing, though, because there is a different set of standards for Antique as opposed to Modern guns, even though some of the words used to describe the various grades overlap. A "Fair" gun accurately graded using the Modern grading system can be in considerably different condition than a "Fair" gun using the Antique rating system, so you have to be sure what standard is being applied.

To make things more complicated, some very popular price guides have established rating systems of their own, at least one of which uses the exact same condition terms used in the NRA Standards, but defines them differently. The bottom line is that while condition ratings can be useful, you need to know exactly whose standards are being applied before you can know what is meant when someone says that a gun is "Very Good."

Condition Rating Systems Revisited

Please remember that condition ratings are very subjective, even those based upon a "percentage of original finish" system.

A friend of mine tells an illuminating story. During his early years as a collector, he had the luck to be seated at a table with four or five of the country's foremost gun experts — all of them highly experienced at grading guns. My friend had a nice pistol with him and one of the people at the table suggested that it might be fun to have everyone try to rate the case colors on a percentage scale, secretly writing their judgement on the back of their napkin.

When the results were revealed, the ratings at the table ranged from "90% fading" to "40%" and were fairly evenly distributed within that range. Interestingly, the two most famous experts at the table were the ones with the extreme high and low estimates. Does this mean that these folks were incompetent? Heck no...it just means that different people judge guns differently. For instance, one person might judge entirely by coverage, while another person might put extra value on the intensity and brightness of the finish that remains.

Grading guns is a little like a beauty contest — every judge can legitimately have his or her own favorite, because beauty is in the eye of the beholder, no matter how scientific we try to make it.

When in Doubt, Ask!

Always ask a seller if he has done any restoration or repair work on anything you are about to buy. You will be surprised what you might learn. Most folks are pretty up front about this kind of stuff and will be happy to tell you. And if you encounter a bad attitude at this point, maybe that should tell you something.

While you are at it, ask all the questions about the item's history that you can think of. I don't know how many times I have returned from a show with a new purchase wishing that I had asked such simple things as whether there was any known provenance.

If You Are Spending Lots of Money, Get An Appraisal

I don't know how many times I have comforted collectors who got burned on major purchases because they were unwilling to spend a small percentage of the purchase

Both of these Italian Vetterlis were recently advertised as having about 95% finish. And it isn't a lie. The gun on the right might have rust coming through, and the finish is dull, but it is almost entirely intact. However, the overall condition of the left-hand rifle is quite a bit different, despite their having about the same percentage of finish remaining.

price on an appraisal. Please, if you are going to break the bank and spend six month's pay for a truly expensive gun, protect yourself by getting an appraisal or hiring a well-regarded expert to inspect it for you.

The appraiser should be disinterested (not involved in the deal) and not someone who was introduced to you by the seller...no matter how famous or well regarded he is. He should also be an expert in the specific type of gun you are buying...don't ask a Colt guy to appraise your flintlock.

For smaller purchases, where an appraisal isn't practical, at least have some of your collector friends look at the piece first, unless you are very, very confident in your ability to judge the gun yourself. Two brains, as they say, are often better than one.

The funny thing is that many people resist asking for the help of others. My friend Frank Sellers had a sign on his gun show table for years that read, "Appraisals Ten Dollars." Frank is one of the best appraisers in the business. Prestigious auction houses spend big money to get Frank's values for their catalogs. So you would think that there would be a huge line of people waiting to get his bargain-priced appraisals. But Frank says, "Nope...months go by without a single person taking me up on it. People are strange." Strange, indeed.

The bottom line is that smart collectors aren't scared to admit when they need help. There's no shame in asking for advice...the most successful collectors and dealers do it all the time.

30. Dealers Are a Resource

When I started collecting, it was normal for beginning collectors to establish a relationship with one or two carefully chosen dealers and to make most of their purchases through them. Today, what I am more likely to see is new collectors buying large numbers of items at auction, or from huge Internet sites, and not having a particularly good idea of what they are buying.

While there are lots of great auction houses and Internet sites, I think that it is a mistake for beginners to totally disregard the traditional dealer/client relationship. The best dealers rarely carry fake or "bad" stock, because they are too shrewd to buy it in the first place. If a dealer knows you are a "regular," he will often give you useful guidance and search out items for your collection.

Will you pay more by buying through a reputable dealer? Not necessarily so! Beginners can make a lot of expensive mistakes, and using a nationally known dealer as a "filter" to avoid bad purchases will usually pay for itself. Also, specialist dealers know the value of the guns they have for sale and will often give you a better, more accurate price than a

A good dealer will give you collecting ideas you never would have thought of yourself. This Hill's Patent Self Extractor Revolver was purchased on the recommendation of a well known pistol dealer.

less knowledgeable individual who isn't sure how much the gun is really worth and guesses unrealistically high.

How Do I Find Dealers?

A wide selection of dealers and auction houses that sell collectible guns have ads in our magazine, *Man at Arms for the Gun Collector*. Call 1-800-999-4697 to subscribe or order a single copy.

How Do I Find Gun Shows?

Another place to find dealers is at a gun show. There is a national list of gun shows on the *Man at Arms for the Gun Collector* web site: www.manatarmsbooks.com

While any gun show can be an opportunity to find an exciting collectible gun, beginning collectors are often advised to seek out one of the nation's premier collector gun shows, which do not allow flea market merchandise and offer a room full of possibilities for the budding collector. Look for shows that are nationally advertised in

A list of gun shows can be found by following the links at www.manatarmsbooks.com

While some dealers have fixed prices, most are willing to negotiate, and it never hurts to ask politely.

collector magazines, have restrictions on what can be offered for sale and attract educational displays. Many of these shows are sponsored by NRA-affiliated collector organizations and provide a great way for newcomers to get their feet wet.

How to Negotiate a Price

First of all, don't be scared to bargain. As one old gun dealer once told me when I was a teenager, "There's no such thing as an insulting offer." Some offers might be silly, perhaps, but never really insulting.

While a few sellers, particularly catalog dealers or retail gun shops, have firm prices, most folks like to haggle — as long as it stays friendly. So enjoy the process, do your best, and don't hesitate to suggest a trade if that's what it takes to get the deal done. If the seller wants to make a deal, you will soon come to an agreement.

If you are shy in this regard, you are going to miss out on plenty of opportunities.

Get a Receipt

Especially when you are spending a lot of money, be sure to ask for a receipt, and make sure that it is detailed. If the dealer has made assurances, such as "It's 100% original and I offer a lifetime return policy," make sure this information is on the receipt for future reference. As well as being protection in case something goes wrong, receipts are also great provenance items that will be useful when it is your turn to sell.

Play Nice!

When it does come time to make a purchase, please remember to treat the seller with respect. Sometimes, newcomers don't know quite how to act, especially at gun shows, which have an etiquette all of their own. So here are some pointers for you.

Gun Show Purchasing Etiquette I

Never negotiate with a dealer unless you truly intend to buy the item. It is standard practice that if you suggest a price, you are literally promising to pay that amount if the dealer says "yes." Nothing disturbs dealers more than reluctantly agreeing to a reduced amount and then having the buyer walk off to "think about it."

Beating a dealer down just to learn his bottom line is rude, plain and simple. An offer is an offer and should be treated as such.

However, don't be scared to make offers at gun shows. Most dealers expect some negotiation and most of the time the price tag is not firm.

Gun Show Purchasing Etiquette II

Never pick up or otherwise handle items without permission.

In most situations, you will be welcome to examine guns and swords that are for sale on dealers' tables, but it is generally a good idea to handle them by the

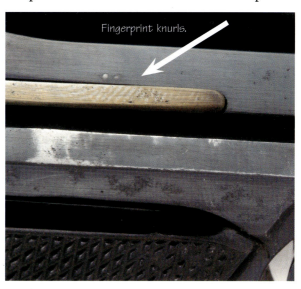

Fingerprint knurls.

Note the fingerprint damage to the straw-colored finish of this Luger. Be careful when handling someone else's gun, because one careless touch is all it takes.

Buying the Smart Way

It is always best to check if a firearm is loaded before handling it. On some guns, like this World War II "Liberator" pistol, you might not understand how the gun functions well enough to do this safely. In these situations, don't be afraid to ask the owner to demonstrate this for you rather than risk damaging someone's property, or worse, having a weapon discharge accidentally.

stocks or grips rather than smearing your fingerprints (or the drippings from your jelly donut) all over the perfectly preserved metal. Sometimes you have to touch the metal when inspecting a gun, and dealers understand this, but grabbing a gun by the blued parts is almost never actually necessary and can easily lead to rust.

Gun Show Purchasing Etiquette III

When handling a firearm, always act as if it is loaded. This goes doubly for guns that aren't your own, because you never really know how fastidious the owner is about such things.

Frankly, it makes me nervous when I hear someone snapping the action of a gun at a nearby table and look up to see the barrel pointed directly at me. I know that guns are usually tied at gun shows and certainly shouldn't be loaded in the first place, but anyone who has seen a gun go off inadvertently will tell you what you should already know: point the darned thing in the air, at the floor, anywhere but at other people. I regularly see sloppy gun handling at shows that would get you kicked off a firing range, and there really isn't an excuse for it.

Gun Show Purchasing Etiquette IV

Don't cock, snap, disassemble or otherwise work the action of an antique gun without permission. Better yet, ask the dealer to do it for you. Some of these items are delicate, and if you break it, you don't really want to pay for it, do you?

Gun Show Purchasing Etiquette V

40 Try not to handle more than one item at a time unless encouraged by the dealer. There has been a certain amount of theft at shows recently, and it just makes it easier for the dealer to keep track of his/her stock if you aren't playing your own version of "the shell game" at their table.

Also, don't stand directly in front of a dealer's table when you are chatting with your friends. He or she is trying to do business and you don't want to block the approach of paying customers.

Gun Show Purchasing Etiquette VI

41 If you are negotiating to buy a gun, please don't rattle off the item's supposed defects in the hope of getting a better price. Not only will this insult the dealer, but it also demeans yourself — because why would you ever want to buy the thing in the first place if it has so many problems. Lastly, when you complain like this, all you are really accomplishing is telling the dealer just how much you want the piece. Real Estate agents will tell you that they always know when a buyer is serious about purchasing a house because he or she will start complaining about the age of the roof, the ugly wallpaper in the bathroom and a litany of other grievances.

If you have real questions about a gun's condition, please ask them. But no one wants to hear you whine about something for which you are about to pay good money.

Lock from a Thomas Manton dueling pistol. When negotiating for fine items like this, it is rude to point out minor flaws.

Model 1895 Nagant revolver, manufactured in 1909 and later refinished by the Soviets. Never ask a dealer to bypass laws when selling you a modern pistol such as this. *(Courtesy Empire Arms)*

42 Gun Show Purchasing Etiquette VII

I know that I shouldn't have to say this, but never ask gun dealers to do anything illegal or even mildly immoral. I've actually stood at tables where people got stomping mad because a dealer wouldn't sell them C&R handguns without the necessary paperwork. This is highly inappropriate. It doesn't take much for a dealer to lose his license or even be incarcerated.

The rules of the show should also be respected. If it is a pre-1898 show, an all-Colts show, or if Nazi items aren't allowed, don't ask the dealer to break the rules or do business in the parking lot. Sure, make other arrangements, but don't abuse the hospitality of the show promoter by carrying out a forbidden transaction at his or her event.

43 Gun Show Purchasing Etiquette VIII

And lastly, if you are wearing dirty cammo gear, just got in a fight, stink of tequila and have on a hat that reads "The Bitch Had It Coming," please, please, for the love of God say "no" when the T.V. News camera crew asks you for an interview. The media knows how they want to portray gun show customers, and they are going to search high and low until they find someone who is willing to get on camera and confirm all of their most unfortunate preconceived notions. Even intelligent collectors with the best of intentions can be made to look foolish by an aggressive reporter and some underhanded editing. So, if you see one of these camera crews, tell the show organizers

Buying the Smart Way

so that they can have someone experienced represent the event.

"Sunday Fever"

Most gun shows are open on Saturday and Sunday. Many collectors, if they haven't found something to buy on the first day, get desperate on the second. Their money is just burning a hole in their pocket, and even though they aren't finding exactly what they want, they want to buy something so badly that it is easy to make a rash or uninformed decision.

Actually, this can work in your favor. I've bought some things under the influence of "Sunday Fever" that actually turned out to be great items, or at least got me interested in fields of collecting that I was never active in before.

The other side of this phenomenon is that people with tables at shows sometimes get more "reasonable" about their prices as the show nears its end. The prospect of loading all those heavy guns and swords back into their cars, trucks and vans starts to weigh heavily on their minds, and occasionally a bargain can be had at the last minute.

Collector shows like this New England Antique Arms Society gun show in Hartford, Connecticut, offer a great opportunity to make contacts, view educational displays and add to your growing collection.

45 Hints for Buying at Auction

There are a number of auction houses in the United States and elsewhere that specialize in collectible firearms. Advertisements for upcoming sales can be found in *Man at Arms for the Gun Collector* magazine and other publications like *Shotgun News*.

Buying at auction is an art unto itself, but here are a few things to think about:

• Read the "Conditions of Sale." They are very important. Also please understand that except for the most extreme circumstances, you will "own" anything you are high bidder for, and it is next to impossible to "undo" an auction sale.

• But what if the gun is an obvious fake or was seriously misrepresented. What recourse will you have? Find out up front.

• Know all expenses before you bid, from buyer's premiums (which are the percentage of the "hammer price" that the auction house charges buyers, and vary widely) to an idea of approximate shipping and insurance charges.

• Try to find out who wrote the descriptions. Was it an expert on the exact type of gun you are bidding on?

• Condition descriptions vary a lot from auction house to auction house. Some barely give condition descriptions at all. If it is possible, ask for a "Condition Report" on the specific gun you are interested in.

• Find out if there are any state, local, federal or other laws that will complicate your receiving the gun once you have bid on it. If the

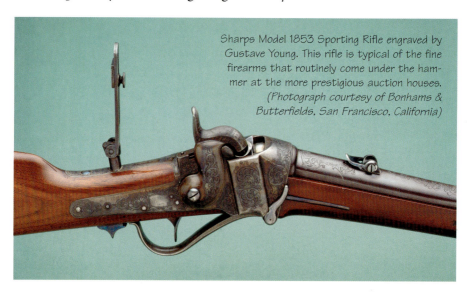

Sharps Model 1853 Sporting Rifle engraved by Gustave Young. This rifle is typical of the fine firearms that routinely come under the hammer at the more prestigious auction houses. (Photograph courtesy of Bonhams & Butterfields, San Francisco, California)

Buying the Smart Way

Collectible arms auctions can be a great opportunity to examine hundreds of fine weapons and are fun and educational even if you don't end up buying anything.
(Photograph courtesy of Amoskeag Auction Company, Inc.)

auction is overseas, you will need to pay attention to things like customs clearance and whether you will need a special import license.

+ If you cannot attend the auction in person, seriously consider hiring a trusted dealer or other representative to do this for you. There is no substitution for personally examining the lots that are up for sale. Catalog photography can only tell you so much. Neither you nor the auction house want the gun to be an unpleasant surprise when you receive it.

+ If you *are* bidding from a distance, seriously consider doing this by telephone if you are not familiar with the auction house. In the "bad old days," there were many alleged instances of auction houses starting the bidding with the top bid of the highest absentee bidder, rather than actually trying to purchase the item for that person at the most favorable terms. This was called "running up a bid." This practice is highly unethical and has not been encountered much lately, but bidding by telephone almost certainly eliminates the possibility.

Hints for Buying Through Internet Auctions

Because the gun cannot be inspected before purchase, Internet auctions offer special challenges for the purchaser. You often do not know the person you are buying from and have no opportunity to inspect the gun in person.

In spite of this, bidders report surprisingly few problems purchasing guns through Internet auctions. It never hurts to be careful, though. Aside from the advice given about traditional auctions listed above, here are some additional considerations:

- The quality of descriptions and condition statements for Internet auctions will vary widely according to the knowledge of the person writing the description. Do not simply assume that these are expert opinions. You might know more about the gun than the person selling it! Condition statements that read like, "It's the best one I've seen in a long time," sound reassuring but don't really mean anything.

- Ask lots of questions of the seller about condition, etc., because you will have no opportunity to examine the gun in person. Be aware that there are lots of guns being sold that have major replacement parts or other obvious defects.

- What happens if there is a problem? Will you be able to return the item, and if so, under what specific conditions. Study these conditions carefully and do not assume extra flexibility on the part of the seller.

- Unless you know and trust the seller, always pay by credit card, PayPal or some other third-party service. This does not always guarantee protection if you are ripped off, but it sure can't hurt!

- If the auction site has a feedback feature where people rate their transactions with sellers, pay careful attention to what is being said. However, be aware that some sellers have been known to "run up" their positive responses by having relatives or friends buy numerous small items from them.

- If you have a problem with a purchase, contact the seller immediately and be nice. A good attitude can get you a long way in this world. Don't start off assuming that the person you are dealing with is a crook. It isn't fair and it won't get you anywhere.

- Lastly, and this is really important, be aware that there are a huge number of internet gun auctions where the "starting bid" or "reserve" is quite a bit higher than the actual value of the gun. A huge number of gun auctions end with no bids at all, because the seller has grossly overvalued his item. Maybe he doesn't know any better or maybe he is looking for a "fish" to come along, but either way you shouldn't assume that you are paying a "fair auction price" in such a circumstance.

In fact, quite a few dealers put items up at auction with the start-

A Model 1911 Schmidt-Rubin Swiss service rifle. These rifles were made from 1912 until 1919. Earlier versions of this rifle system, like the Model 1889, are quite similar. However, all of the Model 1889s are considered antique, while all of the Model 1911s are considered modern.

ing bid being their regular retail price. They aren't trying to fool anyone, they are just looking for a different way to advertise their guns. In these cases, the buyer is usually the only bidder.

What Makes a Gun Antique or Modern?

According to the Gun Control Act of 1968, a firearm whose receiver was made before January 1, 1899, is an "antique" according to federal law. Anything made on or after that date is "modern." State and local laws can and sometimes do add their own wrinkle, but for the federal government that is the current standard as of the time this book was published. Laws can change, though, and it is your responsibility to stay up to date and in compliance. However, as of now, an antique gun is not actually a "firearm" according to federal law.

It is not the model date, the shipping date, the date of assembly, the date stamped on the barrel, the patent date or any other date that matters — just when the receiver, itself, was literally manufactured. Many models of guns have production histories that cover both sides of the cut-off date, of course, which can make things messy and complicated.

When in doubt, just assume that a gun is modern. Even when you aren't in doubt, but proving antique status might require special information or a complicated argument, treat the gun as if it were modern.

Some firearms, like this M1841 Mississippi, are clearly pre-1899, and therefore antique. However, there are a large number of guns where precise dating becomes an issue.

It's the safe way to go. Why put yourself at unnecessary risk?

Replicas of antique guns are considered modern guns unless they copy very old ignition systems like flintlock and meet other standards. This book is not about replicas, so we won't cover them here, but it is worth noting that they are not always categorized in the same way as the antique firearms they copy.

Do Antique Guns Cost More?

Yes. Usually. If there is a type of gun that was made in identical configuration both before and after 1898, the earlier ones that fall into the category of "Antique" will usually sell at a premium, even if they are only days older than the "Modern" ones. This is especially noticeable with Smith & Wesson revolvers, but extends to most other borderline guns as well. This isn't because of the age difference between the guns, but because, for the most part, the antique ones are unregulated and less likely to be affected by any future gun control or registration laws. People are willing to spend more to avoid the potential nuisance.

If there are more gun con-

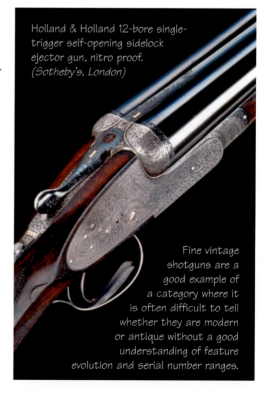

Holland & Holland 12-bore single-trigger self-opening sidelock ejector gun, nitro proof. *(Sotheby's, London)*

Fine vintage shotguns are a good example of a category where it is often difficult to tell whether they are modern or antique without a good understanding of feature evolution and serial number ranges.

Buying the Smart Way

Two early English screw-barrel pistols, which are relatively unusual in that they are not of the boxlock design. The top example is marked "J. WAREN" on the lockplate and bears London view and proof marks. There is no maker's mark, and no London gunmaker named Waren is known. This is perhaps a sign that Mr. Waren was a provincial maker applying fake London proofs to his guns to make them sell better. The bottom example is marked "HALFHIDE" and has real London view and proof with the maker's mark of early 18th-century maker George Halfhide.

trol laws passed, look for this price difference to increase dramatically.

Curio & Relic License — Why You Might Need One

Even if you just collect purely antique guns that are from before 1898, the low price of this license can make it more than worth its cost, even if you only use it once or twice. Depending on where you live, a Curio and Relic (C&R) license allows you to buy many kinds of collectible guns (most particularly surplus military rifles and pistols) through the mail at a significantly lower price than you might pay at your local gun store.

While we will discuss a few aspects of C&R licenses here, this information is going to be pretty general and if you want to make transactions with this license it is your responsibility to learn the rules. Also, laws change all of the time, so the descriptions here might not be valid when you read this. It is your job to act legally and to comply with all laws, whether Federal, State or Local, so avoid unpleasant surprises and do the necessary research before getting started.

What is a C&R License?

The Bureau of Alcohol, Tobacco and Firearms (ATF) is the government agency that issues Federal Firearms Licenses (FFL) for gun dealers. In general, only businesses can get one of these licenses, but there is a watered-down version for collectors called a Curio and Relics (C&R) FFL. This doesn't allow you to act as a gun dealer or to buy or carry modern firearms, but it does give you certain privileges to buy and sell Curio & Relic firearms with other license holders, out-of-state dealers, auction houses, internet auction sites, etc., just as long as you are not violating any state, local or other law.

In fact, some mail order companies will ONLY deal with license holders or will give them special discounts, but you will need to send them a signed photocopy of your license before they will even talk with you about a purchase.

What Qualifies as a Curio & Relic?

Curios and Relics are defined as firearms with special interest to collectors and they must meet specific age requirements or be on the ATF's C&R list. In general, if a gun was made 50 or more years ago, it automatically qualifies as a C&R. There are many other firearms on the list, however, that are less than 50 years old but have been put there because they have particular historical interest or because most of their value comes from the fact that they are collectible (as opposed to deriving from their being working firearms). The list is continually being updated and you can actually apply to have a gun added if you have a situation that meets the ATF's standards. If you have any doubt about how old a gun is, make

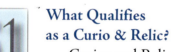

Buying the Smart Way

A Yugoslavian-manufactured SKS M.59/66A1 rifle. Some firearms on the C&R list are less than fifty years old, but are included because of their collector appeal and other factors.

sure that it is on the list rather than making assumptions. You can view the ATF list of C&R eligible firearms at:
http://www.aft.gov/firearms/curios/index.htm

52 Things to Watch Out For

Many military surplus longarms have been put on the C&R list, even if they are less than 50 years old. However, if they have been sporterized (modified from their original historical configuration for hunting or other use) this can take them off of the list. Be sure to check with the ATF in these cases! And I would get it in writing, because a verbal answer doesn't do you much good as evidence if you are ever challenged on this. And I know that I have said this earlier, but be aware of all laws, not just the federal ones. Some states, for instance, have special rules and types of guns that they will not allow you to buy.

53 Basic Requirements to Get a C&R License

The requirements to get a C&R license will probably change over time, so call the ATF for an application/instructions and the latest details (703-455-7801). Currently, you have to be at least 21 years old, a U.S. citizen and you can't be a convicted felon or have broken any gun laws. There are other requirements and exceptions, so be sure to get the full details from the ATF. Also, you obviously should never lie on these applications because you can get into huge trouble.

The license currently costs $30, lasts three years and takes about two months to get. There are plenty of rules about how transactions need to be performed, where you can ship guns, what you do if you move from the address on your license, etc., so be sure to master the details before engaging in your first transaction.

You will also have to notify your local Chief Law Enforcement Officer and give him/her your name and address for their records. My own local police department is quite helpful about this, but your mileage may vary, so you might want to check with other gun collectors in your town before starting the application procedure. As I said earlier, the C&R details given here just touch the tip of the iceberg, so do your homework and stay within the law.

Nepalese markings on a Martini-Henry. In 2003, a large number of 19th-century weapons from Napal were imported for sale as military surplus.

Buying Surplus

If you collect the weapons of the 1880s or later, you really should get to know the major surplus dealers, and monitor their sales lists. While it is true that the golden age of surplus buying (and even the second golden age) are over, new lots of guns still surface from time to time, and you will want to be there when it happens to get the best condition examples. In general, it is worth paying more to get a "picked" gun when buying from a surplus dealer.

Currently, however, there is little action on the surplus market because almost all obvious sources of surplus guns to import have been exhausted. Another factor is currency exchange rates. It makes a lot more sense for surplus dealers to buy guns from overseas governments when the dollar is strong. If the dollar is weak, this severely limits the overseas buying power of American surplus dealers who need to be able to mark their products up significantly in order to cover the many expenses involved in such a transaction.

Import and Re-Import Marks

Have you ever seen an ad for a gun that listed "import marked" or "not import marked" as one of its features? Have

Buying the Smart Way

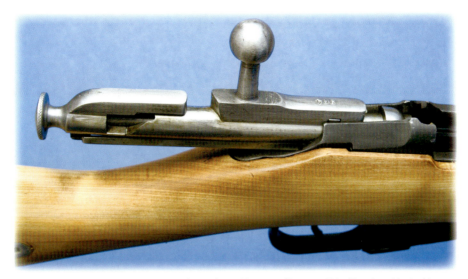

Many recent surplus imports have been from Eastern Europe. This Russian Mosin-Nagant 91/30 service rifle was made in 1943 at Tula and refinished by the Soviet government at a later time. Thousands of these rifles were sold with unmatched bayonets and accessories to American collectors and shooters; prices were inexpensive, generally about $70 for a very nice example and often cheaper. When the ready supply was exhausted in 2005, prices edged upwards, much like they had for imported Finnish Mosin-Nagants a few years earlier.

you ever wondered what it means?

By U.S. law, surplus weapons imported from other countries are required to be marked in the metal with information that usually includes the model of the rifle, the ammunition it takes, the name and location of the importer, and the country of manufacture. The marks are fairly unattractive, and while importers try to locate them in discrete places, most collectors would rather not have their guns disfigured in this way.

Guns made in the United States, like the M1 Garand, can also have

Import markings on recently imported military surplus rifles. The top mark, found on the Mosin-Nagant illustrated above, shows that the rifle was imported by Century Arms International. This mark is relatively large and prominent, being located on the left-hand side of the receiver. The bottom mark is from a Mauser 98K carbine. Found on the underside of the muzzle end of the barrel, it is smaller and more discretely located. While the presence of import marks generally devalue a piece, less obvious ones are usually prefered over large "billboard" marks.

The accessory package that was included with many surplus Russian Mosin-Nagant rifles.

import marks on them. These guns were re-imported from other countries that had been given them as part of Lend-Lease or other military aid programs. Until 1986, it was actually illegal to import these used battle rifles, but with President Reagan's support, Congress passed a bill allowing the importation for collecting purposes of military rifles made before 1945. One of the reasons why many collectors do not like import marks is that the condition of these American rifles, which had often been used by our own forces and then shipped to foreign allies with less than stellar maintenance programs, was not always very good. War trophy rifles, brought home directly by American veterans and never used by other countries, were generally in much better condition and were much preferred by collectors. Import-marked guns came to be considered "junk" by many collectors, even in cases when this wasn't quite fair to the rifle itself, which may have seen some very interesting overseas action on top of front-line U.S. battle use.

The end result, however, is that import marks generally devalue a weapon somewhat, even though the gun itself may be a perfect example of its type with no other defects. In general, import marks are forgiven more on foreign-manufactured guns than on those originally made in the United States.

The Name of the Maker

56 This is a concept that is pretty hard for some sword and gun collectors to accept, but the name marked on the exterior of a weapon (even if it says "made by") isn't always the person or company who made it.

I'll give you a modern example. The department store Sears sells a huge number of washing machines under the name Kenmore. But does Sears make them? No, of course not. Sears is a retailer. They hire another company to do the manufacturing...maybe Whirlpool, for instance. But since Sears wants their customers to keep returning, they insist upon putting their own trade name on that washer. It's simply good advertising. And if your neighbor likes your washer, he or she will see the Kenmore name and take their business to Sears. Get it?

The arms business was no different. Even back in the 1700s, the name on the gun or sword was often the person who retailed it, not the person who actually made it.

The lock of a percussion pistol marked with the name and address of famous American maker Richard Constable. Weapons made by Constable are highly desirable. However, many guns marked with his name (this one included) bear proof marks from Birmingham, England. Constable was able to import guns more cheaply than it would have cost him to make them himself.

Henry Deringer Did Not Make This Gun!

57 Some gunmakers had valuable reputations during their own lifetimes, and copyists often put these famous names on their own guns in order to make a quick buck — kind of like those guys who sell "Rolex" watches at Times Square in New York City. How to tell specific copies apart from the real thing is a subject beyond the scope of this book, but close observation of the real thing can go a long way towards revealing the "no-name rip off."

Here are some gun makers that were most often the target of this kind of copying: Smith & Wesson (especially the top break revolvers),

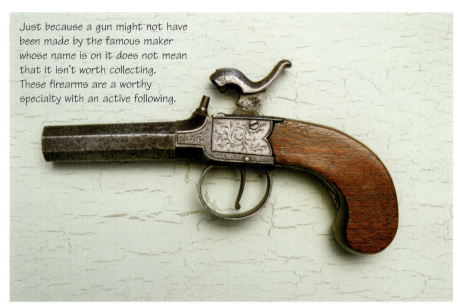

Just because a gun might not have been made by the famous maker whose name is on it does not mean that it isn't worth collecting. These firearms are a worthy specialty with an active following.

A percussion pocket pistol engraved with the name and address of revered London gunmaker Durs Egg. Since Egg went blind in 1822, this pistol is too late to have been his product. The pistol's low overall quality and Birmingham proofs help to confirm this. Egg's son John traded under his dead father's more famous name from c.1841–65, and it is presumed that this is actually one of John's weapons that he marked "Durs Egg" to promote sales.

Henry Nock (look for Birmingham-proved guns made after his death), and Henry Deringer (his real production is always marked in very specific ways; copies are often signed De<u>rr</u>inger).

Remember the Subcontractors

Back when the city of Birmingham in England was trying to get its own proof house in the early 1800s, there were hearings about the gun trade and how it worked. The testimony is very informative. For instance, it was explained that something like thirty different specialist workmen or workwomen (there were a lot of ladies and girls in the gunmaking field) were required in order to make a single high-end gun.

Wow! That's a lot!

What this tells us is that it would be a pretty unusual craftsman who could make every single part of a weapon himself. And even if he did somehow have the skills and tools to do it, it probably wouldn't be very efficient. Barrel making is a great example of something that just wouldn't make much sense to do in a small workshop. These trades were highly specialized and benefited from efficiencies of scale. Don't think of pre-factory era gunmakers like studio artists who were single-handedly creating a painting all by their own hands. Heck, even the famous painters and sculptors didn't always work that way...many of them employed teams of apprentices and assistants.

Trade Names

Particularly during the late 19th and early 20th centuries, there were lots of inexpensive guns sold in the United States using "trade names." These look a lot like company names and were marked on countless guns that were sold in hardware and department stores, but they are not the names of real manufacturers. It was all just for marketing. So if you find a name like "Buckeye," "Avenger" or "Favorite" on your shotgun or revolver, you might have a bit of trouble figuring out who actually made the gun and when.

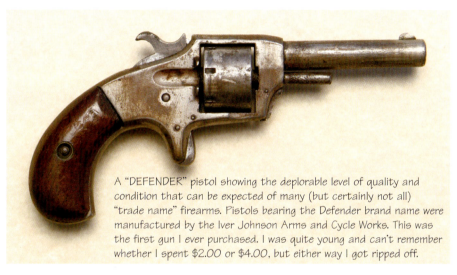

A "DEFENDER" pistol showing the deplorable level of quality and condition that can be expected of many (but certainly not all) "trade name" firearms. Pistols bearing the Defender brand name were manufactured by the Iver Johnson Arms and Cycle Works. This was the first gun I ever purchased. I was quite young and can't remember whether I spent $2.00 or $4.00, but either way I got ripped off.

Luckily for us, arms curator and author Herb Houze has compiled an extremely useful list of trade names used on American firearms, and when possible, he explains who the real manufacturer was. You can find this list towards the end of the *Standard Catalog of Firearms*®, which is a popular price guide edited by Ned Schwing. If you strike out there, I would also recommend the excellent directory *American Gunsmiths* by Frank Sellers.

Accessorize

Everyone will agree that gun and sword prices have gone up tremendously in the past decade. Many collectors can only make purchases a couple of times a year. It's pretty

A Colt's Patent percussion mold. This accessory might seem like a good buy to a beginner, but experienced collectors will immediately notice that the bullet cavities were reshaped at a later time with a file or other metal working tool. This devalues the mold almost entirely.

Some typical accessories, including Vetterli cartridges, a powder measure and a 17th-century musket flint wrapped in lead.

hard to stay excited about a collecting hobby where you can only add to your collection every now and then.

What to do? Keep your energy level up by purchasing smaller, less expensive accessory items that go with your collecting interests. Some ideas? Cartridges, cartridge wrappers, period artwork, advertising, old photographs, belts, holsters, trench art, buckles, uniforms...anything that relates to your collection but won't break the bank.

Chasing after these smaller accessories will keep you excited between major purchases, and will give you the material you need to mount great displays.

 Old Picture Warning
This is just a quick warning that gun and militaria shows are currently overflowing with fake "antique" photographs of people carrying guns. These often show Indian Wars or Wild West scenes and are usually cabinet cards or CDVs. The quality of

Buying the Smart Way

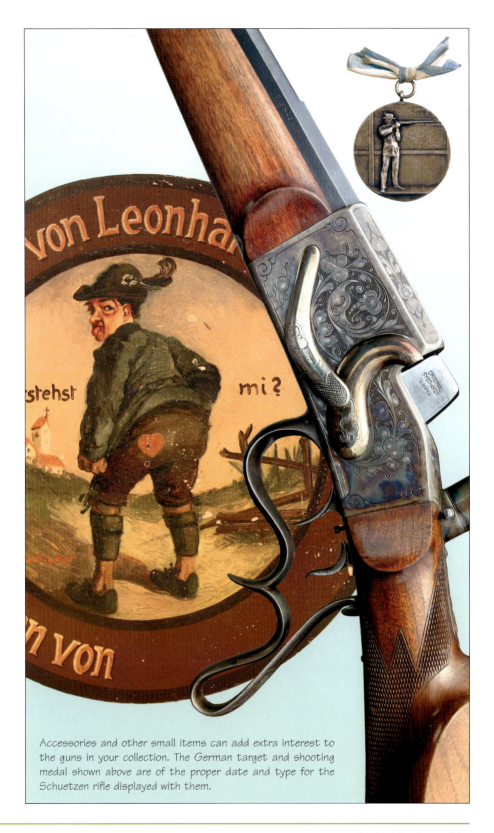

Accessories and other small items can add extra interest to the guns in your collection. The German target and shooting medal shown above are of the proper date and type for the Schuetzen rifle displayed with them.

An original photograph of German soldiers with Gew. 71 Mausers. The bicycle adds interest to the scene, which seems to be a rifle repair shop. Since what you are holding in your hands is a book, and therefore a reproduction, if you look at this picture under magnification you will be able to see that the photo image is made up of a complex pattern of small dots.

many of these fakes is quite low and they would never pass muster at an image show, but sometimes gun collectors can be fooled.

Really well-made fake images are tough to spot, but most fakes are actually made from printed post cards or are simply copies made with a color laser printer or color laser photocopier. To identify these low-cost frauds, just look at the picture itself under magnification. The image portion of cheap fakes will usually be made up either of tiny parallel lines or little dots (sometimes in rows, sometimes not) that cannot be seen with the naked eye. Real antique photograph prints should have totally smooth tones and should not be made up like a mosaic from shapes of any kind. Of course, there are better fakes out there, but most of the current crop being sold to gun collectors fall into this category.

What About Bayonets?

A lot of gun collectors are confused by bayonets... if it fits, they are pretty much happy. I must admit that I, myself, fall into this category. But this is not the smart way to collect.

Buying the Smart Way

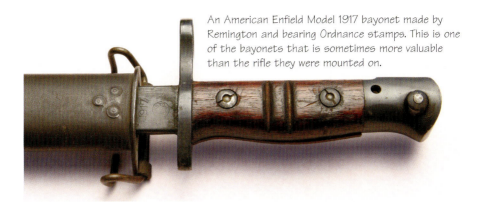

An American Enfield Model 1917 bayonet made by Remington and bearing Ordnance stamps. This is one of the bayonets that is sometimes more valuable than the rifle they were mounted on.

In the past decade, bayonet collecting has exploded. I know plenty of military guns where the bayonet is now worth more than the rifle itself! Other bayonets, like the one for the Model 1941 Johnson rifle, may look cheap and ugly (in this case, almost exactly like a tent peg) but are worth plenty, and there are very convincing reproductions that could easily fool the unsuspecting.

So it is important to know which bayonets are rare, if only because you might be buying a real bargain if an otherwise normal gun comes with a bayonet that is somehow special or rare. When collectors sell guns, they sometimes fail to consider how much the bayonet should contribute to the price and often they practically throw it in for free.

Those of us who don't do the research in this area and fail to stay informed are sure to pay for our ignorance down the road.

Cast Steel

Lots of old gun barrels have the words "CAST STEEL" stamped in them. This has caused plenty of confusion.

With almost no exceptions, these barrels were *not*, I repeat, *not* cast in a mold. Cast Steel refers to how the steel itself was made and has nothing to do with how a gun was constructed.

Tanker Garands & Jungle Carbines

There are some categories of military longarms out there that just never existed in real life. There are other types that were made for the military in limited numbers, but later on, more were "made up" than ever existed in the first place.

They are neat, handy and look fun — but they are modern-assembled commercial products that should not be considered overly histori-

These are the two types of proofs that appear most often on guns that seem to be American products but were actually made elsewhere. To the left are the post-1813 view and proof marks for Birmingham, England. Above is the proof mark for Liege, Belgium. These two cities supplied a huge number of guns exported to the United States.

cal or collectible. Some folks have been fooled by these, but experienced collectors usually know better. There is nothing wrong with them...they just aren't "real."

Learn Your Proofmarks

Even if you just collect American weaponry, be sure that you have a working knowledge of the proofmarks of all the world's major arms making cities and countries. For instance, Liége, Belgium and Birmingham, England, made many guns and swords that were later marketed in the United States with American names on them. But they often bear the proof marks of their original makers. If the item was imported rather than being of domestic production, this can have a significant impact upon value.

Barrel Lengths

For factory-made guns with standard barrel lengths, measure the barrels exactly before making a purchase. If the barrel has been cut down for some reason, it will almost certainly reduce the value of the gun. Deviations can also indicate rare variations, so be aware of any special barrel lengths that you should be looking for.

Buying the Smart Way

When is Bore Condition Important?

On some guns, bore condition doesn't mean anything. On other guns, it can have a huge impact on price. Before shopping for a collectible firearm, it is worth learning what category you are dealing in.

In general, flintlock and percussion weapons do not fluctuate much based upon bore condition, unless it is pretty extreme. Neither do many civilian revolvers, regardless of their ignition system. A selection of guns where bore condition is more important might include single shot rifles, target weapons, military firearms of the 20th century, semiautomatic pistols and fine vintage shotguns.

"Factory Original"

For factory-made guns and military weapons it is particularly important to their value that the guns be in the condition in which they left the factory or were issued to troops. Replacement sights, restocking, sporterization and refinishing almost always reduce a gun's value significantly. An exception to this rule might be military guns that were government altered for reissue. Rolling blocks converted from rimfire to centerfire, arsenal refinishes, etc., often reduce but don't destroy a gun's value. Indeed, a particularly rare military alteration can sell at a premium. Also, in some cases practically all the guns were altered, so "factory original" examples are not available.

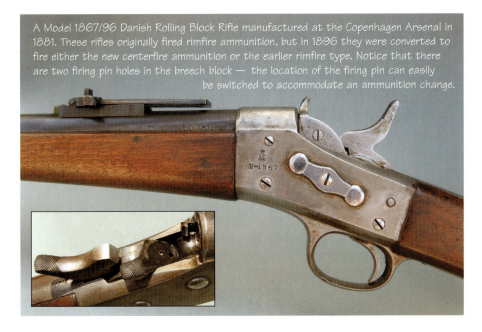

A Model 1867/96 Danish Rolling Block Rifle manufactured at the Copenhagen Arsenal in 1881. These rifles originally fired rimfire ammunition, but in 1896 they were converted to fire either the new centerfire ammunition or the earlier rimfire type. Notice that there are two firing pin holes in the breech block — the location of the firing pin can easily be switched to accommodate an ammunition change.

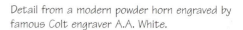

Detail from a modern powder horn engraved by famous Colt engraver A.A. White.

69 Aftermarket Engraving

While often very attractive, aftermarket engraving is not valued as much as factory engraving — especially if the work was not done when the gun was new. Poor workmanship, or modern engraving on an antique gun, can actually devalue the piece significantly. This is particularly true for Colts and Winchesters. All that matters to many of collectors is whether the work was done by the factory. Even if an engraver who used to work at the factory does the work, it is almost always worth less than the same craftsman's work while he was employed at the factory. And it might, in some rare circumstances, even be worth less than a factory-original, unengraved gun.

A few modern master engravers like Al White and Howard Dove have such a cult of personality that their work can be an exception to just about any of these rules, but this is truly unusual, and it is uncertain whether these values will survive over time as their names perhaps become less well known.

70 Engraving on Pre-Factory Guns

Lots of flintlock collectors talk about the "style" of engraving used by famous gunsmiths, as if these guys were whipping out engraving tools and doing it themselves with their own unique artistic sensibilities. For the most part, this is pure rubbish!

Yes, it is true that huge concerns such as Colt and Winchester had factory engravers who used a recognizable "company" style. But for almost everyone else, engraving was something that was done by outside establishments. So, to talk about an individual gunsmith's engraving "style" usually doesn't make much sense. He might have consistently used a particular outside engraver who had a style of his or her own, but in most cases this had little to do with the gunmaker's individual tastes.

Buying the Smart Way

Engraving on pre-factory guns, like this London dueling pistol, was normally done by outside specialist engravers rather than someone in the gunmaker's shop.

Here is a great example. From the mid-18th century until 1812, there was a very active London engraver named William Palmer. And guess who was sending him guns to engrave? Henry Nock, Durs Egg, John Manton, William Jover, Joseph Manton, Robert Wogdon and many more. It reads like a "Who's Who" of famous London gunsmiths! And they were all using the same guy.

Low Serial Numbers

In general, very low serial numbers will add to the value of guns by widely collected makers. How much depends on how popular the model of gun is, how many were made, etc. But be sure that you understand how the serialization system works for the particular firearm you are looking at.

Some serial numbers are actually cut down or abbreviated versions of much longer numbers, and your supposedly "low number" might not mean anything at all. Also, many firearms (pepperboxes in particular) were produced in batches, and when the maker reached number 50 or 100 or 200 or 500 or whatever, he would just start over again at number 1. There are some gun models with many existing serial #1s, most of which aren't particularly special at all.

On the other hand, in my own collection I have a pair of duelling pistols that are serial number 1001. This doesn't seem very special until

Buying the Smart Way

Single shot Mauser 1871s were altered by St-Denis in France to take the 6.5 mm Daudeteau cartridge on contract for Uruguay. Although these rifles were rebarreled and assembled from unmatching parts, they are still considered a legitimate military weapon as assembled.

An American stocked and U.S. surcharged musket from the period immediately following the Revolution. Most of the parts are French. Although this is an assembled musket, the fact that it was put together during the historical period for military use gives it added value.

you realize that the maker of those particular pistols started numbering his pistols at number 1000 or 1001, much like some folks start their check book at a high number so it doesn't look like they have a new account. So it would seem that I have either the first or second numbered gun, depending on how he decided to start.

Learn to understand how the numbering systems work for guns that you are liable to purchase, because it is easy to get fooled or miss out on something special.

Parts or Assembled Guns

In general, be aware of guns that were made-up from parts. Mixed serial numbers, parts from different eras, etc., are all a problem. Parts guns with documented military use, however, might be interesting collector's items. For instance, there are the French-made Daudeteau-caliber military rifles assembled for sale to Uruguay, mostly made up from surplus German Model 1871 parts that were refinished and assembled for export. While often ugly, these guns can have significant collector interest.

73 Parts Guns — The 20th-Century U.S. Military Longarms

Among collectors of 20th-century U.S. military longarms, it has become quite common to assemble weapons entirely from loose parts or to take guns that were updated at arsenals and revert them to their original, earlier (and more valuable) configurations. The question "is this the correct part" has become a cliché of the modern gun show.

M1 carbines are perhaps the most notorious example of this phenomenon, made even worse by the fact that some early books about these guns gave incorrect parts information, leading to the careful assembly of thousands of historically impossible weapons.

If these guns are correctly assembled, they are usually accepted by collectors, although this may change in the future.

74 Mixed Serial Numbers

The serial numbers on most longarms and pistols should match, but this isn't always the case. On some guns, the parts were actually assembled with no regard to keeping like-numbered parts together. On other guns, particularly some military rifles, just certain parts should match. On yet other military guns, they originally matched when shipped from the factory, but after years of service, government arsenals dismantled all the guns and then reassembled them later with mismatched numbers. In a case like that, matched numbers might even be reason to suspect that the gun is a fake!

As usual, knowledge of the weapons you collect, and the configurations in which they should appear, is key to becoming a successful collector.

75 How Much to Pay for a Name or an Inscription

One of the great joys of collecting is when you can trace an item in your collection to an identifiable historical owner. The evidence for such an identification usually comes in one of two forms: documentation and inscription.

This Belgian-made double barrel boot pistol was purchased by my father directly from a Civil War veteran who claimed to have carried it as a "last ditch" weapon throughout the war. However, while interesting and almost certainly true, this story does not add much (if any) monetary value to the piece. The provenance is entirely oral and depends upon the accuracy and honesty of two men, both of whom are dead and one of whom was extremely old when the story was passed on. Stories like this should definitely be preserved, but it is generally unwise to pay too much money for them in the absence of further proof.

Unfortunately, most documents offered as proof that a certain individual owned a particular gun only indicate that the person owned "a" gun, rather than "the" specific gun in question. In some cases, we get really lucky, and the serial number is listed in the document. However, unless the document in question is a probate record, court record or some other place where a serial number would normally appear, we must ask ourselves why the serial number appears on that piece of paper. For instance, if a gunfighter is writing to his mother and says that he recently purchased a new pistol and includes the serial number, we have to ask ourselves, "Why in the world would he have mentioned that?" This would call the document, itself, into question.

In the case of inscriptions, we have to ask ourselves two questions. First, are we sure that the name inscribed can be satisfactorily tied to the historical individual in question? For instance, if a gun is inscribed "John Brown", it might have been owned by the famous abolitionist — or maybe by some other John Brown who was perhaps a rural house painter. Supporting documentation and provenance can sometimes answer these concerns, but often they cannot.

Secondly, is the inscription itself genuine? This is a tough one. While most fake inscriptions are laughably easy to catch, there are some excellent master engravers/fakers out there, and their work is frighteningly good. Thankfully, work like this doesn't come cheap and generally doesn't appear on any but the most expensive of weapons. Costly collectibles tend to have strong provenance including illustrated publication. If a very expensive inscribed arm doesn't have a firm provenance, you have to ask yourself why. Lack of provenance isn't totally damning, but it is a concern that needs to be addressed.

For the less masterful fake inscriptions, look to style and condition. The style of lettering should be consistent with the period of the alleged inscription. Modern type faces, for instance, should not appear on Federal-era flintlocks. Also, if an inscription is old, it should share the condi-

(below) The Webley-Greene revolver carried by Lancelot Lowther, the Earl of Lonsdale, in the First World War. He served as a King's Messenger, bringing dispatches to the front, and was highly decorated. A famous fox hunter, Lowther is shown above in a prewar sporting scene. The early war inscription makes this revolver especially interesting.

Buying the Smart Way

tion seen on the rest of the weapon. If an inscribed sword scabbard is heavily corroded, but the inscription is nice and fresh, this is a problem. Use lots of light and high magnification...are there fine signs of age inside the strokes of the lettering? If so, this is a very good sign. Watch out, though. Some fakers use acid and other methods to age a new, fake inscription. High magnification often reveals this method because it is difficult to accomplish without affecting adjacent areas of flat surface.

So, after all these warnings, how much is a legitimate inscription worth? That's a darned good question, actually, and there isn't a firm answer. In general, an inscription to a researchable individual who doesn't happen to be famous or particularly interesting warrants roughly a one-third premium over the normal cost of the gun or sword. The more interesting the historical figure is, the higher the value gets. Weapons owned by truly famous individuals can command amazingly high premiums, especially if the item is solidly provenanced and was used in a well-known event. You have to decide for yourself whether the questions brought up here have been answered to your satisfaction when determining how much that inscription is worth to you.

Join Clubs

Joining a collecting club is highly recommended. Nowhere else can you learn so much and make so many valuable contacts. Clubs tend to be either dedicated to a single type or manufacturer of gun, or represent all gun collectors in a state or region. Consider joining both a local club and national clubs covering the types of guns you collect.

The National Rifle Association maintains a list of affiliated clubs. Check it out on the internet at http://www.nationalfirearmsmuseum.org/collector/gun_club.asp

Not all clubs are affiliated, but this is the best single source of information on collector clubs nationwide.

What's It Worth?

Legendary dealer and author Norm Flayderman recently told me something that he has learned in his many years as a leading force in this hobby. It doesn't matter what it has sold for in the past, it doesn't matter what your friend says it is worth and it doesn't matter what is on the price tag. The only time you know for certain how much a gun is worth is when someone pulls out his or her wallet and pays for it. And that, at that exact moment, is what it is worth. He was kidding around, but there's some truth to it.

Commemorative Values

There have been many commemorative firearms, both firing and non-firing, offered over the years by companies that specialize in these types of items. Many collectors have bought these because they are attractive for interior decoration, because they have a special respect for the person or event being commemorated, or because they enjoy the workmanship of the commemorative weapon itself.

While these guns can be very enjoyable to own, it is worth noting that these guns have not increased in value over the years in the way that most original-production collectible firearms have. Some sell better than others, but as a group, used commemoratives go for less than their original retail cost.

Another related category are factory commemoratives. These are guns made in modern times by Colt, Winchester and other gun makers, copying famous historical firearms made by the same company. While there aren't many factory commemoratives being produced today, they were quite popular thirty years ago, and some models were made in staggering quantities.

As a group, factory commemoratives retain their value better than the non-factory types, and many models have increased in value over the years. Others have lost value, and still others have stayed the same, but overall, there is an active market for buying these guns used.

One thing worth knowing about commemoratives in general is that their value usually plummets if they are not in perfect, unfired condition with their box and all the original paperwork, etc.

Firing Replica Values

Another category of guns similar to commemoratives are the firing replicas. These are usually guns used by historical reenactors and are working replicas of famous antique firearms.

Since these products are usually sold continuously and in unlimited quantities, firing replicas can usually be purchased new and, therefore, are less likely to increase in value over the years. However, there is definitely an active secondary market for these guns, and in excellent work-

An early firing replica. Among replica firearms, custom-made pieces tend to be valued the highest, with factory-made pieces coming in second and customer-assembled kit guns third.

ing condition, they tend to sell for two-thirds of their cost new.

Toy Guns

The mock weapon, along with the mock baby, were probably the first toys ever invented. They doubtless date back to caveman days. Scaled-down guns made as toys are popular collectibles, especially if they are antique, accurately represent a full-size weapon and function properly. Note that most of the older "toy" guns can really work as small weapons and should be handled safely like any other firearm.

Functioning toy guns were rarely made in large quantities and are difficult to value today. Prices tend to have more to do with the manufacturing quality and age of the piece than anything else, although these are just general guidelines. Also, be aware that there are a few Cadet guns out there — the best ones are government issued, scaled-down

A child's Brown Bess musket, made to almost exactly half size, including a bayonet. It is marked "TOWER" on the lock, bears Tower proofs on the barrel and is fully functioning.

versions of service arms. These are a different category entirely, with their own prices, often quite strong.

 Final Word I will sum up this chapter with advice from Erik Goldstein, curator of firearms at Colonial Williamsburg: *"If you've never bought a bad gun, you aren't buying enough."*

In other words, don't be disillusioned by your mistakes. They happen to everybody. Just be sure that you learn from them. And please, don't pass them on to someone else without identifying the problem.

"The Little Volunteer," a Currier & Ives lithograph depicting a boy in U.S. military uniform with a functioning toy-sized longarm. While no longer considered proper playthings for children, such guns are a popular collecting topic today.

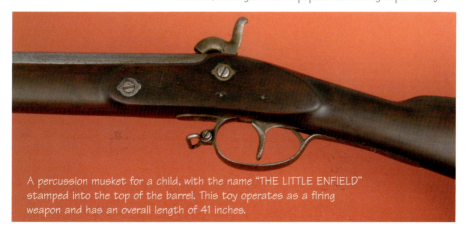

A percussion musket for a child, with the name "THE LITTLE ENFIELD" stamped into the top of the barrel. This toy operates as a firing weapon and has an overall length of 41 inches.

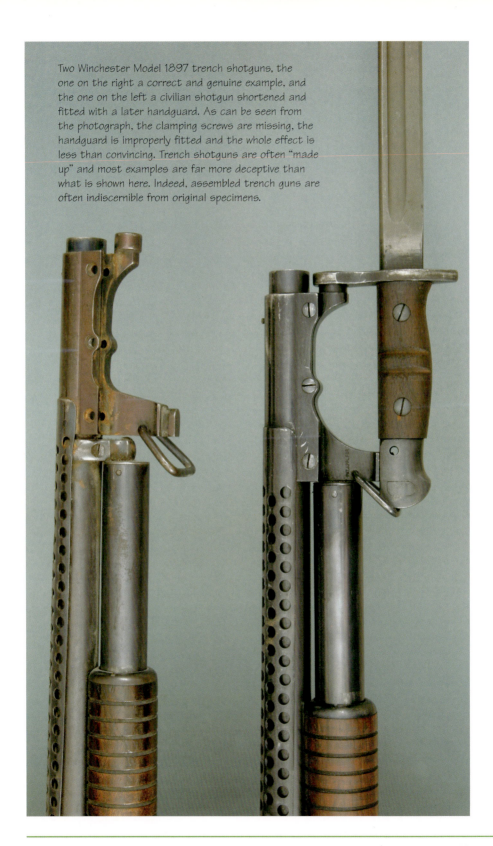

Two Winchester Model 1897 trench shotguns, the one on the right a correct and genuine example, and the one on the left a civilian shotgun shortened and fitted with a later handguard. As can be seen from the photograph, the clamping screws are missing, the handguard is improperly fitted and the whole effect is less than convincing. Trench shotguns are often "made up" and most examples are far more deceptive than what is shown here. Indeed, assembled trench guns are often indiscernible from original specimens.

Warnings and Suggestions

An Ounce of Prevention

In my job as Editor of *Man at Arms for the Gun Collector* magazine, I hear about the fallout from just about every type of bad experience that collectors can have in this hobby. So, while most people get nothing but joy from gun collecting, it is worth going over some of the most common pitfalls that you might encounter, especially for the beginners amongst us. Most bad experiences can be prevented with a little homework and by asking the right people for advice and help.

And please, don't let any of the information in this chapter scare you off. The whopping majority of people in this field are friendly and honest. In fact, *nearly all* of them are friendly and honest. Unfortunately, the few "bad apples" get a lot of attention, but this

Marine Corps rifle instruction at Parris Island (600 yards with sandbag rest) during World War I. Just as yesterday's soldiers needed to train and prepare for battle, today's collectors need to be ready for any potential challenges that await them.

is true of any collecting hobby, and I can say with confidence that there are fewer shenanigans in gun collecting than in any other collecting field that I can think of.

Major Frauds and How They Are Perpetrated

Just like in any other field of antique or art collecting, there have been a few isolated instances of outright fraud within the gun collecting world. Most of us aren't going to be spending enough money to attract this kind of attention, but it is still worth knowing the basic types of scams — if only for entertainment. Usually, the game revolves around misrepresenting the value of the gun or group of guns in question. In recent years, the F.B.I. has become increasingly involved in policing the collecting world and exposing illegal activities of all kinds. Perpetrators have gone to jail, and many observers feel that scams of these types are quickly becoming a thing of the past.

Exotic Major League Frauds and Deceptions
Part I: Inflated "Letters" and Appraisals

Collectors naturally get nervous when buying commonly faked guns like engraved Colts and Confederate weapons. Because of this, a small industry has developed selling "Letters of Authenticity" for these items. Almost all of the experts who write these letters are upstanding individuals who do this work as a public service

A military longarm by Potts & Hunt of London, England. A generation ago, guns of this type were often represented by sellers as having been imported during the Civil War for Confederate usage. While in a few cases this might have been true, the whopping majority were actually manufactured for volunteer companies in England and imported to the United States in modern times.

Warnings and Suggestions

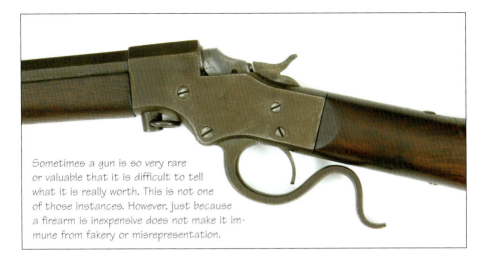

Sometimes a gun is so very rare or valuable that it is difficult to tell what it is really worth. This is not one of those instances. However, just because a firearm is inexpensive does not make it immune from fakery or misrepresentation.

and often spend more money preparing the letters than they actually charge their customers. However, purchasers should always be aware of any relationship that exists between the seller of a gun and the writer of the letter that is being used to authenticate it.

I know people who have been offered as much as $10,000 to write letters of authentication on guns that are notorious fakes. While these experts naturally refused to go along with such offers, there might be others who decide to take the money. It is always worth considering how much you should trust letters written by people who are either involved in business with the seller or are not known to you personally — especially if the letter was paid for by the seller and not yourself.

Exotic Major League Frauds and Deceptions
Part II: Creating a Fake Auction Record

Some collectible guns are so very expensive that no one really knows what they are worth. There aren't any price guides for $100,000 guns! So, often, buyers use past auction records in order to establish an idea of current value. They either look for a comparable item that has sold at another recent auction or they look at how much the gun for sale sold for when it last changed hands.

Want to drive up the price of a gun before selling it to a well-heeled buyer? No problem. What you do is put it up for auction and have a friend buy it. Then wait six months and have the friend put it up for auction again, at which time you and two other friends drive the price way up and you buy it for a large amount of money against seemingly vigorous competition. Of course, you already own the gun and are really buying it from yourself. The auctioneer's premium is an expense you are willing to pay in order to create a paper trail of escalating values.

Then you can document that you bought the gun at auction for umpteen dollars and offer it for "only" a ten percent markup. Sounds like good work if you can get it! But it's awfully dishonest.

This is reportedly very, very common in the world of collectible automobiles, but it is also seen in the antique gun world from time to time.

Exotic Major-League Frauds and Deceptions
Part III: Buying Through a Dishonest Agent

Many wealthy collectors hire representatives to make their purchases for them. These experts get to keep about 5% to 30% of the purchase price as their commission (depending on how expensive the guns are and what services are being provided), in exchange for locating the items and assuring their authenticity.

This sounds like a great situation for everyone involved until the "expert representative" gets greedy. You would think that 15% of a million dollars or more per year would be enough to satisfy anyone's needs, but apparently this isn't always true. A few of these agents have allegedly found ways to get more than their fair share.

Since the commission percentage is based upon the purchase price, the easiest way to make more is to convince the client to spend more. This is sometimes done by representing the guns being sold as more valuable than they really are — and then taking a kickback from the seller as well.

Another method that has supposedly been used by aggressive agents is to sell the collector something that the agent owns himself...once again at an inflated price. Of course, the collector would become suspicious if he knew his agent was the actual seller, so the gun often passes through some third party who is paid a commission in exchange for appearing to be the actual owner.

Exotic Major League Frauds and Deceptions
Part IV: Selling Through a Dishonest Agent

Perhaps one of the most common kinds of fraud in all kinds of collecting is when you are selling through an agent, and he or she misrepresents the selling price. This kind of fraud can happen to anyone, regardless of how expensive or inexpensive the item is, and is worth protecting against. How does it work? Here is an example from the fine art world:

There was once an old lady who owned a number of excellent works of art — paintings mostly. She was approached by someone who said that he had ready buyers for these items and would act as her agent in exchange for 20% of the purchase price. Being an appraiser, he helped her to establish values for all of the things that needed to be sold. After a couple of weeks had gone by, he called her on the phone and said he had found a buyer, but that the buyer would only pay 90% of what the items were worth. He was, however, willing to pay in cash. The lady, wanting to be done with the situation, agreed.

This all seemed well and good, until it was discovered years later that the items had actually sold for more than twice the appraised value, and the appraiser had pocketed the difference.

This kind of fraud can

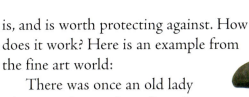

be hard to detect and prove, so it is very important to know as much as you can about the reputation of the person you are working with. Also, ask for copies of all receipts and make sure the terms of your transaction and the percentage being kept by the agent are clearly recorded in writing. Lastly, on particularly important deals, it can't hurt to ask to talk with the actual buyer. There is no need to insult the middleman by saying you don't trust him. Just say that the gun has a history and you want to be sure that you are doing your duty by passing on all relevant information and answering all of the buyer's questions. If, during this discussion, you confirm the purchase price, it wouldn't seem unusual, would it?

By the way, none of the above is meant to discourage you from selling through an agent or dealer on commission. It's actually a great way to sell collectible guns and is highly recommended…just make sure that you either trust the person implicitly or have a way to confirm the details of the transaction. The last thing you want is to send someone your guns to sell and then, months later, have them look you straight in the face and ask, "What guns?"

Auction Games

Some varieties of fraud revolve around the auction world — almost always without the knowledge of the auction house itself. Here are some of the better-known variations on this theme.

Auction Games and How They Are Played
Part I: The Straw Bidder

Auction fraud has been around just about as long as auctions themselves. And most of the tricks played on the unsuspecting are just as old.

The first dirty trick we will talk about is the "straw buyer." Let's use an example. Say that I'm a guy who wants to sell a very expensive gun, and I want to really drive the price up. What I might do is have a friend or two sit in the auction room and bid on my gun — even though they have no intention of buying it. They are there just to drive up the price and make the honest bidder, who really wants to purchase my gun, pay as much as possible. As soon as the bidding slows down and the real bidders seem to be reaching their limits, these "straw bidders" will drop out and leave the purchaser with a significantly inflated bill. This is

Auction pools generally require a set of bidders with specialized buying patterns. More generic guns, like this Indian Trade Gun by Wilson, are unlikely targets for such activity.

against the law in most jurisdictions, but it does happen from time to time and is very difficult to prove.

90 Auction Games and How They Are Played Part II: The Pool

The next game we need to talk about is the "auction pool." It is illegal in most states and works like this. Suppose a small group of dealers or collectors discovers that they always seem to be bidding against each other on the same items. For instance, they all deal in fine Winchesters, and given that there are a limited number of these guns available, they all bid on every one that comes up for auction. One of them always ends up winning, but they are driving up the price on each other. If they are sneaky, they might do this:

They meet together in a hotel room the night before the auction. They go through the auction catalog and circle any items where at least two of them intend to bid. Then they designate one of their group as the buyer. He shows up the next day with a wad of cash and buys all of the circled items. The prices seem strangely low, because none of his friends are bidding against him. At the end of the day, he pays his bill, collects his guns, and heads back to the hotel.

Later that night, another auction is held, but in the hotel room between the members of the ring. They bid until someone wins, and this is called the "knock-out." They do this for every item that their buyer purchased. Then, when they are through, they all split the difference between what the buyer had to pay at the auction and what the items really sold for in their hotel room. Even if you end up buying nothing, you still get your split because you were in on the arrangement.

This kind of ring is rare in the gun world compared to other fields of antiques and art. But when an auction pool is operated correctly and with "heavy hitters" participating, it can result in significant losses for the auction house and its consignors. However, laws against pool bidding are very hard to enforce, not only because it is difficult to prove but because auction houses are sometimes unwilling to offend people who are probably among their most active customers.

Auction Games and How They Are Played
Part III: Devalue It, Then Buy It, An Old-Time Classic

This one only works if you are a well-known author or another kind of recognized expert. It also helps if the gun is in a category that is often faked, like Confederate weapons, for example. What someone does is go up to the gun before the auction and handle it at great length. Every now and then, the person will make a highly audible sighing noise, like he is disgusted. Then, as he turns to walk away, he chuckles to himself and shakes his head, as if amused by the duplicity of the world in creating such a convincing fake. Then, he arranges to be a phone bidder and purchases the gun from down the street — after having destroyed its market value without saying a word.

This trick used to happen every now and then, but doesn't work very well today because there are so many absentee bidders who aren't there in person to be swayed by such a person's antics. And if you think this sounds like fun, think again. If you are noticed by the consignor, and are caught saying untrue things about the item, you could actually be sued for slander.

A Mannlicher M.95/30, which is a shortened and rechambered version of the venerable Model 95. While it looks like an original carbine, it is not. These altered incarnations of the M.95 are a legitimate military weapon, but generally have lower values than full length versions.

More Common Problems Encountered by Collectors

Now that we have covered some of the more exotic problems that some collectors have faced, it is time to cover situations that normal people are more likely to encounter. However, even these more "common" problems are still pretty darned rare. Considering the large number of transactions that take place in the gun collecting world, it is surprising that customers do not encounter more difficulties with sellers. This is a great credit to our hobby and the many wonderful people who deal in it.

We will now explore some of the ways that a buyer might become misled about the true value or identity of a gun.

Greed is the Enemy

Aside from the truly unlikely risk of being swindled by an unscrupulous individual, we also have to watch out for guns that simply have defects or that have been manufactured or altered to confuse or defraud us.

In so very many cases where collectors end up purchasing guns that aren't what they seem, greed is behind the mistake. In the excitement of getting a great gun for less than its going price, collectors will sometimes overlook all kinds of faults that become apparent later. It is almost a kind of selective blindness. I understand that sometimes you have to move quickly to avoid disappointment, but believe me, the disappointment of a "fish that got away" is nowhere near the disappointment of a "fish that stinks" once you get it home.

In the next chapter, we will spend some time discussing how to identify these fishy problems and inspect questionable guns, but as an introduction to that topic we should explain the difference between outright fakes, fraudulent alterations and over-enthusiastic restorations.

Outright Fakes

Believe it or not, outright fakes are actually very, very rare in the gun collecting world. There are plenty of guns that have been changed somehow to increase their value, but very few guns that have been made up from scratch to fool collectors. The only really significant group of totally fake guns that I can think of are Walker Colts. These revolvers have been valuable for a very long time, and some top experts in this field believe that more than half of the current Walkers on the market are outright fakes. This, however, is a very, very unusual situation.

One other category that comes up often is when replica firearms made for the reenactor or shooting market are altered to appear genuinely old. Most of these replicas are pretty easy to tell from the originals if you have any experience at all, but some working copies are pretty convincing. Especially if you collect items of Civil War, Revoluntionary War or Wild West vintage, be sure to keep up with the replica guns and accoutrements being offered by popular catalog vendors. For other categories of guns, World War II military rifles for instance, you are quite likely to encounter fake/replica bayonets and accoutrements but highly unlikely to encounter fake firearms themselves.

If you do collect a gun that has been accurately copied, make careful comparison and find the features where the copy differs from the original. There always are some. Of course, almost all firing replicas are marked with the name and location of the modern manufacturer (usually in Italy), but troublemakers sometimes grind this information off and then use acid to "age" the metal. (Occasionally, you can still smell the acid months later, so sniffing never hurts.)

You used to be able to look for the grinding marks where the manufacturer's name was taken off, but these days the scar is often patched with welding, so stay aware. In actuality, though, very few guns have been convincingly copied, and most of us need not be concerned.

Last, but not least, if you are looking at a supposedly American-made revolver of the 19th century and it has metric screw threads (there are tools to check), something is almost definitely amiss.

Most Fakes Aren't Entirely Fake — The World of Fraudulent or Deceptive Alterations

There is no way that I can give this topic the full attention it needs, but I will take a shot. There may be very few entirely made-from-scratch fake guns on the market, but there certainly are plenty that have been "improved" over the years, occasionally with benign intentions. But the end result is the same. This generation's restoration quickly becomes the next generation's deception.

Since the difference between an average gun and a great one is often a small marking, a special barrel length, different grips, a rare sight or some other easily added feature, mechanically minded people have often been tempted to alter guns for financial gain, sometimes making a full and profitable career out of it. For this reason, it is good to know the

Some collectors seem to think that there is a large supply of guns out there that are just as fake as the battle scene in this First World War postcard. But it just isn't true.

basic techniques for recognizing when this "work" has been done on a gun, because this may affect its price. The next chapter will outline some of these recognition techniques.

Even though it is obviously wrong to make a gun more valuable by "changing it" into a more desirable type, what should we think about other kinds of work that can be done to guns? Perhaps it is time for a general discussion of refinishing and restoration.

Refinishing & Restoration I
A Definition

This whole topic is a quagmire and a controversial one at that. Some collectors feel that if a gun has been abused, it should be returned to its original beauty — looking just like it did when it was shipped from the factory. Other collectors believe that if a gun shows some wear, then that damage is part of the gun's legitimate history and evidence of its use. They argue, for example, that if a gun has been through a war and shows some battle scars, it is wrong and almost sacrilegious to remove them today.

There are many layers of opinion about restoration. Some typical opinions might be:

1. All restoration and repair is wrong. The gun's precious historical record should not be altered in any way.

2. It's OK to fix broken parts and make the gun work again, but the parts should not look deceptively original.

3. Refinishing the metal and replacing parts are fine, but the gun should still look old and show its true history.

4. I want all my guns to look brand new, and that's fine as long as I'm just returning it to how it used to look.

5. I can't afford a special/rare gun so I'm going to make one. It's my gun and I can do whatever I want with it.

6. I want to make a big profit creating an expensive gun out of an inexpensive one, and I'm going to hire a gunsmith to help me.

Amongst collectors, the most common opinion is probably #2. Amongst dealers, the most common opinions are probably #3 and #4.

Refinishing & Restoration II
What Do They Do

As can be seen from the typical opinions listed in the previous entry, different people have different ideas about what constitutes proper restoration. For some, proper restoration might mean a light cleaning. For others, it might mean fixing broken grips using whatever is left of the original parts. Or, it might mean going whole hog.

Some new collectors might wonder what can actually be accomplished by a professional restorer. The answer, perhaps unfortunately, is just about anything. The only real limit is how much money the cus-

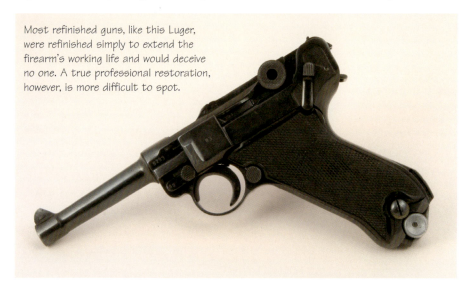

Most refinished guns, like this Luger, were refinished simply to extend the firearm's working life and would deceive no one. A true professional restoration, however, is more difficult to spot.

tomer is willing to spend. Restorers that I have met are capable of making new parts, filling the deepest rust pitting, making the whole surface of the gun look brand new, recutting all of the edges so they are factory sharp, recutting all of the engraving and stamps, changing the serial numbers, putting on fresh bluing, replacing gold inlay, applying the patina of age — and if they are good enough, you won't be able to detect any of it without laboratory tests.

Interestingly, custom-made replacement parts are often chosen over fixing the old parts because there are no welding marks to hide, and the restoration cannot be detected by x-ray.

Refinishing & Restoration III
How Good Can It Be?

Here is an example. I once saw a pair of duelling pistols for sale in an English gun shop. The dealer told me that one of the locks had been lost over the years and he had replaced it with a brand new one made from scratch. Grinning, he challenged me to tell which pistol had the replaced lock. Now of all the guns I collect, I'm probably the best at English duelling pistols. This should have been a piece of cake for me, but it wasn't. Both locks were perfect. Eventually, I guessed, and I guessed wrong.

Now you might be thinking that I just wasn't looking hard enough, but this simply isn't true. I know of three seperate gun restorers who have purchased guns, thinking that they were in original condition, only to discover days later that the guns were completely refinished. How did they know? They had done the work themselves!

Refinishing & Restoration IV
Our Saving Grace

Many dealers and collectors (perhaps more dealers than collectors!) will read the above story about the replaced lock and figure, "If you can't tell the difference, why would you care if it's replaced?"

However, most collectors do care, and fortunately for them, truly artistic gun restoration is expensive and relatively rare. Most restoration is pretty awful and easily identified, usually being limited to unconvincing replacement parts and a thick, dull re-blue. This will be discussed more fully in the next chapter.

Remember that the person wishing to fix a gun up for profit has to be able to add the original cost of the imperfect gun to the price of the restoration, subtract that from the final purchase price when he sells it, and come out with a profit. Most high-end restoration costs thousands of dollars, which often makes such projects impractical. However, I would warn that people often spend money in silly ways and, sometimes, handy folks practice their skills on cheap guns. I've seen $5,000 restorations on $500 guns, so while economics do play a role in whether a gun was likely restored, it isn't a foolproof test.

100 Refinishing & Restoration V
The Moral Question

A good deal of restoration work seems to have been done with the best of intentions. The owner sees that the beauty of his or her gun has been diminished and wants to save the weapon so it can look pretty again. This is an honest impulse, and perhaps even a noble one. And remember, quite a bit of refinishing, for example, was done a few decades ago when many of today's collectible guns were still being used and shot. The owner just wanted his tool to keep doing its job. He wasn't trying to fool you any more than a car owner is when he puts a new coat of paint on his beat-up old Buick.

But, unfortunately, even if the owner who paid for the work tells the next purchaser exactly what was done, eventually this information is going to be lost. Someone is going to buy the gun and think it is in original condition. Whether this happens because of forgetfulness, death or dishonesty, it will happen and there is no way to stop it.

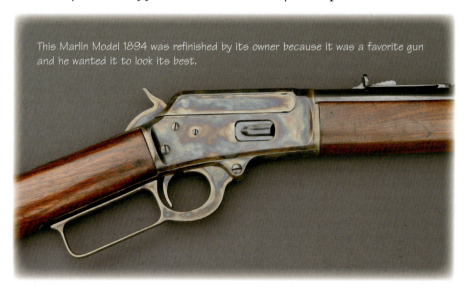
This Marlin Model 1894 was refinished by its owner because it was a favorite gun and he wanted it to look its best.

If we are looking for some authority on what is right and what is wrong, perhaps we should find out what the National Rifle Association has to say about all this? Among other things, according to the NRA's "Code of Ethics for Gun Collectors and Dealers," the following are "practices considered unethical":

The refinishing (bluing, browning, or plating) or engraving of any collectors weapons, unless the weapons may be clearly marked under the stocks or elsewhere to indicate the date and nature of the work, and provided the seller unequivocally shall describe such non-original treatment to a buyer...

It is worth noting, however, that according to Norm Flayderman in his essential and highly recommended book, *Flayderman's Guide to Antique American Firearms...and their values*, refinishing is almost never recorded under the grips, and even if it was, it could easily be removed with a little sandpaper.

Refinishing & Restoration VI
Don't Ask, Don't Tell

Unfortunately, many sellers disposing of refinished or heavily restored pieces follow what gun dealer Jim Supica disparagingly calls the "Don't Ask, Don't Tell" rule. If the buyer doesn't ask, they won't tell. In response to this, some restorers have begun placing a small stamp bearing their initials or some other mark never used by a gun factory in a discrete place on the gun, perhaps under the grips. This is a practice that should be encouraged, and I commend these folks for taking the responsible route of signing their work for future generations to recognize.

However, you should always, always ask if a gun you are buying has been worked on. If you hesitate, this quotation from an article in the 1974 *Gun Collector's Digest* by a gun restorer of the last generation should steel your nerve:

When a firearm is restored for the sole purpose of selling it, should the seller inform the buyer that the gun has been restored? In all cases in which the buyer asks if the finish is original, he should be informed that the gun was restored to original condition. On the other hand, the author feels that ethics do not require that one hang a sign on a gun reading "restored." If a gun is correctly restored, it should stand on its own merit. The buyer will not find it necessary to inquire about its authenticity.

Refinishing & Restoration VII
The Question of Value

One of the reasons why some sellers end up following the "Don't Ask, Don't Tell" rule described above is that the vast majority of collectors do not want heavily restored guns. Perhaps this will change in the future, but right now when a gun is auctioned and advertised as restored, even if it bears the mark of a highly skilled and well-regarded restorer, the market will be limited and the value could be quite a bit less than what the gun would get if it were in similar but original condition.

And this is for an excellent, excellent restoration. Poor restorations can almost totally devalue a gun to the point where no collector would buy it. Sometimes restored guns do go for more, depending on the rarity of the model and how hard it is to find new-condition original specimens, but these instances are quite rare in today's marketplace.

In general, the purchasing of heavily restored guns, no matter how good, is difficult to recommend from a financial point of view.

Refinishing & Restoration VIII
The House of Cards Effect

Be particularly wary of deluxe and highly decorated guns that have been refinished. Let's take, for example, a beautiful, engraved Colt revolver. The gun looks great, but you have determined that the blued finish is a modern restoration. What does this tell us about the rest of the pistol?

Well, for one thing, if the engraving is in great shape and looks perfect, then it was either recut or is totally fraudulent. Otherwise, it would probably have been severely worn and degraded by the pre-refinish polishing. And what about those wonderful, perfect grips? If the gun is refinished, then it was probably in somewhat worn shape to start out with. So how could those mint grips possibly be original to a gun that had seen that kind of use? It's like a house of cards. Once one part of the revolver comes into question, all other aspects of the piece also have to be looked at with suspicion.

Let's move on to the serial numbers. Like the engraving, serial numbers would likely have been softened during buffing. So if they look consistent with the rest of the gun — in other words, crisp and new —

This is the deluxe plated and engraved Henry rifle given by the factory to President Abraham Lincoln. Famous weapons like serial number 6, shown here, are often so well documented that we know where they have been since they were manufactured. It is more common, however, that we have to act like detectives and study a gun's physical condition to confirm its originality.
(Smithsonian Institution Collection)

then they probably aren't in original condition either. Maybe they were recut or restamped. Maybe they were even filled in with welding and had completely fresh stampings done. If so, maybe the serial numbers themselves aren't original, and the factory letter that came with the Colt refers to a completely different revolver altogether — one that is supposed to have fancy grips and lots of engraving. Yours might have left the factory as a completely plain pistol and the real deluxe gun (sharing the same serial number that yours now has marked on it) is sitting in someone else's collection.

Can you see how it is hard to trust a high-end piece once you know it is refinished? What about the parts of the revolver, itself. If the serial numbers might have been reapplied, who is to say that they were matching numbers in the first place? Maybe this is a parts gun. And remember, buffing can cover up all kinds of evidence of repair, alteration, patchwork and outright incorrect parts.

Once it is learned that a deluxe gun has been comprehensively refinished, it calls into qustion absolutely everything about the gun. Even laboratory tests might never be enough to make you trust this revolver completely. Then again, most of the gun could be totally correct. But how will you, the collector, ever know for sure?

104 **Refinishing & Restoration IX**
Original Finish Seals in Authenticity

Conversely, even a small amount of original finish can be like historical Saran Wrap®, sealing in the true, "factory fresh" features of a gun. Just about anything covered by original finish almost *has* to be right, unless the part itself is a replacement.

105 **Refinishing & Restoration X**
Is Refinishing Always Modern?

Nope. Lots of guns were refinished by the original factory, government arsenals or independent contractors during the gun's original period of use. Often, when this was done, the gun was stamped to show who did the work and when, as discussed below.

106 **Factory Refinish Marks**

Some of the very best refinished or refurbished weapons are those that were returned to the original factory or arsenal that manufactured them. Since these guns were fixed-up by the very same people who made them, using the same tools and machinery, all the correct dies and with perhaps a near limitless supply of original-production replacement parts, it is no wonder that a collector can get fooled.

If that is the bad news, then the good news is that factory and arsenal refinishes do not degrade the value of a gun quite as much as commercial work does. In general, guns that were refinished in the historical period are worth much more than guns that were refinished last week, and if they were done by the original manufacturer, then all the better. There are also many military arms in particular where original finish examples are just about nonexistent because they were all recalled for identical refurbishment before storage or reissue.

Some arsenals and factories marked the guns that had undergone such treatment, and a knowledge of these marks can be of particular use to collectors. For instance, during much of their history, Smith & Wesson struck a star in front of the serial number on pistols that were refinished at the factory.

The bolt and a portion of the butt stock from a German 98k carbine that was captured by the Soviets during World War II and then refinished at a later time. Note that both parts had new "matching" serial numbers put on them when they were imported into the U.S.A.

107 Low-Quality Arsenal Refinishes

While many arsenal refinish jobs are quite collectible, there are others that are pretty rough and severely degrade a gun's collector value. One example would be the Russian refinishes that we are seeing sold on the surplus market today. After World War II, the Soviet Union put countless bolt-action military rifles into cold storage in case they were needed for a future conflict.

These rifles were mostly Russian Moisin-Nagants or captured German k98s. These guns were dismantled, reworked and rebuilt by the Soviet government during the 1950s, and while they are refinished, the work isn't always as good as the original arsenal product.

Warnings and Suggestions

Does this mean that these guns are uncollectible? Actually, no. They saw lots of action during World War II, can have very interesting marks showing their history and are a fun relic of the Cold War. For the price, they are great. But because of the sheer quantities involved, they did not receive the same amount of attention given to many other arsenal refurbished guns.

108 Refarbing — A Different Flavor of Refinishing

Earlier, we introduced the topic of firing replicas that are good enough to make new collectors believe they are antique. Beginner collectors should be aware that even these replicas can be refinished. It has become increasingly common amongst military reenactors and Cowboy Action Shooters to try to make their modern firing replicas as accurate as possible — including all the correct markings and inspection stamps.

For many years now, it has been common practice amongst these folks to grind off the Italian marks on their modern imported guns to make them look "more correct." This, of course, left a scar in the metal, which collectors learned to look for and were able to detect easily. What we are seeing more of now is that these grinding marks are getting sophisticated and harder to spot, following the contours of the gun more accurately and sometimes even being filled with welding. Then, of course, they add the "correct" inspection marks and proofs.

Some collectors find reenactment appealing, but want an activity that is more firearms oriented. The North-South Skirmish Assn. holds uniformed live-fire matches that might just fit the bill.

Another aspect of this "make it look real" trend is that reproduction guns are being given increasingly accurate finishes, often including intentional signs of fake aging — sort of like acid-washed blue jeans. Faded finishes, flaked plating, rust pits and holster wear are all being added to these guns to meet the demands of their customers.

As always, we commend the Cimarron company for putting a mistake in their barrel address to help identify their Colt copies as reproductions. Veteran specialist collectors are unlikely to be fooled in any case, but those with less experience should learn what is out there, because some of it is starting to get very, very convincing.

Doubt me? Just go to the Internet and search for "Defarb," which is the reenactor term for making a piece of reproduction gear look more original. It's a real education.

Stretched "Artillery" Colts

Sometimes, gun owners and restorers have chosen to take a gun that was altered during its period of historical use and do work on it to return it to its "original" configuration. In the process, the true history of the gun is lost, and very often, the original parts are substituted with modern replacements. This is a highly controversial activity, but it is very profitable because the earlier configurations of these guns sell at a high premium. One of the most famous examples of this are the stretched "Artillery" Colts.

John A. Kopec is the world's most respected expert on Colt U.S. Cavalry revolvers, so let's quote him directly on this topic:

In an effort to combat the epidemic of fakery that is currently on the rise, I would like to take this opportunity to warn your readers of what is going on in the Colt U.S. Cavalry collecting field.

The most recent craze of today's "restorers" is the re-conversion of the lesser-valued Colt Artillery revolvers into all-matching Cavalry revolvers. This is especially prevalent when these fakers find an Artillery revolver with a desirable serial number. Most commonly encountered are those revolvers with "Custer"-era serial numbers.

These revolvers are prime targets for the "handiwork" of these restorers. All serial numbers are made to match, a newly manufactured 7.5-inch barrel is attached, a facsimile address re-rolled, and a set of beautifully cartouched grips fitted. In many cases, the underside of the revolver's frame is milled flat and the original serial number re-applied. This is accomplished to assure the proposed purchaser that the exact same stamping dies were used in all three major positions. Now we have an "all-matching" U.S. Cavalry revolver!

Many honest old Artillery revolvers are being ruined by these practices. In fact, some of these revolvers are found to have Colt factory records indicating that they had been altered during the Spanish-American War era. Oh, what greed will do!

Our thanks to Mr. Kopec for these comments. It is worth mentioning that this kind of fakery has been going on for nearly fifty years, although the older techniques were quite a bit more primitive, usually being limited to welding on a new section of barrel to make it come up to the full Cavalry length.

A Funny Story

Since we are talking about stretched Artillery Colts, here's a true story for you. A bunch of Colt collectors were standing around admiring a Cavalry Colt. It was beautiful and everybody was envious of the lucky guy who had just bought it.

Until they looked down the barrel with a bore light. Part way down the barrel, the rifling changed direction! The last two inches of the barrel were a patched-on addition to bring what had been an Artillery up to the proper Cavalry barrel length. Be careful out there folks!

Flintlock Reconversions

This is another politically charged topic involving a gun being returned to its "original" condition by throwing away real parts and replacing them with modern ones. When the percussion ignition system was invented, many gun owners and government arsenals wanted to update their existing guns for the new technology.

This process was called "conversion" and could be as crude as driving a percussion nipple into a pistol vent or as sophisticated as completely replacing the breech and lock. Conversions allowed guns, many of them family heirlooms, to continue their working lives for decades after they would otherwise have been rendered obsolete.

While this was seen as a wonderful thing during the period of the gun's use, many modern collectors have been less than pleased with converted guns. Original flintlock guns sell for a lot more money than

U.S. Model 1817 "Common Rifle," converted from flintlock to percussion. This example was made by Nathan Starr of Middletown, Ct. Note that the nipple is brand new.

converted examples, and many collectors think that conversions, as a group, are ugly. Because of this, many of these converted guns have been "reconverted" back to the flintlock system by throwing away the percussion parts and replacing them with salvaged or newly made flintlock parts — in essence, returning the gun as closely as possible to its original appearance when it first left the maker's shop.

Are reconversions ethical? That's a controversial question. Reconversion changes a gun's history, making it look like something it isn't. It also replaces real parts with associated or replica parts, often in a way that isn't entirely consistent with what the actual flintlock mechanism probably looked like in the first place. Because there is no absolute way to know what the original flintlock parts looked like, the gunsmith doing this work must guess, and many of these guesses are wrong. As the number of reconverted guns grows, it could become more and more difficult to tell what the real, original flintlocks really looked like for a particular maker, because truly professional reconversions are quite difficult to detect. Lastly, reconversion, if unreported, increases a gun's selling price and might be seen by some as a form of fraud.

On the other side of the coin, supporters of reconversion point out that the gun was originally flintlock and that they are only returning it to its original configuration as the manufacturer envisioned it. Also, they usually think that the profile of converted guns is awkward and inferior, and view conversions as defects that need to be "fixed."

A 1953 advertisement for military rifles, some of which have been turned into "custom sporters." Rifles that have been fixed up in this way are called "Sporterized" by collectors, and unless they are of particularly high quality they rarely fetch the prices of unaltered examples.

Regardless of how you feel about reconversions as an ethical practice, you will certainly want to be able to know one when you see one. There are sometimes ways to detect a reconversion, and this will be covered in great detail in the next chapter.

Sporterized Military Rifles

After each major war, there has always been a large surplus of military weapons, usually resulting in sales by the government. The customers for many of these weapons were hunters whose needs were different than those of a soldier. Today, we see many classic military rifles that have been "sporterized" by hunters or the companies who supplied them. For instance, there are a large number of Johnson Automatic Rifles on the market whose stocks were checkered by dealers selling the rifles for deer hunting in national magazines. This made them more appealing to hunters at the time, but today they usually are worth only a fraction of such a rifle that is still in its original "factory shipped" configuration.

Fake or Incorrect Attributions

Many guns have old tags on them saying that they were owned by a famous person or a soldier in a famous engagement. Sometimes, there aren't even tags...just stories told by dealers and previous owners. Many of these stories are true. Maybe even most of them are true. But quite a few are also false, and it doesn't always mean that someone is being purposefully deceptive.

Family history is a particularly messy business, and legends that accompany family heirlooms often become more and more distorted with each passing generation. So, even if a gun comes with a notarized letter from the family that originally sold it, there is no guarantee that the information in the letter is actually correct. The same goes for records and identifications from small museums and historical societies.

Try not to pay too much extra money for stories such as these. Always keep in your mind what the gun would be worth without the attribution. Also, check the story as much as you can. For instance, I was once interested in purchasing a pair of duelling pistols being sold by a highly regarded auction house. The pistols were advertised as having

Family stories about weapons passed down through the generations can be enticing, but they aren't always something that you can hang your hat on. Here's a very recent example from my own family. The Walther shown below was given by my father to my mother as a Mother's Day present. (I will not comment on dad's gift choosing skills!) If my parents were famous people, this might make it an interesting relic a hundred years from now. But even though only one generation has passed at this point, the story is already beyond proving. Was I there when the gift was made? No, I was at college. Am I 100% sure that this is the gun in question? Nope, my dad also owned a very similar pistol and they could have gotten switched over the years. I'm 99% sure that the gun and the story are correct, but...

been presented by a famous Revolutionary War general to one of his close comrades. The family of the general was the consignor and provided substantial documentation. However, based upon the birth date of the gunsmith, both the general and his friend were dead for twenty years before the pistols could possibly have been made, so a presentation of this type was (how shall we put this?) — highly unlikely. The pistols were legitimate items, and quite beautiful, but were probably owned by a later generation of the family.

Other Tricky Documentation

Pension records are often used to document the illustrious military career of a gun's original owner. For the Civil War and earlier, however, these accounts were routinely exaggerated. Before the era of comprehensive record keeping, veterans would usually be asked to submit details of their war service in order to substantiate a possible pension, but these accounts are often highly questionable and should be taken with a grain of salt.

Pension acts were usually passed by Congress decades after the conflict had ended, when memories were fading and refuting claims would be difficult. Here is a good example. In the 1880s, the G.A.R. had enormous influence in Congress and was able to encourage passage of extensive benefits for disabled veterans. Well, guess what? Nearly everyone who had served in the Union Army, and many who hadn't, showed up to claim injuries and disabilities brought about by their military service. Investigators came to different conclusions about how many of these claims were fake, but valid claims of disability were probably less than 20% of the sample. All the rest were fraudulent. The Congressional Record is full of outraged reports of investigators who snuck up on veterans who had "lost both legs at Gettysburg," only to find them perfectly whole and healthy, working full time at physically demanding jobs.

Guns of the Gunfighters

Even more care needs to be taken when buying the firearm used by a notorious Western gunfighter or lawman. Records in the early West were shaky at best, and lies were being told about these guns before the original owners were even dead. Newspaper accounts were little more than fiction, and fake documentation, both old and new, abounds.

For instance, Jesse James' mother reportedly sold scores of cheap pis-

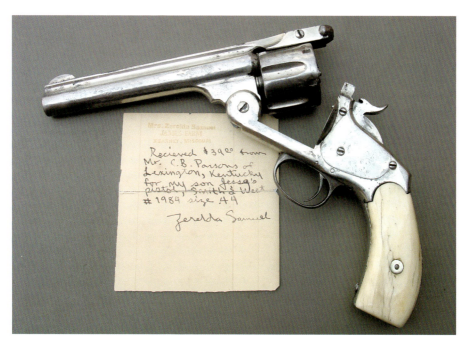

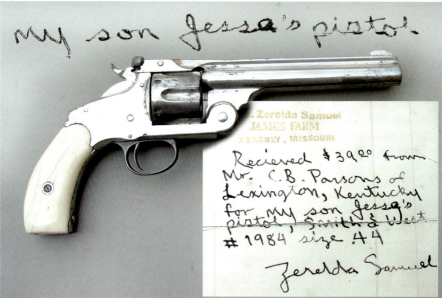

An awesome example of a "Zerelda Gun," sold by Jesse James' mother. These guns have a collecting interest all of their own. *(Jim Supica Collection)*

tols to journalists and other curious visitors, each one supposedly being "Jesse's favorite." It's good paying work if you can get it, and I'm sure that with a son like that she deserved all the compensation she got, but let's just say that there are a lot more outlaw guns today than the desperados themselves ever carried and used during the historical period.

116

Veterans' Encampments and Other Variables

One of the best ways to be certain that a gun or accoutrement was used at a famous battle is if you can purchase an artifact that was actually dug up there. Almost all of these items are totally legitimate. However, there are sometimes other possible scenarios.

Let's say that a Union veteran joins a veterans' group in his retirement. He wants to look good at the big encampment, right? Of course he does! But he has gained some weight over the years, and his old rig doesn't fit. So he goes out and purchases a new one, perhaps from an original supplier or from a surplus dealer. There was a great demand for Civil War guns and dress items during the final decades of the 19th century, and much of it was purchased by veterans to use at their events.

So, our nameless "old soldier" dresses up for the big battlefield encampment, and he and his regimental buddies meet up exactly where they had originally pitched their tents during the war. Off he goes to a campfire party, and having perhaps indulged in a drink or two or twelve, he loses his pistol and his belt while staggering around in the woods to relieve himself. A hundred years or more pass by, and an enthusiastic fellow with a metal detector makes an amazing discovery — an original belt buckle and revolver, rusty but original…right where the soldier dropped them in flight or death. The gun looks about right, but the buckle is a type not known to have been used until the postwar era.

It's an amazing discovery, proving that belt buckles of that type were actually used in the war, much earlier than anyone had ever suspected… or is it?

A Belgian 18-shot percusion self-cocking pepperbox revolver, c.1845. Notice that the chambers are numbered in gold around the collar. I have no real excuse for showing this gun here — it doesn't really illustrate anything in the text — but who needs a reason to show a great picture of a wonderful gun? (Courtesy Sotheby's, London)

Let's Get Down to Brass Tacks!

117   Collectors with an interest in the West are always attracted to Indian weapons. Unfortunately, with a few notable exceptions, the guns that the Indians used are no different than the guns used by everyone else in the West. This makes testing for originality difficult. Adding to this challenge is the fact that Indians tended to use their weapons into the ground with little thought to maintenance. One of the few distinctive indicators of Indian use on a longarm is if it is decorated with brass tacks arranged in geometric or symbolic patterns.

However, it is quite easy to take a worthless piece of junk shotgun or carbine and turn it into an "Indian Gun" simply by applying some brass tacks. Years ago, these frauds could usually be exposed, because the crooks used modern tacks, which have differently shaped shanks than genuine 19th-century tacks. Unfortunately, the current crop of fakes often use antique tacks, which are not that difficult to acquire. In fact, they are often given an extra "patina of age" by literally burning them off the box or trunk they are found on.

One thing that complicates matters for the fakers is that wood covered by a tack is protected and ages at a different rate than the exposed portions of the gun. Tacks also attract quite a bit of muck and filth that often collects around and under the edges of the metal. Therefore, if you pull off one of these tacks, the wood underneath should look somewhat different and you should expect some debris. But just try to get a dealer or auctioneer to let you pull off a few tacks to check the wood! Let's say that it isn't going to happen very often.

Because of this, provenance or expert authentication should be an important part of any high-end transaction of this type.

Things Marked "1776"

118   Many older collectors remember how excited folks became about Revolutionary War weapons back in 1976. Well, the same thing happened in 1876 — only then they often had great-grandpa's musket in the attic, or at least thought they did. Sometimes when you see

1776 marked on the escutcheon of a Colonial fowler converted into a musket. This example appears to be genuine.

the date "1776" marked on a weapon, it was put there at the time of the Centennial, not the Revolution itself. This doesn't mean that the date is inaccurate, just that you have to be careful. Many War of 1812 weapons were marked 1776 during the Centennial, not out of duplicity but in innocent confusion and overenthusiasm.

119 Testing the Hardwoods

For many years, in order to determine whether a flintlock gun was made in America, collectors placed a great deal of emphasis on having stocks tested to determine if the wood was of American origin. While this is still of value in some cases, according to researcher Joseph V. Puleo, it must be remembered that hardwoods were one of the major export products of the American colonies and the United States. In the 18th century, British military muskets were stocked in shops located along the London waterfront because the materials were arriving by ship from overseas, and in the early 19th century, there was even a brief fad among the best English gun makers for using tiger-striped and bird's-eye maple stocks! The origin of stock wood is still a factor to be considered, but not one as foolproof as was once thought.

American maple stocks on a pair of fine London duelling pistols. Exotic American woods were exported to England, which poses an extra challenge when identifying unmarked guns.

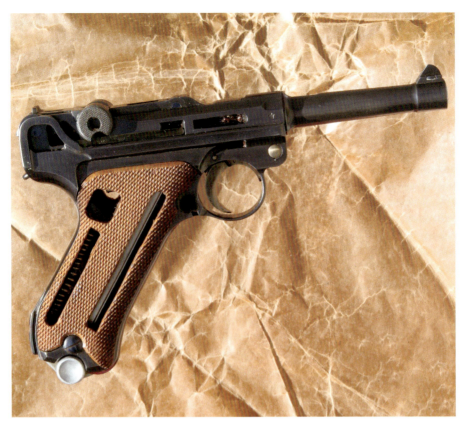

As explained below, many "cutaway" samples were made in modern times to satisfy collector demand. This is a rare, genuine example of a cutaway Persian Luger. (Hansen & Hansen)

The Ten Riskiest Collecting Categories

As would be expected, the things most often faked are what we want to buy the most!

1. Kentucky Rifles in original, flintlock condition.
2. Any Confederate item…especially one marked "C.S.A.", as well as Dance Brothers revolvers.
3. Walker Colts and martial Colt single actions.
4. Any weapon with a Little Bighorn association or a with brass tacks in the stock indicating Indian usage.
5. Tiffany-gripped Colts.
6. Civil War "Enfields" attributed to American use.
7. 20th-century military sniper rifles.
8. "Cutaway" pistols supposedly used as salesman's samples.
9. Engraved Henry Rifles.
10. Early or rare Lugers in mint condition with original finish, special markings and matching serial numbers.

The genuine barrel signature of New England gunmaker Henry Pratt. Interestingly, these signatures were etched rather than engraved. Unfortunately, signatures of the more popular makers were widely faked during the 1950s and 1960s. *(Joseph V. Puleo collection)*

Barrel Signatures on New England Flintlocks

Of course, this kind of trickery was not limited to historical times. For instance, New England rifles were not usually signed by their makers, and the signed examples quickly became valuable. In fact, at least one prominent early collector would not buy a New England longarm unless it was signed. Demand always creates supply, so during the 1950s, there were a couple of fakers known for taking unsigned New England rifles and putting names on them in order to make a quick sale.

An old timer in the region, who knew these characters, was once asked by a friend of mine why Silas Allen (the famous New England gunmaker) used a few different signatures. The old timer responded, "Well...we didn't know the names of too many gunsmiths back then. It's funny how many rifles ended up with those names on them." Enough said. The numbers of rifles involved were probably few, but watch out.

Military Sniper Rifles

Without solid documentation, most sniper rifles are just about impossible to authenticate. Many, like the M1D, were converted by the government from existing rifles, and the surplus barrels needed to convert them today are still available. So, how do you tell an original M1D from one assembled last week? The cruel answer is that you cannot.

Another example, also a variation of the Garand, is the M1C. This is the Garand sniper rifle that goes for the most money, and there are so many fakes out there (perhaps even a majority of the extant examples) that without serial number verification you are probably going to get burned. Even this isn't foolproof, though, because proper, loose M1C receivers have also been reassembled using unrelated parts to recreate an "original" rifle, often in a way that defies detection.

The bottom line is that unless a sniper rifle is heavily documented, it can be risky to spend more on the gun than what the sum of its parts would be worth if sold separately, plus the cost of labor for the assembly. However, sanity of this type is rarely found in the collecting world and prices for questionable examples continue to escalate.

123 Provenance

As collectible gun values continue to rise, it seems inevitable that there will be more and more aggressive restoration and outright fakery. This has happened in collectible furniture, collectible art, collectible armor, numismatics and just about any other mature collecting field.

So what is the answer? For these other collecting fields, the answer became an increased reliance on provenance. Provenance is the record of where a gun has been over the years and who has bought and sold it. If a gun appeared in a book in the 1950s and looks the same today, odds are that nothing fraudulent has happened to that gun.

I expect that provenance will become more and more important in gun collecting in the coming years, and deluxe or exceptionally rare guns with surviving provenance will be considerably easier to sell than those without a full and accurate record of past ownership.

124 Keep Records!

If provenance is becoming an increasing factor in determining values, then the obvious step is for all of us to keep better records.

As fake artists get better at their

In collecting fields like armor, items of provenance like this catalog illustration from the 1890s have become increasingly important.

craft, collectors will want to make sure that they can prove that their collectibles are genuine. One way to help do this is to keep careful records of where guns and swords have been in the past, including any documentation that can show that a specific item existed before the era of aggressive fakery began.

So keep those receipts, catalog illustrations, auction listings and other materials. And store them in a rational way, so that when you pass away, your inheritors will be able to take advantage of this provenance and pass it on to the new owners.

125 Age is No Absolute Guarantee

While provenance is a very useful tool in researching authenticity, it is not a sure thing. Just because a gun dates back forty or so years in its current configuration does not mean that the gun was not "messed with" before that time. It cuts down the odds, but there is no guarantee.

Some examples? As early as the 1960s, Colt Model 1860 Armys with fluted cylinders were being fraudulently created by adding fluting to the standard types with the round cylinder. These fakes became so highly publicized in books and articles that some people think it actually held back the value of high-condition examples.

Examining a Gun

126 **Be Observant**

I cannot stress this enough. Successful collectors succeed by seeing more than other collectors do. Most "rare finds" are purchased after they have been picked up and examined by scores if not hundreds of collectors who did not recognize what they were handling.

127 **Be Forgiving**

This is something else that can't be stressed enough. Most of the guns that we collect are either very old or have literally been through wars. It is unrealistic and unfair to expect perfection.

Sometimes a great gun has the wrong sight on it or has been refinished. Most of us will choose to ignore those weaknesses if the gun has other strengths or points of interest. The older a gun gets, the more forgiving we need to become.

This chapter will give you

Be observant. Unit markings like this can increase a gun's interest and value substantially — even if the weapon itself has serious condition defects.
(Bill Ahearn Collection)

A Chillean M1895 Mauser in abolutely perfect, unissued condition. Just look at the crispness of the markings on the bolt handle. You should not expect this kind of condition on all of your purchases.

lots of ideas about how to inspect guns for signs of damage and alteration. By all means, try to know exactly what you are buying. But sometimes you just need to turn a blind eye. You shouldn't ignore the gun's weaknesses, but you also shouldn't let a gun's flaws stop you from enjoying it properly.

This situation is kind of like family. Most of us have relatives who aren't exactly perfect. Maybe they are rude or dress funny. But we don't kick them out of the family reunion because of those faults and we still try to find a way to love them — for what they are. The same goes for guns. If you can't find a way to love them for what they are, you will forever be disappointed and will miss out on a lot of the fun of being a collector.

Flashlights and Magnifying Glasses

Dim lighting is a problem at many gun shows, and savvy collectors usually carry their own sources of illumination and magnification. Flashlights can be essential in determining the true condition of a gun. Be sure to carry one, but always remember that a flashlight is going to make a gun look worse than normal lighting, so you need to apply a different standard.

The same thing goes for magnifying glasses. All too often, buyers struggle to see tiny markings that are crucial to their purchasing decisions. I even go so far as to carry a flashlight with a built in mini-microscope, which shows me a very bright view of a small section of the gun at 16X power. This is really too much enlargement to view most markings, but it is great for identifying refinished metal.

If you would like some specific suggestions along these lines, refer to the "Tools" chapter later in this book.

The "TRAF" marking on the buttstock of this M1897 Winchester trench gun indicates that it had a secondary career in the traffic division of a police department. Often, markings of this type have become filled with dirt or otherwise dulled with age, and can only be seen with proper lighting and careful examination.

Don't Let Any Marking Go By Unexamined

Study and identify any marking that you find on the guns in your collection. You may have a sleeping rarity on your hands. I will give you an example.

I have a friend who wanted a representative example of a particular Winchester longarm. He wasn't picky about condition and was able to get one at a bargain price because the wood was "carved up." Winchester collectors are usually extremely picky about condition, and the carving on the stock made the gun inexpensive. The gun was also dirty and showed few signs of its original finish.

When my friend got the rifle home, he carefully cleaned it (something none of the Winchester's previous owners had done) and discovered that the carving on the stock was readable. It was a list of animals, and there was a name, date and a town in Wyoming carved in small letters at the bottom.

It turns out that the name was one of "Buffalo Bill's" best friends, and the date and animals listed corresponded to the details of a hunt they had gone on together. My friend had purchased an amazingly interesting and historical weapon for the price of a piece of junk. But he only learned this by taking the extra step of revealing and researching those otherwise undesirable carvings.

Quality is Job One!

Very often, we are put in the position of having to examine a firearm that we do not know very much about. Perhaps it is a one-of-a-kind weapon, like a flintlock fowler or a revolver by a maker with whom we are not familiar.

In these situations, it is helpful to concentrate on quality first. Is the gun well made? Does it have "extra" features that set it above other simi-

Sometimes quality is easy to see. Other times, you need to use your imagination.
(Bonhams and Butterfield)

(left) Attractive wood is a good sign of quality. *(below)* Another thing to look for are silver mounts, like this particularly fine escutcheon by silversmith John King.

lar weapons. Are there engraving or inlays? Does the wood have a fancy grain?

The devil is in the details. Learn to recognize fine quality just like you have learned to recognize fine condition. Sometimes, even though a gun is in horrible condition, it is valuable because it was elaborately made — even though you might have to use some imagination to appreciate it today. If you can look past the rust and damage, you might see something truly special.

Be Aware of Commonly Missing or Replaced Parts

For every class of collectible weapon, there are specific parts that tend to get lost or damaged with use and age. For a revolver, it might be the grips. For a flintlock, it might the cock's top jaw. For a bolt action rifle, it might be the bolt.

Examining a Gun

(left and above) Missing top jaws and missing grips are common faults on old guns.

For a semi-automatic pistol, it could be the safety lever.

Whatever the commonly missing or replaced parts are for your collecting theme, be aware of them and make them the first thing you look at when examining prospective purchases.

Perennial Weaknesses & Common Faults

132 Some firearm designs have weak spots and are often broken in what would otherwise be unlikely areas. For instance, the Chaffee-Reese had a poorly designed magazine system in the butt. They are often found today with cracks near the toe of the butt, and the magazine pieces having been removed by dissatisfied users. Because of this, a cracked butt toe is almost *expected* in one of these guns. You should examine for repairs in that area, and examples with uncracked wood and a fully intact magazine system will command a premium price. A similar phenomenon is when almost all examples of a particular gun are "flogged" (the Ward-Burton carbine comes to mind), and truly fine specimens are able to command an unexpectedly high

(right) Cracked butt toe on a Chaffee-Reese rifle.

109   Examining a Gun

value, while beat-up examples are tolerated because you probably won't do much better without spending a fortune.

133 Does the Gun Operate?

In most cases, even if you do not intend to fire your collectible firearm, you will want it to be in proper working condition. Sometimes you have to compromise in order to acquire a particularly rare or precious example, but for the most part, it is a big plus if the gun actually works.

134 Uniformity of Condition

One of the ways to identify replaced parts and other alterations to a gun is to look for uniformity of condition. In other words, if the frame is all pitted by old rust, then perhaps the barrel should be pitted, too. Of course, this only applies to the exposed portions of the gun. Protected or covered parts of the gun might not show much wear or corrosion.

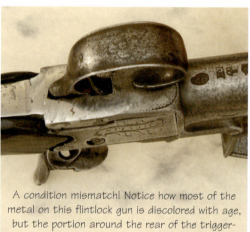

A condition mismatch! Notice how most of the metal on this flintlock gun is discolored with age, but the portion around the rear of the triggerguard is shiny from a recent sloppy repair.

Keep in mind, however, that sometimes different gun parts are made with metals of different hardnesses and will be affected by rust to different degrees. This is where you have to be aware of the particular guns you collect and how they were made. For instance, on many flintlock pistols, the lock parts are made of harder steel than the barrels. So, although the barrel may be more corroded than the hammer, this doesn't necessarily mean that anything is wrong. However, if you have a semiautomatic pistol and the slide is brand new but the rest of the gun is in extremely poor condition, then you probably have a replaced part on your hands.

135 Learn Common Patterns of Wear

Each type of collectible gun has a normal wear pattern. Learn to recognize this pattern! If a gun is in used condition, then it should show wear in the spots where it comes into contact with the hand, as it is pulled from the holster it is kept in, where moving metal meets other surfaces, etc.

One of the best places to look for wear in a used gun is on the grips, which are often made of softer material than the rest of the firearm and are most often subject to handling. New grips on a well-used gun are something that should immediately get your attention.

136 Patina — A Good Sign

A promising thing to look for on an original condition gun is patina, which is a darkening of metal or finish brought on by exposure to the air over a long period of time. It is generally difficult for modern technicians to replicate the exact look of genuine patinated finishes. Patina on unfinished steel is often gray, patina on brass is often dark brown/orange. Note that the colors are not even. This effect is difficult to describe, but collectors quickly learn how really old metal should "look" — especially if it hasn't been kept in protective storage over the years.

This part from a military rifle .22 caliber conversion kit shows a classic wear pattern where the finish has rubbed off of the edge areas but is intact on center areas that are handled less often.

Common patina colors on brass and steel gun parts.

Examining a Gun

Old wooden gunstocks crack and break. This is an unfortunate but unalterable fact of life. Every new collectible firearm purchase should be examined for wood damage. In the photo above, notice the obvious seam where missing wood has been replaced. Most expert repairs will be much more difficult to spot than this. In the photo at right, see the missing piece of wood along the terminal of the barrel tang. Wood is often damaged or missing in areas where it meets metal. Small wood repairs and minor damage do not usually devalue a gun much, unless it is modern or in particularly fine overall condition.

137 Pull the Ramrod

Almost all repairs are easier to see from the inside than the outside. Always ask to pull the barrel if you suspect cracks or other stock damage. If it is a muzzle-loader, simply removing the loading rod will often reveal any problems. Learn as much as you can about work that has been done to a gun *before* you make that big purchase. Repairs shouldn't disqualify a weapon as a collectible, but they do affect price, as well as structural integrity, and are worth spending some time to discover.

138 Quick Epoxy Test for Wood Repairs

Some broken gunstocks have had portions replaced with epoxy. Usually, it is just filling a deep dent here or there, but sometimes these repairs can be quite extensive and can be difficult to notice because it is easy to tint epoxy to just about any color that you want, or even mix it in with ground wood to add an extra-convincing bulk and texture.

Examining a Gun

The easiest way to discover repairs of this type, of course, is disassembly. Patchwork repairs almost never look as good from the inside as they do from the outside. However, this is not always possible, and collectors sometimes find themselves in the awkward position of trying to make a purchasing decision without knowing for sure.

An epoxy repair.

There is, however, a quick test that doesn't require disassembly. Epoxy has a different density than wood and if you tap it with a pen cap, pencil, paper clip or other similar item you may be able to notice a difference in the sound it makes. This trick takes a little practice, but if you get good at it, you can usually tell nine times out of ten.

Wood Finishes & Sanded Stocks

Many collectors are especially concerned that the stocks on their guns have original finish. However, this is often almost impossible to determine for sure. Original wood finishes on certain brands of guns (especially those that were varnished) can, indeed, have distinctive appearances, but these are almost

This M1866 French needle gun has a sanded and refinished stock.

Markings on a sanded gunstock. Notice the lack of crispness and areas where the stamps have been entirely scrubbed away.

all relatively easy to replicate today.

For most guns, the truth is that over the generations the wood has been covered with countless layers of wax, oils and sylicone. A tung oil finish applied today is almost impossible to differentiate from a similar oil finish applied a century ago. Don't waste your time by getting too carried away on this topic.

In most cases, collectors would be advised to pay less attention to the originality of the finish and more attention to whether the stock has been roughly sanded. Coarse grit sanding rounds out a stock's edges and rubs off the markings. This isn't always a horrible problem, but if you are going to concentrate on any one thing about a stock's finish, sanding should probably be it.

Silver Wire Inlay

Many antique guns feature silver wire inlay decoration. Thin channels were cut into the wood and silver wire applied in attractive patterns and shapes. This is a great feature to find on a gun, but inspect such pieces carefully for damage because the wire has a habit of coming loose over the years.

Silver wire that has escaped its channel is like a loose end on a sweater — eventually it will catch on something and pull out more. It is sometimes possible to fix this with glue (use a transmission syringe), but it tends to get messy. On some guns where a large proportion of the wire has come loose, the owner has chosen to have a restorer pull it all out, recut the channels and put in new silver wire. This can be very dif-

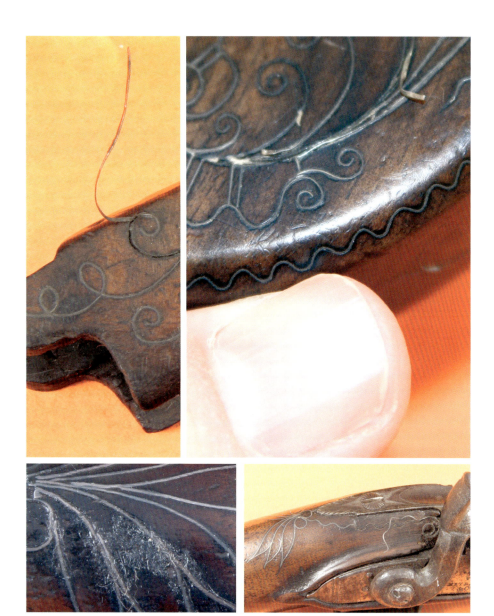

(three views, clockwise from top left) Examples of silver wire coming loose. (middle, left) Silver wire that has been reattached using glue — a messy proposition best left to an expert. (below) A modern example of silver wire that has been added. Notice the patch in the wood and how the wire goes right through the repair and into the new wood.

ficult to detect.

As with other kinds of precious metal inlays, some modern workmen have "improved" previously plain guns by adding silver wire inlay where it doesn't belong. These instances are rare, however, and can often be detected because the artistic style is not appropriate for the age and design of the firearm in question.

141 Is the Caliber Accurate? Is the Bore Relined?

For some types of guns — single shot target rifles come to mind — it was quite common for the original owners to reline the barrels and put in new rifling during the gun's working life. Usually, this was either because the bore was shot out or in order to alter the barrel to a different caliber. This can seriously reduce a collectible gun's value.

How do you tell? Well, sometimes, on more modern guns, you get lucky and the original caliber of the barrel is stamped on its exterior. So a good start is to measure the bore, compare it to the marking and see if it matches. On older or unmarked barrels, it is helpful to know what calibers were factory standard and to see if the exterior dimensions of the barrel are appropriate for the caliber that you see in the bore.

Sometimes, a worn barrel is reamed out and a fresh lining of the original caliber installed. If the rifling is done in a proper factory-appropriate manner, it can often be difficult to detect such a repair, although a seemingly unfired bore on a well-worn rifle might be a good warning sign. On liners installed by shooters, you can usually see the seam at the muzzle where the two pieces of metal were joined. On more careful jobs or restorations done to deceive, this seam is usually removed with polishing and/or welding.

Repairs of this type tend to devalue rifles of major manufacturers with "standard" product lines, like Remington and Winchester, more than those of non-factory craftsmen.

142 Measure the Barrel

On truly early guns this can be meaningless, but for factory-made guns, it really is a good idea to measure the barrel exactly and make sure that it matches the proper specs. as found in factory catalogs and other reference books.

Lots of guns wore out at the muzzle edge during their years of use, losing the proper crisp shape, and a common gunsmithing trick was to cut the barrel back a little to give the piece a new life. Often, the front sight was moved back accordingly. While totally legitimate, these kinds of structural repairs might devalue a collectible firearm.

143 Check the Muzzle Shape

Another sign of a shortened barrel is if the shape of the muzzle's lip is not correct. Many, if not most, guns have a crowned muzzle lip...meaning that the barrel isn't just cut off flush. The barrel walls usually terminate in a slight dome shape, while others, such as many target weapons, do not. Other types of guns almost always have a beveled edge where the muzzle face meets the bore. Learn what to expect here for the classes of guns that you collect.

144 Inscriptions

Since guns engraved with the names of their original owners and other historical details are valuable, some unscrupulous individuals have taken unmarked guns and added exciting names, unit designations, or other rare details to them. Back when I was a teenager, a friend and I were walking around a Connecticut gun show when a man behind a table, who was blatantly engraving the backstrap of a historical Colt revolver, suddenly shouted "Hey, Bill! How do you spell Burnside?" We laughed, but today that Colt is out there and a Civil War general's name is marked on it. That's why I don't usually pay a huge premium for inscribed guns that come without provenance. I want to see some pretty solid paperwork showing that the gun was marked that way back into the historical period. As a general rule, the less famous the name, the more likely that it is legitimate, but this is not something that you can depend upon. Since solid provenance is a rarity, physical inspection of the inscription, itself, becomes important.

145 Inspecting Inscriptions

Despite some exceptional fakes that could fool anyone, it is actually very difficult to put convincing false

This inscribed escutcheon, or thumb piece, has been shown before, but we will discuss it again here in a different context. Notice how the wear and staining all falls quite obviously on top of the letters and designs.

inscriptions on guns. A close examination of the marking in question will usually reveal the fraud unless the perpetrator is especially good at his craft. The only real tools that you need to make such an inspection are light and magnification. Good, bright light is difficult to find at many gun shows. I personally prefer to take questionable guns out of doors because natural light works best for me.

The problem that the fakers face is that new engraving looks nothing like old engraving, which becomes soft and loses its edge over the years. Fresh engraving on a well-worn or corroded gun should be easy to spot, even for beginners. Differences in condition such as this are a good way to spot many kinds of restoration and fakery. Needless to say, if the inscription "falls" into a pitted or ground-out area, then this is a good sign that the inscription was put on after the gun saw a great deal of use and age. While not all guns were inscribed when they were factory new, we usually do not expect extreme corrosion damage or wear under an inscription.

In general, guns inscribed during the historical period will show the same signs of age on and in the inscription that are present on the surface of the metal into which it is cut. If a gun is lightly corroded, for instance, then the whole gun should be lightly corroded unless there is a good reason to think otherwise. So, if the gun has a regular corrosion or wear pattern, then we should also see it in the inscription. Is the inscription worn like the rest of the gun part where it is located? If you look at the inside (or trough) of the engraving cuts themselves under high magnification, do they show the same corrosion or patina seen on the metal next to the

See how the inside cuts of these letters and shapes show the same patina and corrosion as the rest of the metal on this rifle.

inscription? Remember, the corrosion and wear happened after the inscription, presumably, so anything that happened to the gun happened to its inscription, too. If the surface of the gun is lightly pitted with corrosion, then the edges and insides of the engraved cuts should also show the same pitting.

Because of this, the fakers often treat the inscribed area in some way in order to create the necessary effect of wear and age. This, however, tends to create problems of its own. Once again, look for inconsistent wear. Is the part bearing the inscription worn or finished in a way that is inconsistent with the remainder of the gun? Can you see where acid, perhaps, was used to soften the appearance of the inscription, and in the process changed the color of a distinct area of metal around it?

An illustration of well-known Western personality Calamity Jane. Any weapon inscribed to a famous individual should be approached with a healthy amount of caution.

Also, I should add that most fake inscriptions on guns are just awful work and look nothing at all like historical originals. The more originals you see and handle, the easier it will become for you to spot the fakes. The most difficult fake inscriptions to detect are actually those on crisp, mint-condition guns where differences in condition between the gun and the inscription will be less pronounced.

One last comment. Many collectors "prove" that an inscription is genuine by researching the name on the gun and discovering that it matches a genuine person from the historical period or conflict. This is a false proof. It is great to learn about the person who owned your gun, but if you can look up the name, so can the faker. I mean, why use a contrived name when it is so easy to dig up a real one?

Type Styles on Inscriptions

While this is not a surefire method, it is certainly helpful to be aware of various type styles (often called fonts) and when they were popularized. For instance, the little hook-shaped squiggles that extend from the ends of letter shapes are called serifs. Fonts that have these extensions are called serif fonts. This is an example of a serif font. Fonts that do not have these extensions are called sans serif fonts. This is an example of a sans serif font.

Sans serif lettering was not popular until the early 1900s. However, sans serif fonts were actually invented in the early 1800s. So it is less likely that a Civil War gun will have a name engraved on it using sans serif lettering, but there are many legitimate examples.

"Old School" Type Games

Many of the earliest fakes involved the names of famous and desirable gun makers being applied to previously unmarked barrel tops and lockplates — almost always with inappropriate lettering styles. The stamps, especially if they were on lockplates, were usually too shallow, unable to penetrate the hardened steel of a finished firearm. In fact, many of these fraudulent markings were actually put there with simple die kits purchased in hardware stores or even (believe it or not!) with the metal keys from manual typewriters. This one-size-fits-all approach to maker's-mark fakery almost always fell absurdly short of a convincing result.

One way to detect fake markings of this particular type is that the letters in a word often will not line up with each other on a common baseline. The letters will bounce up and down, each with a mind of its own, whereas genuine stamps usually have one die for the entire name or address, and the letters are, therefore, struck all

Part of a fake marking, perhaps made with the keys of an old manual typewriter. For marks like this, sometimes fakers create the impression of age by burying the metal in manure.

Examining a Gun

Beware of inscriptions or markings with historically inappropriate type styles or which do not share the condition characteristics of the surrounding metal.

"Kill notches" on Western guns are often fraudulent modern additions. Look inside the cuts themselves for signs of age that are consistent with the rest of the gun. Rust pits and other irregular signs of corrosion are especially reassuring. From its condition alone, this example looks genuine, but as a general rule I am suspicious of such marks.

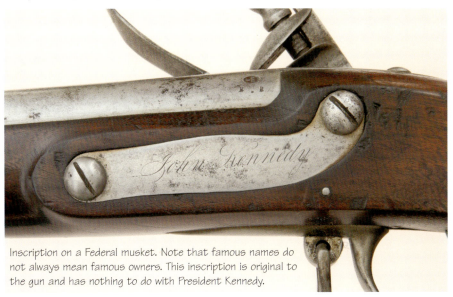

Inscription on a Federal musket. Note that famous names do not always mean famous owners. This inscription is original to the gun and has nothing to do with President Kennedy.

A Webley revolver with the owner's initials "E.P." inscribed on the frame. English revolvers very often have initials marked on them. Notice the rust pit on top of the engraved "P". Generic inscriptions of this type are almost always genuine.

Examining a Gun

If a gun is attributed to a highly regarded maker, the workmanship itself should reflect the expected level of quality. This fine cased set was made by Pirlot of Gent in Belgium.
(Douglas Collection, Royal Military College, Canada)

at once with no variation in position.

Lastly, remember that such fake markings are trying to convince you that the gun was made by a great maker...so expect the gun to be of a quality consistent with the name that is marked on it.

148 Outright Fake Engraving

For those with higher budgets and an interest in Colts, Henrys, Winchesters and other "top drawer" American guns of the 19th century, fake engraving is a legitimate worry and something to educate yourself about. Most of

Engraving should be of an appropriate style for the historical period. Notice that the color and texture of the metal is even throughout the entire engraved panel — a good sign. Fake engraving is rarely a worry on inexpensive weapons like this one.

Some maker's prefered very distinctive styles of engraving.

the techniques for identifying fake engraving are identical to those described for fake incriptions already listed above, so they won't be repeated here. There are, however, some additional things that you should be looking at.

Study the styles of engraving that were used by the factories you are interested in. Learn who the factory engravers were and what their work looks like. If a "factory engraved" gun shows up that has unusual engraving or a pattern that is not factory standard, be on your guard. Most guns engraved by the larger factories have fairly standard engraving patterns that are quickly recognized by experienced collectors. Also, the depths of engraving by shops or workmen are usually fairly consistent. If engraving

Examining a Gun

In many cases, genuine historical engraving is understated and tasteful, rather than exhibiting outrageous amounts of coverage. (Roy Marcot photograph)

for a particular type of shotgun, for instance, is always shallow, then a deeply engraved specimen might deserve some scepticism.

As always, inconsistency is another thing to watch out for. Perhaps you might encounter a gun that has been "improved" by having the "empty," unengraved portions filled in — thereby giving the gun a higher grade of coverage than when it originally left the factory. I recently saw this on a Henry rifle's receiver. Does some of the engraving on a gun look different than the rest? Does it have a different artistic style? Is it thematically inconsistent? Is the depth of engraving not quite the same in some spots? Do areas seem crisper than the rest, like it isn't quite as old? Does it have less filth in the bottom of the cuts than the rest?

As with fake inscriptions, lots of fake engraving simply looks too crisp and fresh for the gun it is being applied to. It even feels unnaturally rough when you run your finger over it. In order to combat this, engravers will sometimes lightly buff the new engraving or wash the area with acid, but this often makes the metal with the new engraving on it have a slightly different color than the rest of the metal on the gun. Watch for this, but don't obsess. Fake engraving is expensive and therefore rare.

Look for Scratches

You can often spot fake engraving by looking for scratches that pass through the cuts. On engraving done when the gun was brand new, any scratches should pass right through the cuts. On more recent engraving, sometimes you can see where there were scratches underneath the engraving...in other words, the engraving cuts through the scratches, rather than the other way around. Look at the little "lips" at the edges of the engraving cuts… any post-engraving scratches should cut into these lips, which are called the burr. If the burrs (which sometimes appear on both sides of the cut, and sometimes on just one side) are intact, then the scratch likely pre-dates the engraving. Some legitimate historical engraving was done after a gun was used for a while, so this does not prove that the engraving is modern, but it is certainly a useful warning sign to look for.

The burrs, as described above, are often polished down so the engraving won't look so raw and fresh, but any pre-existing scratches will still stop before the lips of the cuts and not run through them. This is best seen under magnification. The only way around this that I know of is to polish out all the scratches, which will either give the metal a different color and texture in that area or require refinishing to cover it. Either way, the evidence will usually be there when you look for it.

150 Uneven Surfaces

Factory engraving, and even period-of-use aftermarket engraving, was almost always performed on a perfect metal surface. If the area of the gun being engraved was flat, then it is helpful to imagine that the gun was perfectly, absolutely flat when the engraving was done. There may be exceptions to this, where favorite guns were engraved after years of faithful service, but they are the exception to the rule.

Most original engraving should not fall into pitted areas or other dips in the metal. If the surface of the gun is no longer perfectly flat

It is often more difficult to tell if a scratch is under or over a stamping than it is for engraving, because engraving cuts leave a distinct burr.

Major flaws like the corroded dent in the center of this picture should be expected to cut into the engraving (or in this case, etching) rather than having the pattern descend down into the lower surface of the damaged area.

and even, then the engraving should almost always be strong in the higher spots and weak in the lower spots. The same goes for barrels and other curved areas that may have had their shapes changed by rubbing over the years. Any damage or wear that happened to the gun should also have happened to the engraving. In other words, the engraving should follow the contours of the gun's original surface, not the contours of any defects that presumably took place many decades after the work was supposedly done.

This Remington New Model Police has genuine factory engraving. Notice that the engraving has been rubbed and worn over years of service and cleaning. The condition of the engraving and metal surface is entirely consistent across the gun. However, the cylinder has shiny, fresh metal and crisp, clean engraving. This cylinder, and its engraving, are obviously much newer (or better preserved) than the rest of the gun. Notice also that the style of engraving on the cylinder is not consistent in pattern or quality with that of the pistol frame. This cylinder is a modern replacement. (Photo courtesy of Roy Marcot)

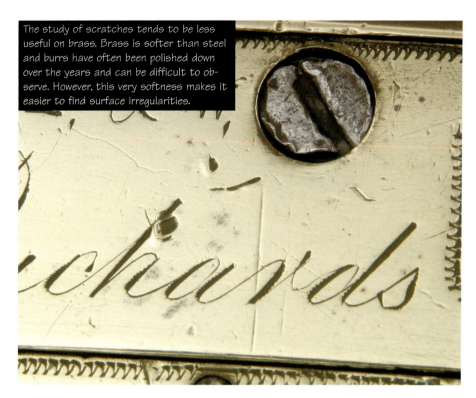

The study of scratches tends to be less useful on brass. Brass is softer than steel and burrs have often been polished down over the years and can be difficult to observe. However, this very softness makes it easier to find surface irregularities.

151 Factory Records — A Great Resource

If there are factory shipping records, do their listings for the gun indicate the quality and quantity of engraving that you see on the gun today? Be particularly suspicious if the gun is a Winchester and the factory record shows that your engraved gun should not have any engraving at all. Winchester records are unusually accurate and complete, and while a disparity between the gun and the records may not totally condemn the piece, it certainly is a huge "red flag."

152 Refreshed Engraving

Be aware that some collectors, dealers and collecting associations do not believe that it is dishonest to refresh engraving. But I think they are wrong.

Notice how this engraving looks like it was engraved right over the corroded metal surface of the lockplate. Examine such engraving very carefully.
(Courtesy of the Colonial Williamsburg Foundation)

Examining a Gun

This is a much more deceptive example of refreshed engraving that carefully follows the contours of the original cuts and would be almost impossible to spot. In this case, the owner sent the gun in to have a stock crack repaired, and the workman decided to refresh the engraving and perform other unrequested restorations "while it was in the shop." This was a very generous thing to do, but it was not what the owner wanted. I am aware of numerous times where these kinds of unauthorized "improvements" have been done by overenthusiastic gunsmiths, and would recommend that customers ordering repairs be very specific in their instructions. *(Bill Ahearn)*

What "refreshed engraving" means is that the original engraving (usually markings, like maker's name and address, military units, etc.) became faint with wear, and a modern engraver was hired to trace over the original engraving to make it clear and readable again.

Most veteran collectors and dealers, myself included, strongly disapprove of refreshed engraving. On the surface, it sounds harmless because it is not misrepresenting anything critical about the gun. However, once the engraving has been refreshed, how can you tell for sure what was under there in the first place. In the end, it makes me distrust what would otherwise be perfectly true and important information.

153 Detecting Refreshed Engraving

Thankfully, most refreshed engraving is shockingly easy to identify. This is because, in order for the gun to require refreshing, it was probably in pretty poor condition to start out with. So what you end up with is a totally worn gun with brand, spanking new engraving. This is really, really easy to spot once you start looking for it. It is most common on Brown Besses and other flintlock and percussion military longarms that bear regimental or other important marks indicating where they were made or who used them.

Of course, sometimes refreshed engraving is just part of a comprehensive restoration and refinishing job, in which case a low-condition gun is significantly altered to make it look factory new. This is an entirely different topic, which will be covered in some detail later on in this chapter.

Wood, Too!

The inconsistency between the condition of a metal surface and the condition of engraving as discussed above can also apply to markings in wood. For instance, if you are looking at a martial revolver with an inspector's cartouche in the grip, compare the condition of the cartouche with the overall condition of the grip itself, especially in the exact area where the cartouche was applied. If the grip's wooden surface is worn down but the marking struck into it is unbroken and perfect, you probably have a problem.

Stamping is Stamping, Engraving is Engraving

Some marks on factory-made guns should be stamped from dies, other markings are normally engraved. Learn the difference. For instance, if the serial number should be stamped, but the example you are looking at is

The serial numbers on most firearms should be stamped, rather than engraved. Engraved serial numbers are often a warning sign to inspect such firearms further. Also notice in this photograph the scratch on the right-hand side, which cuts through the finish and exposes bare metal — which is normal for weapons with original finish. Also, notice that the edges of the cylinder flutes have had their blue worn off. The finish on sharp, exposed areas is often rubbed off from repeated polishing. This is to be expected, even on fine condition firearms.

Examining a Gun

engraved, something could be very, very wrong.

Once you become experienced at studying the physical surfaces of guns, you will almost immediately recognize the difference between a stamped mark and an engraved one. You might get fooled with the naked eye in a dim room, but with good lighting and magnification, you will quickly master this critical skill. Look, in particular, at the lips and the side walls of the marks. Sit down with some guns where you know for sure which were stamped and which were engraved, and learn the difference in appearance between the two. It isn't very tricky and it might save you a pile of grief down the road.

Pantograph Engraving

Some of the worst fake engraving is done using pantograph engraving machines. If you want to see a pantograph, just visit one of those quick-engraving shops that puts initials on belt buckles, etc. They probably use one.

Work done with these machines can sometimes look pretty raw, choppy and lack the proper depth, especially when it is used to copy die stamping (like serial numbers). Perhaps the most noticeable feature of inexpert pantograph engraving is that all the cuts are at an identical and shallow depth. The human hand, even the hand of a master engraver, can't replicate this. The hand will always cut at varying depths — sort of like how you push down harder on certain strokes when writing in script with a pen. Most pantograph work doesn't look like that and has no dynamics. It is shallow, and all the cuts are at an absolutely level depth. The width of the strokes doesn't vary much either, the way traditional engraving does. It almost screams "fake" at you.

However, there are a few expert pantograph technicians out there producing moderately convincing copies of period barrel addresses, etc., either on newly made parts or to refresh the engraving and stamping on heavily worn or refinished guns. I won't tell you how, because I don't want to spread the problem. Luckily, even the best fake/restored pantograph engraving tends to look kind of sharp-edged when it comes out of these machines, and manual polishing or acidic washes are necessary to give the letters a properly aged look. These treatments leave behind their own kind of evidence.

The use of pantograph engraving is most common on medium-priced guns — like many Colts and Lugers — where markings are an important part of the value but where custom, hammer-driven hand-engraving by a master craftsman might be too pricey.

Computerized Laser Engraving

It used to be considerable extra work for deep stamping, like most serial numbers, to be replicated. A custom die with a limited life span would be required. Effectively copying stampings was, therefore, relatively expensive and often was not very convincing. Unfortunately, these deep stamps can now be copied at full depth and shocking accuracy with a laser engraving machine. These laser engravers have been used to forge some of the rarest die stamps in gun collecting, such as Confederate marks.

If you get a chance to examine a fake stamping that has been created with a laser engraver, take advantage of the opportunity and study it under high magnification. Depending on how the work was done, the inside walls of the "stamping" might look either melted or unnaturally straight, with very sharp corners at the floor of the marking, as if the mark had been cut rather than stamped. This, of course, is exactly what a laser does. Laser cut "stampings" also do not affect the area around the mark in the way that a die stamp will. When you pound into metal with a die, the metal right around the mark will be disturbed slightly. Since the laser cuts right into metal, there is no "splash" (so to speak) with a laser engraving.

Despite the tips just mentioned, these fake marks can be really tough to spot. Perhaps the biggest challenge presented by these machines is that they can be used to replicate broken letters from old dies, which is a way that Colt collectors in particular assign dates to some of the rarer models of revolver. However, under magnification, the edges will not appear as smooth as genuine die marks and the shapes of the letters often lack complexity. Of course, gun restorers often make dies of their own, but that's another story.

How Do You Know It's Refinished?

I won't deny it — there are some pretty deceptive refinish jobs out there. The most skilled restoration artists take off all the old finish, recut all the edges so they will be sharp, have an engraver clean up all the markings, or even apply fresh stamps from their own custom-made dies, and then they apply a finish that is perfect for the age and manufacturer of the weapon in question. Some of them even go so far as to add damage, stains, scratches, dirt, grease, etc. to the gun so that you will be fooled into thinking the finish is old. This is similar to how antique furniture con artists have been known to fire shotguns into their fake furniture so that it will look like worm holes. (The trick to detecting this, by the way, is to stick a toothpick into the holes in the wood…insects don't generally bore in a straight line, but shotgun pellets invariably do.)

Expert collectors and dealers seem to know instinctively whether a gun has been refinished. But it isn't instinct or magic that they are using — it's simple observation.

159 Look "Under" the Blue

Here's a great trick for you. When you look at really old blued finishes with a flashlight or strong natural lighting, you will often notice that the blue itself is not solid — even on guns that might otherwise appear to have perfect 100% finish under "normal" interior lighting.

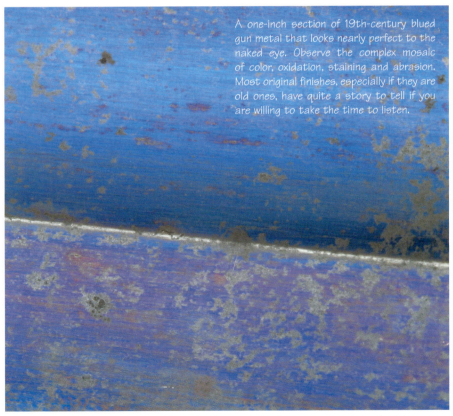

A one-inch section of 19th-century blued gun metal that looks nearly perfect to the naked eye. Observe the complex mosaic of color, oxidation, staining and abrasion. Most original finishes, especially if they are old ones, have quite a story to tell if you are willing to take the time to listen.

Most antique gun finishes are less "solid" than you think they are — as shown by this extreme enlargement. Good light and magnification often reveal a purple color coming through the blue, and this should not be regarded as a bad thing because it would be difficult to fake.

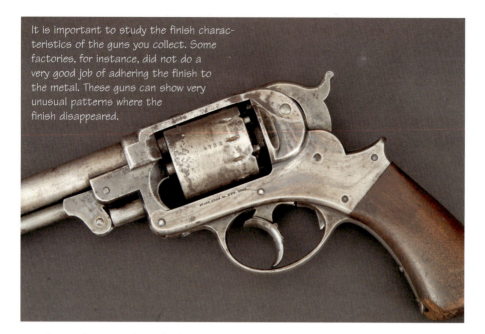

It is important to study the finish characteristics of the guns you collect. Some factories, for instance, did not do a very good job of adhering the finish to the metal. These guns can show very unusual patterns where the finish disappeared.

Sure, the metal might be more-or-less covered with finish, but the really bright, reflective color of blue might only be preserved in spots here and there. The rest of the finish often looks purple and certainly not as shiny as the better-preserved spots — almost as if the purple is a coating under the bright blue portions. On higher condition guns, this effect will be reversed, with the purple spots being in the minority and most of the finish consisting of bright, shiny blue.

This is not a problem with your gun! It is a natural part of the ageing of the finish, and in fact, is a good indicator that the finish is original or at least a very old period-of-use refinish. It would be quite difficult for a modern refinisher to reproduce this effect.

The Layered Look

For beginning collectors, this is almost certainly the single most important entry in this book. *So pay attention.*

Let's start with the concept that things happen to a gun in succession. Think of a gun in layers — imagine the walls of the Grand Canyon. Recent additions have to go on top of earlier ones. Just like an archaeologist who can date recovered artifacts by how deep down they were found in the dirt, a gun collector needs to do the same thing when examining guns. Pay a great deal of attention to what is either under or on top of a gun's finish.

A Model 1897 Winchester shotgun in very nice, little-used condition. Notice bare metal coming through in the areas of wear or damage. Also notice that even guns that are in excellent shape usually have slight variations in finish color due to age and use. For the most part, only firearms with absolutely perfect condition and flawless storage from the time they left the factory should have totally solid finish with no variations in tone. This M1897 is yet another example of how bright, neutral lighting can make even the best gun look a little ragged.

(left) Serial numbers on a refinished Marlin.
(above) The dent along the top edge of this pistol has been filled with refinish.

For instance, if you see worn, old-looking engraving under a brand new blue finish, how could it possibly have gotten there unless the finish is a modern restoration? The engraving is worn, so it seems to be old, but the finish on top is brand new! Why isn't the finish scratched up and rubbed off like the engraving? It just doesn't make sense.

Likewise, if there are pits, dents, scratches or other signs of damage under the finish, then the finish itself must surely have been applied after the damage took place, and is, therefore, a telltale sign of refinishing. With remarkably few exceptions, factories did not apply finish to their guns unless the underlying surface was more-or-less perfect. Understanding this one concept is almost sure to save you a huge amount of money over your collecting career.

A refinished gun — up close and personal. Notice that the edges are softened from buffing.

Examining a Gun

Very close view of the original finish on a M1917 Colt revolver. The actual "naked eye" appearance of this pistol is a lot darker than what you see here. Notice the numerous small scratches in the thin layer of black-colored finish. Red-colored oxidation is beginning to show through the scratches. All of the pistol's edges are crisp and sharp, but even though this gun is in excellent condition these edges have had the finish rubbed off of them. The points of the checkering on the thumb lever also lack finish, and the checkering tips are appropriately rubbed down.

161 Buffing and Stripping

In order to remove signs of corrosion and damage before applying a fresh finish, restorers will usually grind and polish the metal surface. This removes one form of evidence that the gun is refinished but at the same time creates another. This buffing will blur or remove depth from engraving and stampings and make the edges of the gun itself dull and rounded rather than sharp and crisp. There is no way to heavily polish metal without removing some of the surface, and often this work is done in a ham-fisted manner that anyone will spot immediately.

And remember, if you are going to put on new finish, you usually have to remove what is left of the old...which means more buffing or erosive chemical treatments that take away plenty of the original surface metal, leaving yet more evidence that something has been done. That's why the high-end restorers often end up re-grinding the surface of the whole gun, making the edges sharp again, and then having all of the markings and engraving recut so that they will look consistent with the brand new finish that they are about to apply.

When guns with close manufacturing tolerances are refinished, often the buffing will make the refinished parts reassemble too loosely — showing gaps between parts where they should not exist. On some pistols where the exterior dimensions of the parts are well known and reliable, collectors have been known to measure parts that often see the most buffing to see if the thickness of the metal has been reduced.

Fit and Refinish

When inexpert workmen perform the buffing and stripping described above, they often create a gun whose parts no longer fit together properly. This is especially true of high-end revolvers. A truly well-made revolver, like a Smith & Wesson, should assemble almost seamlessly. The different parts should butt up against each other with no noticeable space between them... metal fitting perfectly against metal.

The buffing performed during refinishing often removes enough material at the edges of a revolver's parts to create noticeable spaces between them when reassembled.

Close-up area of a gun that was buffed before refinishing.

Examining a Gun

Flat areas, especially if they are made of very hard metal or have deep corrosion, can be difficult for refinishers to keep perfectly smooth. Notice the "waves" in the metal between the "03" mark and the "byf" mark that are evidence of uneven polishing. Another thing to note on this refinished Luger are the remains of numerous buffed-out rust pits filled with refinish.

163 Check Out the Flat Surfaces

Another thing to look for is that unskilled refinishers will often buff the gun in an uneven manner, so that the flat areas of the gun aren't quite flat anymore. Almost all factory guns will have nearly perfect flat areas...you should not expect to see undulation in the metal. When a gun has a reflective finish, this kind of irregularity can be highly noticeable, and on bright bluing this sometimes makes areas of the finish appear darker than other parts — especially when viewed in good light at an angle.

Screw holes aren't the only part of a gun that can get "dished" during refinishing. Notice the misshapen cylinder flutes on this refinished M1895 Nagant revolver. Also notice the rough polishing marks on the metal, running in various conflicting directions, and the deep gouges that are filled with fresh black refinish. Test your observation skills on rough, utilitarian refinishes like this one before trying to identify the work of a skilled professional firearms restorer.

164 Dished Screw Holes

Another area that should usually be flat but can be affected by buffing are the edges of screw holes. Buffing materials will often enter the hole, widening the opening and hollowing things out a little. If this happens, the screw hole is described as "dished" and it is yet one more thing that might indicate refinishing.

165 Are the Barrel Edges Straight?

On guns made during the modern era, the exterior sides of the barrels are usually pretty darned straight. When guns are refinished, it is difficult to buff the barrel sides in a perfectly even fashion, and shallow areas will often develop. Put a metal ruler along the edge. Are there dips and undulations? This could be a warning sign that work was done here.

166 Dings

Sharp edges on guns almost always pick up dings. These little dents can actually go quite deep into the

(top) A ding that has been filled with refinish along the edge of a pistol. *(bottom)* Another edge on the same pistol. Notice that these dings took place after the refinish and show damage through to the bare metal. Nearby scratches also took place after the refinish. "Good" scratches and dings do not prove that a gun has original finish, because the damage could easily have taken place afterwords. You cannot use evidence of this kind to prove that a gun has original finish — it only works the other way around.

Another example of dents filled with finish, this time in an extreme close-up photograph of a refinished World War I military rifle. Notice white scratches from after the refinish.

metal from two directions, and this makes them challenging for a refinisher. Because of this, many refinishers choose to let them go and they end up being covered with the newly applied finish. Dings made on guns with original finish should not usually have finish inside of the wound, so looking for dings with finish in them can be a great way to identify refinish jobs. However, be aware that some folks have done spot repairs for dings and scratches, in which instance the overall finish might actually be original. Spot repairs of this type are almost always easy to detect and do not properly match the rest of the gun's finish.

Also, some refinishers, especially those working on guns with octagonal barrels, try to bang the dings back into place using a hammer and a flat-nosed tool like a punch, rather than grinding them out. This pushes the metal back where they want it to go, and they clean the spot up afterwords using a file, but this tends to leave scarring of its own on all but the most careful work. Because of their numerous sharp edges, opportunities for pitting and usually the presence of many stamped markings, octagonal barrels remain an excellent place to look for evidence of refinishing.

167 Excellent Condition Guns Should Have Crisp Markings

When a gun is ground and polished prior to refinishing, this wears away at all engraving and stampings. On truly comprehensive refinishing jobs, these markings will be restamped or reengraved. However, on garden-variety refinished guns, the markings will be left shallow or "mushy" and not be recut before the new finish is applied.

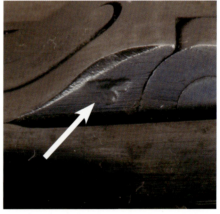

Whoa! Look out! Stampings that have been almost entirely buffed out like this are a sure sign that the gun was refinished. A refinished gun might be acceptable to you, but you should know before you buy.

So if you see a gun with a new finish but smudgy or shallow markings, it is time to pay attention. Be especially aware if one portion of the lettering lacks the depth of the rest. Sometimes the whole tops of letters will be buffed out. On barrel tops, it is often the very center of the letters that are ground down the most.

This is a classic way to identify refinishing, but it can be more complicated than you think. Are the letters really just filled up with crud rather than actually being shallow? Were the marks irregularly stamped or shallow in the first place? This is when knowing from experience how a factory-original gun's markings should look comes in handy. If you don't have this kind of experience, then shallow markings might just be a reason why you should look for more difinitive signs of refinishing on

Stampings on a barrel top that were thinned out by polishing during the refinishing process.

other parts of the gun.

In general, the best markings to look at are stampings that were applied at the factory or by government inspectors after the original finish was applied. When you run your finger over these stampings on guns that are in well-preserved condition, you should feel the crisp, raised edges of the letters rather than perfect smoothness. This is a good sign that the markings were not buffed for refinishing.

168 Price Cannot be a Conclusive Guide

If you think that only really expensive guns can have serial numbers and other markings restruck as part of refinishing, think again. There are companies out there that are refinishing mismatched, inexpensive 98k carbines, including restriking all of the serial numbers to match and applying fresh waff-enampt marks that are correct for the carbine's date and location of manufacture.

169 Signs of Heavy Use

It is much more work to replace missing metal with welding during restoration than to simply buff it down and apply a new finish. For each category of gun, there are places where regular use will corrode or wear away the metal. It might be the touch hole area on a flintlock or the cone on revolvers. If a gun is supposed to be in unfired condition and has perfect finish to match, you should not see inconsistent damage in these areas.

Similarly, if the bore is shot out, the exterior of the gun should not be brand new and appear unfired...it just doesn't make sense. I am sure that there are some scenarios where this could theoretically happen, but they would be unlikely, to say the least. However, do not confuse this shot-out bore condition that we are talking about with guns that were fired once or twice and then not cleaned for years, leaving a mess of corrosion near the breech. This is different, and while unlikely, can theoretically be consistent with an otherwise mint-condition gun.

Look Under the Grips

Restoration and refinishing is a very labor-intensive project. Only the most fastidious workman will go to great lengths to do a perfect job in places that are not immediately visible. On pistols, the quickest spot to look for this kind of sloppiness is under the grips. On a high-condition gun, there should not be pitting or other corrosion damage to the metal surfaces that are protected by the grips — at least not in most circumstances. And there certainly should not be blued-over pits under the grips. Looking for blued-over damage under the grips might be the single fastest way to identify most high-quality refinish jobs.

More from Under the Grips

Another good reason to remove the grips would be to inspect the grips themselves. Many collectible revolvers were shipped with checkered gutta-percha grips. This material is particularly fragile, and lots of these grips have broken over the years. On higher-end revolvers, especially, convincing replacements can be difficult to come by, and restorers have resorted to some very creative and labor-intensive repairs. These repairs usually involve taking two or three broken pieces and joining them together to make one good replacement grip. This might sound like "mission impossible," but with careful matching of colors and a lot of delicate filing, the best of these repairs are totally convincing from the outside. The underside, however, will always show strong evidence of the repair that was done.

Other Hidden Areas

You can learn a lot about a gun by studying the interior nooks and crannies where it is difficult or inconvenient for a restorer to work. Heck, you can even learn a lot by studying the nooks and crannies of the *exterior* of a gun. These

Another look at a sloppily refinished revolver. The white arrow points to a hollowed-out area where two pieces of metal meet. This hard-to-reach area is filled with corrosion pits that were not ground out before refinishing because the tight location made such work inconvenient.

are the places where pitting might have been ground or polished down, but not necessarily filled in to make the surface of the metal smooth again before refinishing. The more complex the shapes are and the tighter the corners of the surfaces, the more difficult it will be for a refinisher to make the interior of the gun look consistent with the brand, spanking renewed exterior. And since few owners are willing to spend the money necessary to make the hidden parts of the gun perfect, even the best refinishing jobs usually fall apart in these areas, unless it is an extremely expensive gun and the intent is purposeful deception.

Also, take some time to inspect the bore. Sometimes, portions of the barrel have been added to achieve a more desirable barrel length. If the work is sloppy, you might be able to see a seam where the rifling does not quite match where the patch was made. Or perhaps the condition and color won't be the same on the patched area as on the rest of the barrel interior. Either way, it is a good idea to examine the bore carefully.

Filth is Your Friend

Even relatively unused guns, unless they are brand new, will build up some oil deposits within the deepest cavities of their mechanisms. Disassemble some of the

A Professional Refinishing Case Study

Veteran collectors will notice that all of the refinished guns illustrated in this chapter fall into the "pretty obvious" category. This was done on purpose. Sometimes, it is easier to explain subtle concepts if you use exaggerated examples. The pistol lock shown here is a more deceptive refinish, but the points of interest can still be demonstrated quite clearly with photographs. The lock is from a Baker Rifle that was rebrowned and had all the engraving recut. At the same time, it was reconverted from percussion to flintlock, which means that all of the exterior lock parts except the lockplate are brand new replacements. The first thing that you should notice is that the brown finish is heavy, monochromatic and dull. It isn't entirely smooth to the touch, either. The engraving shows no wear at all, and is filled with the brown finish. Brown grease has been wedged into the nooks and crannies in an attempt to give the impression of age-old filth, but the color and consistency of the "filth" is too uniform to be genuine. The exterior of the lockplate has been buffed flat to provide a good surface for reengraving and to match the surface texture of the newly made parts, but if you look closely, you can see pock marks from extreme amounts of surface corrosion. On the interior of the lock, there are major rust pits present that are not consistent with the exterior's "new" surface. Some of these pits have been filled with brown paste in an effort to hide them, but they are still obvious if you are looking for them. While the replacement screws used on the lock's exterior are carefully shaped to look original, the interior has a modern machine screw showing.

Examining a Gun

guns in your collection and you will get an idea of what to expect.

What you *shouldn't* expect is a gun off of which you would happily eat dinner. If the interior metal parts of your gun are clean right down to their pores and have no built-up debris in their corners and remote spots, this is not normal. However, it is a great sign that the gun has been refinished.

Before gun finishes can be applied, the metal has to be cleaned and degreased or else the finish will not adhere to the metal's surface properly. In fact, this usually involves literally boiling the metal parts for an hour or more. Do your gun's parts look boiled…sterilized…steam cleaned? If so, then why?

A Photo Finish

When searching for signs of refinishing, good light and magnification are critical tools in your arsenal. If you have the gun at home, however, you might want to make the extra step of taking very high-resolution photographs and then viewing them at extreme magnification on the computer screen.

If your photo is good enough, this will give you an amazingly clear view, and you might see signs of refinishing that you would never have caught with the naked eye. For those of you looking at your pictures with the popular computer program Photoshop®, the setting that you will want to choose for most accurate appearance is "Actual Pixels," which can be found under the "View" menu. For most other programs, 400% is a good place to start.

The Different Colors of Re-Blue

Plum, electric, fire, charcoal — there are lots of colors of "blued" finish. Different factories used different bluing methods during different eras in their history, and it is your job to know what to expect on the gun you are examining. Only handling hundreds of weapons will teach you this lesson, but eventually many refinished guns will look wrong to you immediately and without your having to think about it much. However, be aware that almost all historical factory finishes can be reproduced today if the workman is informed, equipped and skilled. Check out any comprehensive gunsmithing catalog if you doubt this. Even the exact recipes used by London gunsmiths of the 1700s were recorded and are available today…so don't hang your hat entirely on the color of the finish.

Careful study of unquestionably original examples is critical to success in any collecting field. This is a Colt Experimental Shotgun, 1834–1835, made by John Pearson. *(Reproduced by permission of the Elizabeth Hart Jarvis Colt Collection [1905.1025], Wadsworth Atheneum)*

Also, different parts can have different finishes or no finish at all. Should the safety lever be blued or should it be simple, polished steel? Find out, because this stuff is important. Lots of guns that were commercially refinished during the last century were not being fixed up to sell to collectors but to make a saleable product for sporting goods stores. The workmen weren't trying to be authentic, they were trying to make the gun look relatively new and serviceable. It is often very easy to spot these refinishes if you know which color of finish should or should not be on which parts.

176 Your Nose Knows

Many guns from the late 18th and early 19th centuries had browned barrels. This beautiful finish, unfortunately, wears off easily, and quite often a "rebrowning" has been applied. The most inexpensive method of doing this often leaves a distinctive chemical smell. I can't describe the smell, but sniff a few and you will get the drift. "Cold" blue also has a peculiar scent that you will come to recognize.

Another common attribute of many inexpertly rebrowned barrels is that the finish literally feels tacky to the touch and has a heavy, clogged appearance.

Swapped Grips

One of the most common "improvements" found on collectible revolvers is swapped grips. What happens is this. Someone has two almost identical pistols, one in great condition and the other all beat up. Unfortunately, the beat-up pistol has wonderful ivory grips, and the "mint" pistol has plain wood grips. This "problem" is solved by switching grips and increasing the total value of the pistols substantially.

Back in the 1950s and 1960s, certain well-known catalog dealers literally had barrels of grips in their shops, ready to be used for replacing broken grips or upgrading plain ones. This was not considered all that controversial at the time, but today it is a real problem because there are a lot of pistols out there with fancy grips that they should not have, making a deluxe weapon out of what should be a relatively ordinary one. More recently, when the supply of loose grips started to dry up, a large number of entirely new grips were made to serve the same purpose.

How do you tell whether your revolver has the correct grips? Well, in some cases it simply doesn't matter that much. Most pistol models came with just one kind of grips, and if the grips have been replaced. it was not in an attempt to make the pistol look fancier or more valuable than it originally was. As for the replacement grips that "upgrade" the pistol, we are lucky in that many of these are Colts, and the Colt company kept records of which type of grips were shipped with each pistol. Many of these records survive today, and it is usually possible to purchase a letter from the Colt company indicating the pistol's original configuration when shipped. While the cost of these letters has increased substantially in recent years, they are often purchased by dealers and collectors in order to document that the gun is in its original, factory-shipped configuration. Letters of this type can be obtained through the Colt factory Historical Department.

Swapped grips on pistols for which you cannot acquire a factory letter are more difficult to detect, but are often the wrong grips entirely. Learn the proper grips for each model of revolver you collect and the correct grip markings that you should expect on martially marked revolvers. Also, many types of grips are only found in specific serial

Examining a Gun

number ranges. For instance, on some revolvers, early examples had wood grips, and later examples had plastic ones. If you see a plastic grip on an early pistol, it is wrong and historically impossible. On the other hand, some models of Smith & Wesson revolver often work in the other direction, with hard rubber grips appearing on the early pistols and wood grips being proper for the later ones. It is up to you to learn what to expect for the pistols that you collect.

Other parts of guns can be swapped too — most often sights that were changed by the owner to satisfy his own shooting preferences. It is best to be familiar with the original factory configuration of any gun you are purchasing in order to spot alterations of this kind, which often devalue the piece as a collectible firearm.

Grip Fit and Wood Shrinkage

Another warning that a pistol's grips might not be original is to look at their fit. If they don't fit the pistol very well, then this could be an indicator.

Often, when a pistol has wooden grips that don't fit very well, it is suggested that they might have shrunken over the years. Wood does shrink, but hardwoods like walnut often do not shrink very much. Also, the shrinkage should mostly be along the axis that crosses the grain, rather than on the axis that runs parallel to the grain.

Wood shrinks because it loses moisture over time. All wood shrinks at least a little bit. However, the wood fibers shrink much more in width than in length. So the majority of shrinkage should occur across the grain rather than over its length. Even shrinkage, being the same all around, is usually considered a bad sign.

Grip Serial Numbers

Also, on some types of pistols, the serial number should be written under the grips. This is another thing to be aware of. As usual, you will be much more successful in collecting if you learn the critical ins and outs of the guns you are purchasing.

However, it is easy to overthink this issue. Replaced grips, as long as they are of the correct period and type for the gun, are not usually a disaster and often won't affect a gun's price much, if at all.

180 Quick Test for Synthetic Ivory and Pearl Grips

Some replacement grips are made of synthetic materials meant to look like antique ivory or mother-of-pearl. These are almost always unconvincing and shouldn't fool anyone. Heck, they usually don't even fit very well.

However, if you are in doubt, tap your fingernail against it. The synthetic ones will immediately feel different than real ones, and the sound will have a more hollow, plastic quality to it. Some dealers will actually bite mother-of-pearl grips lightly or tap them against their teeth as a test, but this is probably not recommended by orthodontists!

Also, while the newer ivory look-alikes have had a fake grain added to them to give the appearance of natural variations in color, the effect is not convincing on close examination. Another thing to be aware of is that older generations of synthetic ivory would turn solid orange or yellow with age with no variations in the tone. However, since the late 1980s, better plastics have been available, and the newer versions have stable coloring and a more natural appearance.

As a historical note, there was another type of fake ivory common during the 1920s and 30s, and it was made out of milk. It was actually a very convincing copy of the real thing, but it cracked to pieces (in straight lines rather than the curved ones of genuine ivory) after about thirty years and was never used very much on firearms.

181 Grip Checkering is Usually the First to Go

If the grips or stocks have checkered wood, look at the tips of the checkering under magnification. Even on guns that are quite lightly used, there should be some amount of wear on the very tips of the checkering. These sharp tips get rubbed down very quickly.

Next, look in the pits of the checkering. These depths should be rounded out by microscopic filth that has built up over the decades. Nothing stays absolutely clean over long periods of time, and these nooks are especially good at trapping small bits of dirt.

When restored guns have

Wood checkering on used guns should not look like that above. Plastic grips, shown below, will keep their shape a bit longer.

Examining a Gun

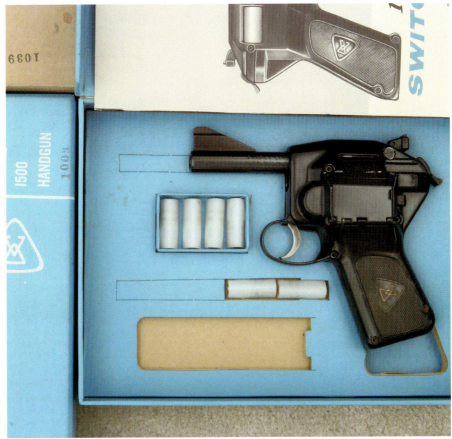

Many firearms manufacturers used very distinctive packaging and casing. This Dardick pistol is in its original blue cardboard case with dummy, triangular "tround" cartridges. In the upper left-hand corner is a portion of the original shipping box with serial number stamped in black.

replaced grips or recut checkering, the wood is often chemically clean and the checkering razor sharp. This is not normal on guns that have seen even a small amount of use or uncovered storage.

182 Is That Case Original?

Since cased or boxed guns are priced at a premium, you are often put in the position of trying to guess whether that box is original to the gun or just something that was added on in more modern times. Often, this can be "mission impossible," but there are a few things you can look for.

First of all, know which types of casings are proper for the manufacturer of your gun. Some gunmakers used very distinctive casings made especially for them, and anything out of the ordinary in this regard would definitely be a signal to be on your guard.

Also, when guns are kept in boxes or cases, they wear away at the casing material. For instance, as a duelling pistol is kept in its box, it will shift and grind away at the lining in the box's lid and floor. When you compare the highest, sharpest portions of the pistol with the wear evident in the lid's lining, they should match. If there is distinctive wear in areas of that lining where there is nothing on the gun that could have caused the damage, then the box obviously spent quite a bit of time housing another pistol than the one that is presently resting in it.

Also look carefully at the wear to the lining or partitions under and around the guns. Is it consistent with the gun's shape? What about the materials themselves? Is the wood, cardboard, baize, velvet appropriate for the kind of casing you are inspecting?

However, I wouldn't always avoid a gun in an unoriginal case just because it is not perfect for the gun. You are usually buying the case as a bonus and are more concerned with the gun, itself. Whether the case is a modern copy or an old case that has been "married" to the gun in modern times, simply be sure that you aren't paying more than the value of the gun, case and any included accessories if purchased separately.

Make sure that a supposedly original case's partitions are logical for the shape of the firearm and necessary accessories. Study wear on the lid and floor for further clues.

Examining a Gun

A Stephen Jenks musket made in Rhode Island in 1813. This musket is in its original flintlock form and shows a properly placed, though large, touch hole. This musket might actually have seen considerable firing, hence the large and irregular touch hole, despite its remarkably good condition. It is probably one of the very rare specimens that has always been well maintained. There is no appreciable pitting on the barrel at the breech.

183 Reconversions

Earlier in this book, we introduced the topic of flintlock reconversions and discussed the ethical dilemma that they present. In this section, we will address some ways that reconversions might be detected. We considered covering the use of bore scopes, x-rays and advanced laboratory tests here, but since these are beyond the budget of the average collector, we will limit ourselves to visual inspection methods.

This is a specialized topic, so I'm bringing in an expert. The whole subject will be addressed by Joseph V. Puleo, contributing technical editor of *Man at Arms for the Gun Collector* magazine. Here is what Mr. Puleo has to say:

184 Puleo on Detecting Reconversions, I
Look For Obvious Warning Signs

Reconversion (the modern practice of returning to flintlock configuration a firearm that was legitimately converted from flintlock to percussion during its working life) has been with us for many years. There are literally thousands of them out there. Whether or not a collector accepts this practice as legitimate restoration isn't part of this discussion. In any case, the neophyte collector should

The touch hole area of a reconverted Model 1795 U.S. musket. The replaced external lock parts may be antique ones and this is a job well done. Nevertheless, note the slight semi-circular seam above and to the left of the touch hole (see arrow). This is probably evidence of the drum hole having been filled with weld. Despite the excellent lock work, the barrel on this gun shows the deep pitting that is consistent with percussion ignition.

be aware of these guns and alert to their signs, because a reconverted arm is invariably worth measurably less than it would be in its original flintlock configuration.

Fortunately, most reconversions have been done by people who seem to have little appreciation for how the flintlock actually works. A glance will often betray some surprising mistakes.

185 Puleo on Detecting Reconversions, II
The Size of the Cock is Important

Look closely at the gun. It is amazing how often the cock isn't large enough to allow the flint to hit the frizzen, or conversely, is so large that there is no room for a flint to fit in the jaws and the frizzen to close.

186 Puleo on Detecting Reconversions, III
Touch Hole Location

Look at the touch hole. Often it will be off center and cleanly drilled. In order to work properly, a touch hole should be very nearly in the center of the flash pan (left to right),

The lock of a North M1813 Navy pistol. Close examination shows that the frizzen and frizzen spring screws are new — as are almost all of the other external lock parts. The barrel of this pistol was deeply pitted at the breech and shows the effects of having been filed smooth. The "touch up" browning solution used to disguise the work isn't the same color as the remainder of the barrel. Also, the touch hole is too near to the front of the pan.

with the center placed so that a line drawn across the top of the flash pan will bisect it. This is ideal, and many arms, especially American-assembled arms made from foreign parts, are not quite this precise. However, the hole should never be right at the bottom of the pan or tucked off into the front or back corner. A touch hole in these locations would hardly work.

In the vast majority of cases, the touch hole would be drilled straight into the side of the barrel. Obviously, the shortest distance the flashing powder has to travel the quicker the ignition will be, so a hole drilled at an angle is often cause for further examination. This does not disqualify a gun, however. The author has seen a very small number of original flint arms where the holes were drilled at a slight angle in order to accommodate a deep breech plug, and according to expert Pete Schmidt, angled vents can also be correct on U.S. martial arms.

Also, it should be noted that British military flintlocks contracted under the Ordnance System will sometimes have irregular touch hole location because the parts were made separately and assembled at a later time, which made exact fit difficult.

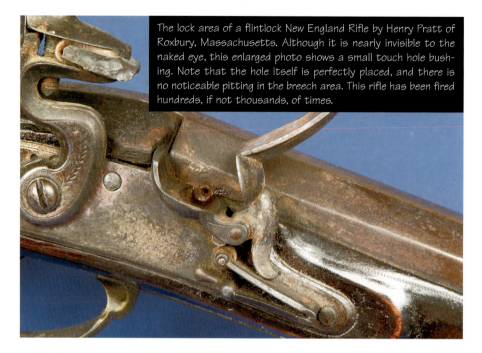

The lock area of a flintlock New England Rifle by Henry Pratt of Roxbury, Massachusetts. Although it is nearly invisible to the naked eye, this enlarged photo shows a small touch hole bushing. Note that the hole itself is perfectly placed, and there is no noticeable pitting in the breech area. This rifle has been fired hundreds, if not thousands, of times.

187 Puleo on Detecting Reconversions, IV
Touch Hole Bushings

Look for a touch hole bushing. Touch holes were bushed in period, but in those cases, the bushing is rarely more than a quarter of an inch in diameter. If the bushing is closer to three-eights or half an inch in diameter, it suggests that the drum of a "drum and nipple" conversion has been removed. Exceptions to this are the gold or platinum bushings used by many of the best English gun makers of the late 18th and early 19th centuries. If you see one of these, you'll know it. They would, in any case, be extremely expensive to reproduce and are suitable for only the highest grade of firearm. Their presence is almost a guarantee of authenticity.

188 Puleo on Detecting Reconversions, V
Touch Hole Shape

Look at the touch hole itself. The burning gasses produced when a flintlock is fired will erode the sides of the hole. The hole itself should look a little irregular and will usually be about 3/32 to a 1/16 of an inch in diameter. Military arms invariably had larger holes than sporting arms, so some judgement, acquired by looking at as many original arms as possible, is necessary.

The bottom of the flash pan may also show some corrosion, but don't be misled by pans that are deeply pitted — this can be done with acid instead of gunpowder and is not normal in well-maintained guns.

189 Puleo on Detecting Reconversions, VI
Pitting on the Right-Hand Side of the Breech

Look at the barrel on the right side. Black gunpowder is hydroscopic, meaning that it attracts water. It isn't otherwise corrosive, so even when a gun is left uncleaned it usually causes only a coating of soft rust to form on the surface of the pan and lockplate. Percussion caps, however, were very corrosive. The fulminates that produced the violent explosion necessary to fire a gun were only improved upon in the middle of the twentieth century. Up until then, they often caused severe pitting unless the gun was very carefully cleaned every time it was used. Our national pride aside, this seems to have happened very rarely. Our forefathers often didn't take particularly good care of their guns. This is a very important point. The right-hand side of a barrel, where the nipple would be located on a converted arm, almost always shows some deep pitting. This is hard, if not impossible,

The lock area of a converted M1817 Common Rifle by Johnson. It is dated 1821. The deep pitting caused by corrosive percussion caps is clear here. The remainder of this rifle shows relatively little use — or at least consistent good care — so it is reasonable to regard this degree of pitting as being fairly normal in converted arms. Black gunpowder does not usually cause this kind of deep corrosion unless it is kept in contact with the metal for a long period of time and allowed to absorb moisture.

to remove, and is the most often overlooked aspect of reconversion. Regardless of how good the lock, touch hole, pan, parts, etc., look, if the barrel is pitted on the right side for about the back half to three-quarters of an inch, be very suspicious.

Puleo on Detecting Reconversions, VII
Off-the-Shelf Lock Parts

Look at the lock parts themselves. In order to produce a reconversion, it's necessary to add a cock, frizzen, pan and frizzen spring to the lock plate along with their necessary screws. These are sold by any number of companies today and are usually made of investment-cast steel. Properly finished, they are difficult for the new collector to detect, though with experience and observation, you will often be able to recognize new parts from twenty feet away. For this reason, there is a considerable trade in original parts since, well-handled, these are much more difficult to detect. To begin with, I suggest that the new enthusiast visit tables at antique gun shows that sell replacement parts. You don't have to buy them, just look carefully and get a feel for what they look like. You'll be surprised how quickly you'll be able to recognize a newly made screw or frizzen spring.

If you point these out to some vendors, they'll allow that the parts are replaced, but the gun is still in "original flint." While this is not impossible, it is very unlikely unless the replaced lock parts we are talking about are the cocks, which often broke at the neck, or the top jaw and top jaw screw, which were often lost. Those immediately noticeable are the ones where no attempt at all has been made to match the style of the cock to the lock. This is actually a good sign that the gun is original (other things being correct also), because the modern "restorer" is unlikely to purposely mismatch the parts like this.

Puleo on Detecting Reconversions, VIII
Study the Frizzen's Face

Look at the face of the frizzen. In order for a flintlock to work, the face of the frizzen (or battery) must be hard. When the flint, which is also very hard and sharp, hits this face, it sheers off microscopic pieces of metal so small that they are heated nearly white hot by the friction. This is what we see as sparks. If the face of the frizzen is soft, the flint will scratch it, but the pieces it rubs off will be too large to be affected by the friction. There will be no sparks.

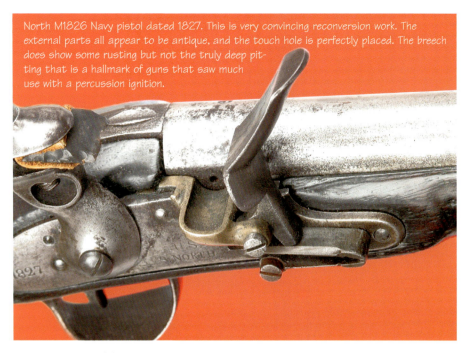

North M1826 Navy pistol dated 1827. This is very convincing reconversion work. The external parts all appear to be antique, and the touch hole is perfectly placed. The breech does show some rusting but not the truly deep pitting that is a hallmark of guns that saw much use with a percussion ignition.

It is unreasonable to expect that a vendor will allow you to snap a flint on the floor of a gun show, but you should certainly examine the face of the frizzen. The marks of the flint on a properly hardened frizzen look more like polishing than abrasions. If there are noticeable deep vertical lines scratched on the frizzen, or more likely, no marks at all, it is possible that the frizzen is soft and of recent manufacture. Original frizzens on well-used arms will often have a slight dent in their faces at precisely the place where the flint strikes. This is a good sign, but it must also correspond to where the flint would actually make contact. Remember, no matter how well a gun has been taken care of, every time it went off, the frizzen was struck. This is one part that MUST show some wear unless it is obvious that the entire arm remains in unused condition.

A good thing to look for on a well-used flintlock is a "shoe" on the frizzen. Since a tiny amount of metal was removed from the face each time the gun was fired, it was quite possible to wear a frizzen out. The hardening process affected only the surface of the metal, and when a frizzen wore out, it was fairly common to repair it by attaching a thin piece of hardened metal to the face in order to restore its sparking qualities. This is a reasonably difficult procedure and one that was only carried out on arms that saw a great deal of use — so a "shoe" on the frizzen is a good indicator (but not an infallible one) that the lock has not been tampered with in modern times.

An example of what to look for on the inside of a reconverted lock. In this case, the brass flash pan insert isn't flush with the inside of the lockplate. This is important, because any gap here would have allowed fouling to get into the works of the lock, which would mean extra cleaning for the gun's owner. Workmanship done during the historical period, when the gun was actually expected to operate as a working firearm, will rarely show a sloppy fit in this area. Also, note that the frizzen screw protrudes through the lockplate, when it should actually fit flush. The lock is from a North M1826 Navy pistol.

Puleo on Detecting Reconversions, IX
The Lock's Interior

If you're still wondering, take the lock out. Very few vendors will object to this, and if they do, have them do it themselves. If they won't, don't buy it. American martial flintlocks had detachable flash pans — iron on the earliest specimens and brass later on. Properly finished, these are difficult to detect. The most commonly overlooked detail is that the section of the pan on the inside of the lockplate MUST be absolutely flush with the double thick boss that the frizzen screw passes through. The whole idea of the thick portion of the lockplate was to keep powder fouling out of the lock mortise. On original flint guns this section should presumably be as flush with and tight against the barrel as is humanly possible.

Nearly all other flintlocks had pans that were forged as one piece with the lockplate. These are not easy to fix and, no matter how good the outside of the lockplate looks, there are often signs of welding and filing on the inside.

193

Puleo on Detecting Reconversions, X
U.S. Martial Arms — Special Considerations

A word about U.S. martial arms. The earliest flintlocks — French arms acquired during the Revolution, the M1795s and the muskets made to supply the states under the Militia Act of 1808 — were nearly all condemned and sold into the civilian market. These almost invariably received "drum and nipple" conversions. The later flintlocks, especially the M1835 arms, were held in storage and few were issued in original flintlock. When the percussion system was adopted, most of them were in new or very nearly new condition and were altered by the so-called "Belgian" or "Government conversion" method, which involved making a new hammer, filling the pan recess with a brass blank to take the place of the flash pan (on some examples the original pan was milled flat and a small insert added to fill up the remaining profile of the pan) and the barrel drilled in a special fixture to receive the nipple. Nearly all of these arms were issued during the first year or two of the Civil War. Grant even makes the comment that at Vicksburg most of his troops were armed "with the old U.S. musket changed over to percussion." These arms nearly always show wear from that service. Since practically none were issued as flintlocks, only a few have survived this way and these are virtually always in extremely good condition. An M1835 showing evidence of having been issued, but still in flintlock, is pretty unlikely. Certainly, a few may exist, but on the whole they should be treated with caution.

Also, in order to alter an arm with one of these "Belgian" conversions, it is necessary to fill and weld over the hole where the nipple was. This necessitates filing the barrel smooth at the breech and drilling a new touch hole. If done extremely well, this is hard to detect with the naked eye, so the overall condition of the rest of the gun becomes a valuable indicator. A bore light that can illuminate the breech area from the inside is very useful in detecting this kind of work. If the gun is a reconversion, there will very likely be lumps of metal from filling up the nipple hole protruding into the chamber. A look at the inside of the lock is also essential, but since these arms also had the removable brass pans, it is easier to disguise work in this area. The bore light is also valuable for examining other suspected reconversions but, given the number of mistakes most reconverters make, is often not necessary. Also, because of where the nipple on one of these Government conversions is located, the breech area is almost always noticeably pitted.

The inside of the lock on the 1827-dated M1826 North Navy pistol. Note that the parts are stamped with a small "P", including the brass flash pan. The stamping on the flash pan, however, appears to have been done with a different die than the other parts — notice the variation in the width of the loop on the "P". The frizzen screw on this lock is below the surface of the lockplate, and everything fits flush against the barrel. The slightly less-than-perfect fit of the brass pan to the lockplate, and the fact that the inside edge of the frizzen appears to have been filed, indicate modern work. However, these are borderline cases. Sometimes it just isn't possible to be completely certain whether a gun is a reconversion or simply an original flintlock ignition that displays some innocent irregularities.

Puleo on Detecting Reconversions, XI
Pistols

All of the above suggestions hold equally true for pistols, except that, because of their short barrels, it is often much easier to examine the inside of the barrel. Where guns show burn wear at the touch hole, which they should if they have seen service, look to see if the inside of the touch hole is worn. The same hot gasses are acting on both ends of the hole, so it's an obvious problem if the outside is worn and the inside is clean and new.

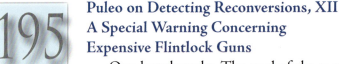

Puleo on Detecting Reconversions, XII
A Special Warning Concerning
Expensive Flintlock Guns

One last thought. The goal of the reconverter, altruistic or not, was to make the arm look as he believed it to look when it was made. There are folks out there who are very good at this, and it would be the rare collector who has never been fooled. Fortunately, the services of mechanics of this order do not come cheap, so it would be unusual to see such work carried out on arms that are not, intrinsically, of great worth. The more expensive the piece, the more careful the collector needs to be.

Slam-Dunk Reconversion Identification

Mr. Puleo's discussion above covers some of the more sophisticated reconversions encountered today. Be aware, however, that plenty of them are just plain awful and won't require that much study.

For instance, many reconversions have barrels where proof markings or manufacturers' addresses have been partially cut off due to the fact that the breech was removed during the percussion conversion process. Naturally, this would not be expected on a genuine original-flintlock gun. Also, we often see reconversions where the percussion touch hole was filled and a new vent drilled to match the new flintlock pan location. Some reconverters make little effort to hide this work, and you will see a circular section of barrel that is a different color or texture than the rest of the surrounding metal. This, of course, is a dead giveaway.

On the other end of the spectrum, there are some classes of guns that have seen extremely high-end reconversion work because of the premium paid for original flint guns. It is doubtful that visual inspection

It is practically never this easy! The reconverter of this M1795 musket has gone to the effort of marking this lock with his name and the date. It is the author's opinion that this is the only really ethical response to the questions raised by this type of "restoration." This approach, however, is not one shared by very many of the mechanics performing reconversions today.

165   *Examining a Gun*

of the gun's exterior will be enough in these cases. U.S. Martial Flintlock pistols and "Kentucky" rifles/pistols immediately come to mind. If you collect in these areas (especially the pistols) you should consider buying a borescope. These devices are covered in a later chapter, and while expensive, they can quickly pay for themselves by saving you from uninformed purchases.

Other Kinds of Reconversions

Flintlocks aren't the only firearms that can be reconverted. We also see this on percussion pistols that were once converted to cartridge and on guns that were rechambered for a new cartridge during their period of use.

Here's a great example from my friend Frank Graves. Frank likes the Winchester 1866, but he has noticed a lot of novice collectors being fooled by guns that were converted from .44 rimfire to .44-40 centerfire during their working lives. The .44-40 was a superior cartridge and lots of old time shooters converted their guns to centerfire by (1) replacing the firing pin with one that had a single protrusion at its center, discarding the "double-firing pinned" original that struck both sides of the rimfire cartridge, and (2) by boring the breech of the barrel to accept the slightly larger-sized cartridge case used by the centerfire cartridge.

As one would imagine, these converted guns are less desirable today than those in original configuration. So lots of them have been reconverted to enhance their value. It is relatively easy to put a firing pin of proper configuration back, but not so easy to return the bore to its original profile. Many unexperienced collectors will look at the front of the bolt, see the proper configuration firing pin and be satisfied — but they fail to check the bore. Experienced collectors carry EMPTY cartridge cases for both types of cartridge so that they can easily check the bores without endangering the gun or their wallets. This is a great little trick.

Learn from Other Collectors

If I have one last hint to go in this section about inspecting guns for purchase, it would be to communicate with your fellow collectors. Most veteran collectors are more than willing to show a polite newcomer the ropes. And it is a lot easier to fool one person than to fool four or five.

When a new kind of fakery is observed, it will be the buzz of the gun show and the hottest topic for club newsletters. But if you fail to communicate and are not informed, you might make yourself an easy target.

Want an example? Sure you do! During the last two decades of the 1800s, and until c.1905, Colt made a series of shipping boxes with a picture of the pistol on the lid. Appropriately enough, these are called "picture boxes." Because they were made from pasteboard, they don't have a high survival rate and are sought after by collectors.

Well, like bees to honey the fakers came along and started to make reproductions that were often sold as originals. These copies weren't very good at all, having two-part construction rather than the hinged lids of the original Colt boxes. Many of them also had incorrect dimensions, most specifically the depth. Almost instantly, these fake boxes became notorious — to the point where they were something of a laughing stock. But believe it or not, despite the fact that they are made wrong and have been widely publicized, there are lots of collectors out there who are still buying them as authentic.

Consult with your friends, talk to dealers, join clubs, subscribe to magazines and sign up for Internet chat groups. Not only will you protect yourself, you will also meet some wonderful people…our hobby is full of them.

Have I Scared You Enough Yet?

Do all of these warnings and tips make you a little sick to your stomach? Are you wondering whether it's really worth getting involved in gun collecting if you have to approach every purchase like some sort of hyperactive Sherlock Holmes? Don't fall prey to those negative thoughts! The vast, whopping majority of guns that you will see for sale by reputable dealers, specialist auction houses and at gun shows are just fine. Some may show a little damage or honest repairs, but nothing that would stop you from making a purchase. If I were to guess, I would say that only about one out of every 500 guns that you will see for sale has been "messed with" in a way that should concern you. Please, take the time to study every purchase and protect yourself, but don't overestimate the situation, either.

Still feeling nervous? Well, some folks would rather reduce the risk even further and not have to worry much at all. The solution is quite simple. Stay away from trendy or popular guns where there aren't enough acceptable pieces to go around. If there is a good supply of the types of guns that you are collecting, then it seems less likely that someone will spend their hard-earned money "improving" the lesser examples.

Another approach that might let you relax a little is to collect guns that aren't in perfect condition. If you are willing to let a gun wear its history on its sleeve, then you probably aren't going to end up with many fakes. Heck, even if you relegated yourself to guns with no more than 85% finish (which can be a very presentable and good-looking gun), you would still avoid the whopping bulk of the refinished, over-restored and fraudulent guns out there. It's definitely worth thinking about.

If you do want to pursue the perfect and the popular, we definitely recommend that you cultivate relationships with specialized, nationally known dealers who are willing to stand behind what they sell. Use their expertise — it is usually worth paying for.

Rust and Other Evils

How the Old Timers Did Things: A History Lesson

Back in the "bad old days," collectors did all sorts of misguided things to their gun collections. Most of these mistakes involved either overenthusiastic cleaning or poor storage.

It isn't that they were being sloppy or lazy — it was just that they didn't know any better. Collectors fifty years from now will probably think the same way about us. For instance, back in the old days, a shiny gun was often considered a good gun. It was entirely common to soak gun parts in Naval Jelly to remove the rust and then buff the heck out of them with an electric polishing wheel. Lots of guns were "cleaned" in this way until they retained few of their original surface details and were so loose that you could see huge gaps between the parts.

The more thoughtful collectors of the day stayed away from these practices, but often did other frustrating things like painting their guns black or covering them with rust-inhibiting linseed oils or lacquers that were not clear or stable. Lots of these guns today have a gummy orange coating on them from this treatment, which can be difficult to remove without strong chemicals, but at least it didn't strip off any of the gun's details and preserved it (if in an ugly fashion) for today's generation.

Removing Corrosion — Easy Does it!

Our job as modern collectors is to learn from the mistakes of our elders. Do you have a collectible weapon that is a bit gray and dull with age but isn't actively rusting? No problem. Leave it that way!

All too often I meet collectors who have polished their guns to the point where markings have been diminished, edges are smooth and (in

It is easy to rub away attractive engraving like this if you aren't careful.

extreme cases) the parts are loose and no longer fit together properly. Those sound strangely like the mistakes of past generations that we just described in the previous entry, don't they? Let's not repeat those mistakes!

Your guns are not the kitchen counter; you don't need to be able to eat off of them or make them shine. Cleaning and preserving is great... polishing or shining is generally a bad idea.

Overcleaning

If you have original finish on a gun, do all you can to preserve it. I know this seems obvious, but some collectors just can't resist the urge to make their guns shiny at the expense of patina. This is a common mistake of beginning collectors. My dad, who was a collector going back to the 1930s, made this mistake on his very first purchase.

Back at the height of the Depression, when my father was eleven, his mother let him buy a Hotchkiss carbine from a local pawn shop for three dollars. The gun was in original condition, but the finish had become dull with age. This did not match what he, as a youngster, expected a gun to look like. So he stayed up until the late hours of the night polishing off all of the original finish and making the gun shiny all over — something that he eventually learned to regret.

Remember, it is better to have a nice dull gray patina than a shiny surface where one does not belong. Every time you shine steel, you are removing some of the original surface...scraping away the firearm's history bit by bit. A gun that has been overcleaned is much less valuable than a gun that has never been cleaned at all. Too many weapons have lost their original surfaces because their owners just didn't think it looked exciting or "presentable" enough.

Rust Removal

So what do we do if there is active rust on our gun that really needs to be removed? Well, this depends a lot on what kind of gun it is and what kind of surface we are talking about. In any case, practice first with an old rusty piece of metal or a broken "junk gun" before risking something that you value. It is easy to damage your gun trying to remove rust. It is a skill that can only be learned from experience, and you cannot pick it up entirely from a book. If in any doubt at all, you should consider having a professional do the job (the American Institute for Conservation does free referrals) rather than causing damage that cannot be undone. I especially encourage reference to a professional if there is fine finish or delicate engraving present. The instructions below assume steel with no finish present, and even then there is always a considerable element of risk involved.

Also, do not automatically be discouraged if the rust appears to be thick. Rust, the byproduct of corrosion itself, can easily be fifteen times thicker than the original solid metal surface from which it corroded. So you can actually see a considerable surface of rust without having lost very much of the original metal. Sometimes you get lucky.

Less Drastic Rust Removal

If the rust is fairly new and restricted to the surface, you may be able to get away with just wiping it down with mineral spirits until it is clean. But remember, mineral spirits is a combustible chemical that should be used with a lot of ventilation and by carefully following the instructions on the container. Cloths used with solvents like mineral spirits will require special disposal because they give off dangerous fumes and are highly flammable and combustible. Follow the manufacturer's instructions.

Another approach is to use synthetic gun oil and scrape the rust off with a small wedge of soft, clean wood. Teflon spatulas work, too.

Discard and replace wooden wedges often, because if they pick up hard debris you can end up digging into the metal and causing damage. When finished, clean with mineral spirits as described above.

With particularly stubborn cases, some people let the oil sit on the metal overnight to soften up the rust.

205 More Drastic Rust Removal

If the above method doesn't meet your needs, try scrubbing with a nylon or boar bristle brush (some toothbrushes work quite well, but there are stiffer types sold in hardware stores, too) to remove the loose stuff, wipe off the dust with a dry cloth, then go at the scrubbing again, but this time with mineral spirits. Naturally, you will want to wear goggles, work in a ventilated space and follow all manufacturer's safety and handling instructions.

Do not, I repeat, do not use metal brushes. I know that this can be a temptation, and soft metal brushes of brass, etc., are unlikely to scratch steel, but they do leave behind traces of their own metal, which can theoretically cause bimetallic corrosion. In extreme, particularly stubborn cases, you may have to resort to metal brushes, but it certainly should not be what you start out with.

After scrubbing for awhile, wipe the brown, grubby mess off with a clean cloth or a bore patch, and then go at it with the brush and mineral spirits again. Eventually, when you are satisfied with the results, wipe clean with mineral spirits and a cloth, dry it off with another clean cloth, and you are done. Dispose of all rags and chemicals properly.

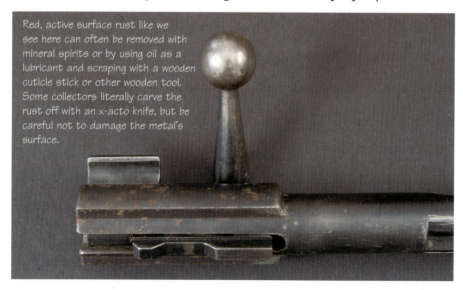

Red, active surface rust like we see here can often be removed with mineral spirits or by using oil as a lubricant and scraping with a wooden cuticle stick or other wooden tool. Some collectors literally carve the rust off with an x-acto knife, but be careful not to damage the metal's surface.

Rust and Other Evils

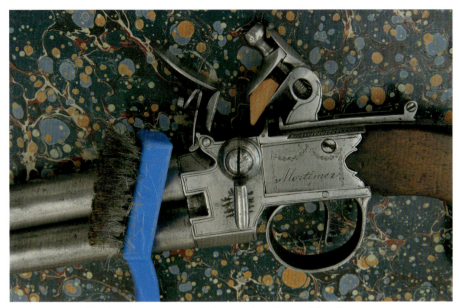

Wire brushes can scratch the metal surfaces of fine firearms.
If you absolutely have to use them, be very careful.

Really Serious Rust Removal

206
If the above methods don't get you anywhere, it is time to try steel wool. This should be in the finest grade available (OOOO) and should not have any detergents, oils or other additives. There are some excellent textile alternatives to steel wool out there that are available at any paint store, but these should also be in an extremely fine grade of grit. It's better to get a sore arm from scrubbing than to strip off the surface of your gun.

We are now working with something that can actually remove the original, steel surface of the gun — so obviously, you need to take care and experiment first on remote areas of the metal that no one will ever see. Be patient and remem-

Steel wool and its alternatives should always be used in the finest grade available.

173 *Rust and Other Evils*

ber that there are no guarantees...it is very easy to permanently damage a gun by doing this. You need to consider whether hiring a professional might be a better choice for the gun in question.

When finished, wash with mineral spirits and dry as described previously.

Heavy Duty Chemicals

Most hardware stores carry chemical rust removers that will work much more quickly than the process described above. All I can say is, "Don't do it!" Some collectors have mastered the timing and neutralization procedures necessary to control these products, and I have seen it done quite successfully. However, for most folks I just think that it is too risky to recommend. I have seen too many "pickled" guns, with the entire surface of the firearm evenly etched away, to encourage that procedure for anyone but the most experienced experts.

On a related note, there are also heavy duty rust barriers/preventatives that you can buy at automotive supply stores. I have seen these applied to collectible arms with disastrous results. Again...don't try it.

Cleanliness is Next to Godliness: Washing Wooden Gun Parts

Even if there is no active rust on your gun, it might just be dirty or have oily residue on it. When wood needs to be cleaned, the usual approach is just to wash it in room-temperature water with dish soap (two drops per gallon). If you have metallic (hard) tap water, spring for a bottle of distilled water. You can buy it cheaply at most pharmacies. Don't soak the wood...just gently wash the outside with a clean, damp cloth. You don't want the wood soaking in the moisture. As long as you don't overdo it, and dry the wood immediately with a clean cloth, most wooden gun stocks and grips will react well to this treatment, as will most finishes.

However, if the grips are painted, you should approach the situation with care. The paint may wash away in the water. And as always, test wash an inexpensive example before jumping in with both feet. Take your time and be sure that you are happy with the results before taking any real risks.

Some folks do a final cleaning with mineral spirits at this time, which cleans a bit deeper and helps evaporate any remaining water. As

Scrubbing with a soft brush can be surprisingly effective.

Wooden swabs make great tools for cleaning and oiling complicated mechanisms and hard-to-reach areas. The ones with wooden sticks are great because the unpadded end can be used to scrape at spots of rust and dirt.

is described in the hint below, this is a dicey proposition, but if done in moderation, can be safe in many situations. Remember...every gun is unique. Learn what works for you and the guns you collect, and remember that the first rule is to "do no harm" rather than take a chance with a process that may be irreversible.

209 Be Careful with Alcohol and Solvents on Wood

I know that it can be tempting, but try not to expose the wood on your guns to chemicals that evaporate rapidly. Your stocks can and will crack if subjected to this kind of abuse. You can also strip off precious original finish if you use these materials. That means take care with alcohol, acetone, etc. If you have to use something, mineral spirits is usually the safest option.

Yes, there are a few situations where you might need to break this rule, but it is always a risk and should be done with caution.

210 Removing Cosmoline

If you collect post-Civil War military weapons, you will eventually have an encounter with the dreaded Cosmoline. Actually, Cosmoline is great stuff. It's a preservative that keeps guns rust-free in all sorts of challenging storage situations. Government arsenals have loved it for over a century. Unfortunately, it is also sticky, greasy and seemingly impossible to remove.

First of all, let me say that I make no guarantees concerning any of the suggestions about Cosmoline given here. Some of these solutions are pretty brutal, and you can definitely damage guns; all I can tell you is what has worked for me. If something goes wrong, you are on your own. Also, don't assume that a gun covered in Cosmoline is unloaded; it only takes a second to check.

If you have never had to remove Cosmoline from a gun before, let me just pause here to laugh hysterically, because you are in for a real treat! In many cases, the Cosmoline has been on the gun for 100 years, and even if it was put on last week, it isn't going to come off easily. There are different schools of thought on how to remove Cosmoline, most of which involve disassembling the rifle and treating the wood and metal parts separately.

For the wood, many people use oven cleaner (definitely an outside activity!) or try to fit all the wooden parts into a dishwasher. Both of these methods work, but they are fairly brutal. Expect a raised grain and you can kiss any original finish goodby. The dishwasher method, in particular, can crack the wood with its heat. Some folks suggest relatively hot (but not boiling) water and mild liquid dish soap, like Dawn®. After any of these treatments, the stock might be bleached and rough. This can be fixed by some very gentle smoothing with extra fine steel wool and then a light application of oil. I use lemon oil for safety reasons, but

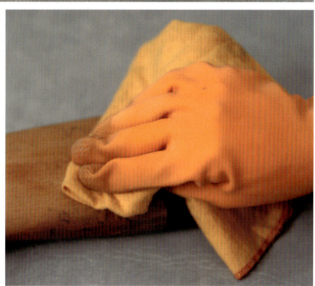

Removing Cosmoline from metal parts usually isn't difficult once the gun is disassembled, but the wood is more of a challenge. The safest method, perhaps, is to allow the stock to heat up in the sun until the grease starts to sweat out of the wood's pores. Then wipe it off with a cotton rag and repeat until you are satisfied. Woolen rags should be avoided because their fibers will snag in the wood's grain.

most other people seem to prefer boiled linseed oil.

If there is a good deal of original finish on the stock, these methods might be harsher than what you want. This is time to use the gentlest methods possible. One product that seems to please people who are trying to preserve stock finish is Orange Clean®. It has worked well for me, but it darkens the wood because it is an oil-based product. If you have a nice blonde rifle stock, this darkening effect is a definite drawback.

If you are looking for the safest and least invasive technique, it is probably to leave the gun in the sunshine for an hour or so until it heats up. The Cosmoline will usually start to sweat out of the wood, beading up on the exterior surface so you can wipe it off with cotton rags. You will probably have to repeat this process many times, but it usually works pretty well. It also helps to clean out any markings and other nooks and crannies with a nylon brush.

For the metal parts, after disassembly I put them in a sink filled with almost-boiling water and then (with heavy dishwashing gloves on) scrub everything down with a nylon brush. I cannot stress how important it is that your spouse not be at home when you do this, because it is going to smell and make a horrible mess. Some people use acetone, but aside from the health concerns of using a flammable solvent in an enclosed space, splashing acetone around the kitchen might just be the difference between sleeping alone and receiving divorce papers the next morning. It's your call.

As a final step on the metal, I pour absolutely boiling water over everything (including lots down the barrel), which should provide a final cleaning and dry the metal with fast evaporation. Because it will be so dry, you will need to use oil or another corrosion preventative on all the metal parts before reassembly. Pushing a number of oiled patches down the barrel with your cleaning rod wouldn't hurt, either. Cleaned and dried metal tends to attract rust like a magnet so don't delay this critical step.

As you can probably see, we are still looking for the ultimate answer to this question. Cosmoline removal is one of the most highly discussed/argued firearms topics on the Internet, and there are almost as many opinions as there are collectors. Experiment on an inexpensive gun before approaching something more valuable, and you will soon find an approach that works for you.

Historical Cosmoline Removal

Ever wonder how they removed cosmoline "back in the day"? Here is a description pertaining to Krags:

There was great activity in...garrisons when issues were made...still in unopened packing cases, and sticky with cosmoline. From the hour of their receipt, until every last vestige of the yellow grease had been removed, the whole of the line of barracks reeked of kerosene. The odor was everywhere, invading the company kitchens and tainting the food for weeks to come. Uniforms and equipment suffered too, especially shelter halfs, and no amount of scrubbing with yellow soap could completely eradicate the stains. Rags, potato sacks, old tentage and particularly old newspapers were in demand, in fact anything to rid the beautiful new weapons of their sticky coating of the detested cosmoline...

Be Careful

No matter what you use to remove rust or clean your gun, test any products on a hidden area of an inexpensive item before jumping in with both feet and experimenting on your favorite engraved Colt. That goes for the rust preventative coatings described below, too. Every situation is different. Just because something works for me does not mean that it will work for you. I make no guarantees, just honestly report what I do in my own collection.

Rust Prevention

Of course, the best way to remove rust is to prevent it from attacking your guns in the first place. There is no rust-removal process that will return your gun to brand new. Corrosion is not a reversible reaction. Rust comes from humidity, so take the steps to make sure that metal and moisture never meet.

In the next chapter, we will discuss climate control, proper storage and other ways to stop humidity at its source. But here we will cover the physical procedures necessary to protect your guns at the very surface of the metal.

Coatings — A Barrier Against Rust

We will talk about bags, cases and climate control later on, but the first line of defense is on the gun itself. With very few exceptions, every gun needs some sort of coating on the metal to inhibit rust. Some guns also need lubricant to

Notice how the barrel band has protected the metal underneath it on this Federal Era musket. Covering metal with coatings is a crucial tool in our rust prevention arsenal.

inhibit wear to their moving parts. This is where it gets tricky, because there are a lot of choices, and none of them seem to work perfectly in every situation. You will have to make an informed decision as to what is best for you.

Remember, though, that no barrier will be effective if there is active rust underneath it. That rust will be sealed in there, probably causing more damage than it would have without the coating. A coating of organic oil, for example, will just sit on top of the rust and will not significantly deter further damage. So be sure, before you take any of these steps, that all active rust has been removed.

"What is active rust?" you might ask. It is the rust that is continuing to do damage. In general, assume that all rust is active unless it is an old black, patinated coating. All brown and red rust should be presumed active. See earlier in this chapter for hints on removing it.

First Things First: Is There Finish Present?

The first thing to do is to determine if any original finish is present. Different finishes, applied by different workmen, during different times in history, at different factories, all react…well…differently.

For instance, many types of otherwise stable blued finishes that have a light case of speckled rust coming through will react well to being soaked in kerosene and then being scraped with a soft wedge of some kind or a fine grade of steel wool. However, other types of blued finishes might get stripped off entirely by such a process, and on yet other guns you could end up removing huge chunks of otherwise saveable blue.

So if you collect percussion-era Colts, for instance, you might want to consult with specialized collectors and conservators in that field before venturing out on your own. The information about coatings below will address bare metal. Many of these techniques and products work just fine with finished metal, too, but I can't take responsibility for every situation and won't be making any promises.

Oil, The Old Standby

Arms collectors of past generations usually coated their guns with organic oil. Singer® Sewing Machine Oil and Hoppe's® Gun Oil were the most common choices. While this probably wasn't too good for the wood, often darkening it, the oil offered a decent protection against rust. In fact, many collec-

Organic oil has its limitations, but this traditional favorite remains useful in many situations.

tors and dealers still use it and swear by it. In fact, with more complex mechanisms like semiautomatic pistols, and for guns that are going to be used rather than just displayed, oil is an excellent choice.

There are also gun oils containing silicone that offer more of a preservative effect and provide more lasting lubrication. Watch out for these, however, on guns with delicate surfaces, because some collectors have found that they penetrate a little too much. Also watch out for oils that contain solvents. While these are great for cleaning working guns, they probably shouldn't be your first choice for simply protecting collectible firearms against rust.

Synthetic Oils

Still using old-fashioned gun oil to lubricate those revolvers, repeating longarms and automatic pistols? You might want to experiment with some of the newer synthetic products like CorrosionX® and Breakfree®. Just like the synthetic oils that are used in cars, these new oils penetrate better and are chemically designed to stick to metal. They are especially good at getting under moisture, rather than just floating on top of it like regular oils do.

The down side? First of all, because of their penetrating properties, they might not be the safest choice for delicate plated finishes like gilding, silver plating and nickel. Also, while early indications show that they are probably just fine for many gun finishes like bluing, these are

While designed for working modern guns, the new generation of synthetic oils have many promising properties that may also prove useful for collectible firearms.

relatively new products to the hobby and it would be nice to see a little more evidence before endorsing them completely. For instance, according to Smith & Wesson expert Jim Supica, some collectors report problems with Breakfree® hardening into a varnish-like coating after repeated applications. However, many collectors and dealers are very happy with their performance, and I expect that we will be seeing more of these new oils as time goes by, probably including some special products formulated particularly for the collector market.

Also, please remember, oils are for metal, not wood. Most wood is better off with a high-quality wax product.

So When Is Oil A Bad Idea?

As will be described below, museum professionals generally prefer wax over oils (whether organic or synthetic) because liquid coverings tend to pick up dust and lint, which in turn pick up moisture from the air and promote spots of rust. The other problem with oils is that they are liquid and will eventually dry up or flow towards the ground with gravity. This means that they need to be reapplied occasionally, which can result in the gun becoming "greased up" with sticky old oil...a messy proposition.

For most museum experts and many of today's private collectors, these are reasons enough to avoid oil in many typical situations.

219 Wax

While oils are sometimes useful for preserving complex mechanisms like repeating firearms (especially if you are going to be working the actions every now and then), and are still the best choice for guns you are going to shoot, most museum conservators promote the use of wax for preserving the metal parts of collectible guns. Sword collectors, our "brothers in arms," have led the way in the use of wax, especially on blades. It's great stuff because it is inert and you can take it off easily with a gentle solvent.

Some waxes can be used on both metal and wood (an advantage over oil, which can only be used safely on metal), and since it is a solid, it doesn't flow "south" with gravity. In a static situation, a wax preservative can last a very long time. It is not, however, a good choice for firearms that will ever be used — just for display pieces.

220 If Wax, Then What Kind?

Just like with oil, with wax there is a choice between the organic and the synthetic. The waxes usually preferred by experts for protecting metal are synthetic microcrystolene waxes...the most popular being the Renaissance Wax® and Curator's Choice® brands. However, this is expensive stuff, and many people compromise with the widely available Butcher's® brand bowling alley wax — a high-quality organic wax made mostly from carnauba.

For protecting wood, pigmented carnauba wax is often suggested. Many fine paste furniture waxes have high concentrations of carnauba. Do not use spray waxes or other non-paste wax products, which do not offer the same protection and might even dry out your wooden stocks.

In case you are wondering, the reason that microcrystolene wax isn't often suggested for wood is because it is inefficient from a cost/benefit point of view (wood is unlikely to rust and doesn't need the fancy stuff) and because, like some other "clear" waxes,

Renaissance Wax® is one of the most popular brands of inorganic wax for preserving the metal parts of collectible firearms.

it can give the wood a "frosted" white appearance that many collectors find objectionable.

Applying Wax

First of all, never wax a dirty or oily surface. Wax does not mix well with oil or other greases. Wax applied on top of these substances will make a dull, white mess. So start out with a clean surface.

It helps to heat the item up slightly before waxing it (putting the gun in a sunny location for an hour works great), and a couple of thin coats work better than one thick one. Also, be sure to very gently buff out the wax completely...and I mean completely. You don't want unpolished wax on your gun. What we are looking for is a thin, hard protective coating. Four coats are not better than two...you will never buff all of that wax completely enough and will only be creating a tasty meal for fungus and mold.

Applying wax.

A shoe brush is often a useful tool for buffing wax on gun stocks.

Applying wax to the exterior of a firearm is usually a pretty easy job. The interior, however, especially the mechanism, can be another story entirely. All those springs and little pieces can make it a nasty job.

If you do decide to apply wax to the inside of a gun, the method is to melt some of the wax and apply it with a small nylon brush, then buff

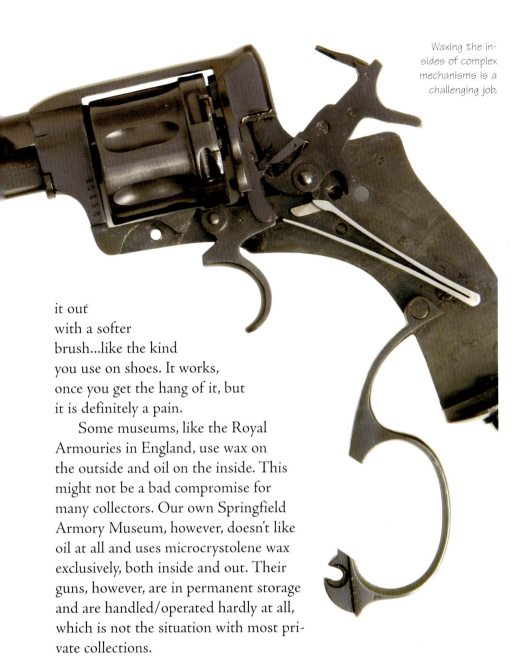

Waxing the insides of complex mechanisms is a challenging job.

it out with a softer brush...like the kind you use on shoes. It works, once you get the hang of it, but it is definitely a pain.

Some museums, like the Royal Armouries in England, use wax on the outside and oil on the inside. This might not be a bad compromise for many collectors. Our own Springfield Armory Museum, however, doesn't like oil at all and uses microcrystolene wax exclusively, both inside and out. Their guns, however, are in permanent storage and are handled/operated hardly at all, which is not the situation with most private collections.

Disadvantages of Wax

The disadvantages of wax? It wears off if you handle the item too much. Also, if you don't polish it out effectively, it can gum up the works of complex firearm parts or interiors, and it will quickly wear off of moving parts if you operate the mechanism. Also, waxing is not a good choice for guns that are still being used.

Rust and Other Evils

What Do I Use if I Have to Remove the Wax?

Many solvents will remove wax. Remember, though, that some of these (acetone included) can remove original finish. Mineral spirits are usually a better choice.

So After All This, What Do You Do?

Personally, I use wax on all the wood. For metal, I use wax on the outside and synthetic oil on the inside, unless the gun is fairly modern or a working gun, in which case I use synthetic oil for all the metal, unless the finish is delicate, in which case I use traditional organic oil.

Sounds complicated, huh? I wish it wasn't, but we are all still feeling our way with this topic, and there will be few single solutions for collectors with varied collections.

Should I Oil My Wood?

According to David H. Arnold, conservator at the Springfield Armory, oil should never be put on gunstocks where you want to preserve the original finish and appearance. I will quote Mr. Arnold here:

Wood is neither thirsty nor hungry. It is usually covered by a finish which may have become corrupted in some way, making it look "dry." The wood beneath the finish does not need to be 'fed.' Never put oil on any kind of an historic finish. There may well be unintended but permanently damaging consequences to ignoring this advice... Applying a modern finish over an equivalent historic finish can forever confuse the finish 'history' of a stock by making it difficult, if not impossible, to tell what (if anything) is original, and what is a restoration material — even with an analytical microscope. Therefore, you would not want to touch up, say, a shellac finish with shellac.

Whack the Shellac!

You might be wondering how to remove the thick coating of ugly shellac that is found on the stocks of that huge pile of World War II Soviet-captured German k98 rifles that were recently imported from the Ukraine. You see the same kind of shellac on Mosin-Nagants. We usually think of shellac as more of a preservative (kind of like Cosmoline), rather than a service finish. In fact, many early collectors coated their guns with shellac to prevent rust and even today you occasionally come across guns that have been treated that way.

If we are following the "do no harm" rule, we should probably leave the shellac alone. It isn't hurting anyone…it just looks ugly and feels sticky. On the other hand, if you do decide to remove the stuff, it is a pretty simple procedure. Denatured alcohol is the answer, and it can be found in the paint section of hardware stores. The packaging should have instructions about safe handling. It isn't tricky to use. It works quickly, and a nylon brush will clean out the nooks and crannies. Be aware

Technical Note: The shellac discussed here is probably mixed with varnish or linseed oil, because pure shellac generally cracks with age rather than discoloring.

The two scenes at the right show shellac being removed from a gunstock. The view below has half of the shellac removed to show the difference.

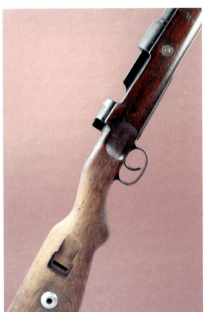

Rust and Other Evils

that it usually doesn't look like much is happening, and you might swear that it isn't working, but when the alcohol dries, the shellac will be gone, leaving a slight orange residue behind. One way to wash off this residue is with a household cleaner called Orange Clean®, which works very well but leaves behind an oily finish; you might prefer dish soap and water.

Should I Use Leather Preservatives or Dressings?

Boy, is this a controversial question! Some people say that leather preservatives, especially if they contain oils, will do no end of damage to your collectible leather. Other folks say that without oil, leather will crumble to pieces. Either way, they often make their arguments with an almost religious conviction. The only thing that just about everyone agrees on is that proper storage, in particular the control of relative humidity and avoiding stagnant, moist air, is very important.

So what's the answer? Personally, I think that it might depend on where you live. Solutions that work well in the desert might not make sense if you live near the ocean. The big benefit of oil and fat-based leather dressings seems to be possible increased flexibility rather than long-term preservation. If the leather is just for display and no longer needs to do its original job and be flexible, then some have suggested that leaving it alone (even if it looks dry) might be the best course. Even wax-based treatments, which many feel are the safest alternatives, reportedly can cause discoloration at the least and encourage biological deterioration of the leather at the worst.

In the end, I guess that we will take the recourse of cowards and quote a trusted government authority — in this case, the National Park Service. Here are some comments from the NPS's internal information sheet about leather preservation:

The indiscriminate treatment of leather with fatty substances is a long-standing tradition... The dressings are usually applied in an attempt to slow deterioration, improve the appearance of the leather, and perhaps restore some of its former strength and flexibility...

The effect of dressings on leather permanence has been studied, and almost invariably the researchers conclude that the dressing has no preservative effect...

One of the major problems with commercial dressings is that people apply them for their immediate results without awareness of their long-term

The muzzle end of this barrel is polished, the part on the left is not. Different collectors have different opinions about which appearance is preferable.

effects. Instability of certain fats or oils, dressing additives, and solvents contained in dressings can be responsible for numerous undesirable and unexpected effects...

It is evident that the dressing of leather is a popular and well-established procedure, yet there is a fair amount of experimental and practical evidence that suggests it has little or no effect on leather's rate of deterioration. The regular dressing of leather is hard to justify in terms of conservation principles since it has little or no preservative effect when applied in a customary uncalculated manner and there are so many potentially dangerous side effects...

It is recommended that park staffs not apply leather dressings to their historical collections on a routine basis. However, in certain individual situations, it may be appropriate for dressings to be applied...under the direction of a conservator.

That %*!@# Tarnish

I'm told that centuries ago, brass and silver didn't tarnish nearly as much as it does today. It's something to do with pollution in the air. Regardless of whether our ancestors shared in our misery, it is hard to escape the fact that tarnish on brass and silver weapon parts can be a real pain in the neck for modern collectors. Many collectors want their brass and silver to look shiny. Other collectors prefer the tarnished look as a legitimate sign of age.

Embrace the Enemy

When in doubt, leaving tarnish alone might be the best course of action. Collectors should hesitate before removing a deep, century-old brass patina. This coating

Brass is often best left unpolished because repeated polishings slowly soften the crispness of the metal's edges and engraved decorations. If you do decide to polish brass, it is best to coat it afterwards so that continual polishing will not be necessary to preserve the effect.

of tarnish is usually quite stable and will protect the brass better than anything you can do. Old, brown brass patinas can go quite deep into the metal, and there is rarely a good reason to remove it. Besides, its very color testifies to its age and originality.

Silver is more problematic. Very often, the best course is to let silver tarnish just as long as it stabilizes. However, silver tarnish is a corrosive action and in certain circumstances can cause gradual damage. For this reason, many collectors who choose to leave brass tarnish alone will take a different approach with silver. The entries below will discuss common methods that are used when a tarnish legitimately needs to be removed.

Brass Tarnish

Brass is a common metal on firearms and can be quite beautiful. However, it does tarnish rapidly, and repeated polishing can cause damage. Non-abrasive brass polishes are available; avoid the abrasive type. Museums often protect the polished surface with a coating called Incralac. This mixture can be purchased from museum conservation supply houses and is applied as a spray or brushed on. If you can remove the brass parts from the gun, use the spray. If you cannot remove the brass parts, you will have to use the brush-on version in thin coats.

Incralac is great stuff and does a super job of preventing tarnish, but if you handle your collection with your bare hands, it might not be the best choice. Oils from your hands have a way of getting under the finish and causing mischief. Also, the Incralac does eventually need to be cleaned off with a gentle solvent and reapplied. For this reason, a coating of wax and a forgiving eye for the inevitable touch of tarnish are probably the best suggestion for typical collections. For those with untouched displays in climate-controlled cases, however, Incralac might be something to explore.

Silver Tarnish

For silver, specialized thin lacquers are used by museums, but they have the same limitations as the Incralac discussed above. Unless you have climate-controlled cases and handle your items with white gloves, they probably aren't for you.

This French, silverplated pocket pistol by LePage shows the discoloration of mild tarnish.

Three views of tarnish removal with Never Dull.® The tarnish sticks to the wadding. Always follow up with a light buffing using a cotton cloth.

There are plenty of products made for collectors of antique silver and coins, but unless you are willing to bag or encase your silver-mounted guns, you are probably going to get regular tarnish. A wax coating will slow the process, but not for long. This eventually means polishing, but most silver polishes are abrasive. Coin collectors seem to like a gentler product called Never Dull®, and I have used it with some success — although it lasts no longer than traditional silver polish does...it's just cleaner and not so abrasive. Just like with brass, a forgiving eye and a less-active approach might be best in many cases.

Silver and Plastic Wrap

Some collectors think that a nice way to delay tarnish on silver is to wrap the item in plastic cling wrap. This is a bad idea; don't do it.

Common kitchen plastic wrap gives off chlorine, which will eat away the surface of your silver, making it dull and lifeless.

Rust and Other Evils

233 What Museums Do With Silver

If you want to go the museum lacquer route, please refer to conservation papers and guides that give specific instructions. It is quite a task and not without its risks. The basic routine is to chemically clean with Thiourea, which is non-abrasive and dissolves the silver sulfide (another word for tarnish). This stuff has to be washed off in the extreme, so this is no good for silver that you can't actually remove totally from the gun. The washing process involves a neutral detergent and an hour of rinsing with deionized water, then drying using cotton cloths and ethanol. After drying is complete, the silver is degreased with acetone because grease from contact with skin stops lacquer from sticking to the metal. Then, the lacquer is either brushed or sprayed on, using two complete coats. Common lacquers for this application are Agateen #27 and Acryloid B-72.

Another method, which is similar but uses more common products that you can buy at a hardware store, is found in the book *Saving Stuff*, by Don Williams, senior conservator of the Smithsonian Institution. It is available at many local libraries.

Needless to say, this process is inconvenient. The simple fact that it requires removing the silver from the gun for treatment can be a problem. It also employs chemicals that might be carcinogenic and otherwise dangerous and requires special gloves, masks, lots of ventilation, etc. In short, I really don't recommend it and only outline the process here to discourage you from exploring the idea more fully unless you are equipped and trained for such things.

234 Silver Plating

Silver plating has been a popular finish for gun parts during many historical periods and can offer beauty and strength at the same time. It poses an extra challenge today, however, because if you use an abrasive silver polish you can quickly wear through to the base metal, losing all the beauty, and if you let active tarnish eat away at it, that's not doing you any good either.

If you do have silver-plated guns, the best option might be to store them in drawers, silver storage bags or glass display cases where the tarnish won't be as active as if the guns were continually exposed to the elements.

A pierced sideplate made with imitation silver. Notice that when it tarnishes, it starts to take on a faintly brass-like color. Guns mounted with these alloys are usually of high quality.

Imitation Silver

While we are talking about the problems of silver, we should note that early gun and sword makers didn't like it much either, but for a different reason. Silver is a malleable and weak metal that fails easily under stress.

It does look wonderful, however, so arms makers were always on the lookout for substitutions that shared its cosmetic aspects but had more tensile strength and rigidity. Most of these substitutes, like Britainnia metal and tutenag, were alloys where other metals or compounds like tin were added to the mix. Today, these substitutes often devalue a gun or sword that is mounted with them instead of pure silver, but when they were new, the price was actually higher because they were an advanced and revolutionary product. Given this fact, perhaps we should be giving these arms more respect and value them accordingly.

How to tell that you are looking at an alloy rather than silver? It's mostly in the appearance, and you will learn over time what you are looking at. However, one old trick that an "old timer" taught me is to rub the metal with your sleeve and then quickly sniff the rubbed area. Since most of these alloys contain at least some brass, they often give off a faint "brassy" smell when they are rubbed. Some people disagree, but it seems to work for me.

236 Gold

What about gold and gold finish? First of all, gold doesn't tarnish (which is why it is a precious metal... the same goes for platinum). You are wasting your time polishing it, and it is such a soft metal that you are almost certainly wearing it off. Unless gold shows a special problem, you probably don't need to do anything to it at all, although a thin coat of wax won't hurt. If the gold doesn't look very good, you might want to try wiping it lightly with mineral spirits...it's probably just dirty.

Gold escutcheon on a pistol grip.

And never, I repeat, never use those gold cleaners used by jewelers and ladies to clean rings, etc. They will remove part of the surface. Likewise, when you are cleaning the iron, steel or other metal around gold inlays, be sure not to touch the gold because it will very easily cause permanent damage.

237 Bronze

Bronze is unusual in firearms, but the general rule is to leave it alone unless there is a problem. It has a self-protecting patina that is, in and of itself, an attractive and valuable feature. Bronze does, however, need to be kept very clean and free of dust or serious damage can result.

Bronze can also cause corrosion in other bronze objects called "Bronze Disease," and can contribute to bimetallic corrosion when stored near other metals, so if you have bronze objects in your collection, you might want to store them separately from other items. If you are interested in learning more about Bronze Disease and the proper handling of this beautiful metal, refer to books and websites dealing with ancient coins.

238 Is Refinishing Worth the Investment?

Rather than following the preservation route described in this chapter, some collectors feel that it would be better to take a worn gun and get it professionally refinished to factory-new condition. The assumption is that its value will be the same or similar to a gun that has actually passed down through time with its original finish intact. With almost no exceptions, this just isn't so.

While repairing a broken gun can easily increase its value, adding replacement bluing, nickel plating, etc., is almost sure to decrease collector interest — no matter how good the work is. Most collectors simply do not want modern finishes on their collectible guns, and are certainly not willing to pay more for guns that many people will literally view as defaced. A worn gun showing patches of factory-original finish is always better than a brand-spanking-new refinish. There may be reasons why you would want to do such work (for instance, if you are using the gun purely for shooting), but value probably shouldn't be one of them — at least in today's collector market as I view it.

"Restraint" is the Word for Repairs and Restorations

If a collectible gun does need to be repaired, try to exercise some restraint. The mechanics who do this kind of work are usually excellent and knowledgeable, but asking them what should be done can be similar to asking a plastic surgeon the same question. In either case, you are likely to agree to more procedures than are really necessary. Part of this, of course, might be that the more work they do, the more money they can charge, but in my own experience it is more likely that they are simply very proud of their abilities and are eager to use all of their talents. It is up to you, the customer, to restrict the work being done to legitimate repairs and not let the job turn into an exercise in making the gun something that it is not.

What About Preservation Records

Just like we keep historical records on our collection, we should also keep track of what repairs and preservation steps were done...and when. Is it time to rewax that gunstock? Don't guess. Keep records and you will do a better job of preserving your collectible weapons.

And remember...regular maintenance, even if it isn't perfect, is better than perfect maintenance done irregularly. Choose methods that you will actually do in a timely manner. Just as long as you aren't actively doing harm, this is better than preserving 40% of your collection "by the book" while 60% of your collection languishes from inattention.

Quick Clean-Up After Shooting Military Bolt Actions with Corrosive Ammunition

Quite a bit of the ammunition used in historical cartridge firearms is highly corrosive, and regardless of whether you are a shooter or not you will probably eventually find yourself needing to clean a gun that has been fired using corrosive ammunition.

For the guys out there, my first suggestion...and this is a biggie, well worth the entire cost of this book...is to do it outside, in the garage, in the basement — basically anywhere except the kitchen. Let me repeat that: *anywhere but the kitchen*. It's a divorce waiting to happen, only surpassed by the notorious "casting lead bullets on the stove top." Having been bagged by my wife doing both of these things, believe me, you simply do not want to go there. There will not be enough flowers in the world to calm her down.

Now let's get down to brass tacks. There are a lot of cleaning solutions, some of which are sold as commercial products, that will cut through corrosive gunpowder residue, but if you don't like these, you could do much worse than simply using three parts water and one part ammonia. Ammonia is a better choice than many more expensive solvents that you can buy in gun shops because these are often aimed at modern ammunition that does not have the salts like those put out by the primers of the older ammunition. You can buy ammonia in the cleaning section of any supermarket. Some folks even go with Windex® brand window cleaner, which has ammonia in a different dilution. However, I'm not in favor of the spray bottles because the spray can get all over the place and hit surfaces that you might not want it to touch.

The best approach is to do this promptly after you are done shooting and the gun has cooled down, because the longer you wait the tougher the job will be. Start by removing the bolt and ensuring that the gun isn't loaded and that the magazine is empty. The next step is running a couple of patches soaked with whatever cleaning mixture you are using through the bore using your cleaning rod.

Always start the patch at the muzzle end and remove it at the breech. You do not want to scrub the patch around it or pull it back through the barrel because all this does is distribute the filth rather than actually removing it. You never push the patch through from the breech because that is the dirtiest part of the barrel and there is no need to soil the muzzle end of the barrel. Please note that this is the opposite of what is normally recommended for non-corrosive ammunition, where cleaning from the breech is usually recommended to avoid wear to the muzzle crown. If you are cleaning a target gun, or anything else where muzzle condition is particularly important, this may be something to take into consideration.

Next, run a dry patch or two through the bore to soak up the ammonia. Ammonia is a solvent and you really don't want to leave it sitting there forever. You also don't want to get it on any finished parts of the gun, because it can, over time, cut through some metal and wood finishes. Next, run a patch with oil on it down the bore because the ammonia has an extreme drying effect on the metal, which can make it susceptible to rust. Make sure you get full coverage with the oil, but you also want a very light coating with no drips or puddles.

The next day, check your bore carefully to make sure that everything is OK. If not, start over.

A More Complete Solution

For more complete cleaning, you can disassemble the bolt and clean the parts individually, although often the bolt face is the only place where this effort is really worth it. What you will find is that different people have different routines that work for them and their guns, but for the most part, they are variations on the process just described. If this particular method doesn't work for you, there are always lots of other ways to do it so don't stop experimenting until you find the routine that accomplishes what you want.

A Dirty Trick

All this talk about using ammonia solutions to clean gun barrels reminds me of a story involving a local reenactment unit. It seems that a sergeant in their ranks had read that Civil War soldiers would sometimes urinate down the barrels of their muskets during the heat of battle in order to give the bores a quick cleaning. There is a strong ammonia content in urine, and it seems that this was effective enough in a pinch.

Anyway, this fellow decided to try this questionable trick out at his group's next battle reenactment. So there they were, firing away at the Rebels from a protected position, and he figured that his gun might be a little fouled so he discreetly "poured ammonia solution" down the

German soldiers cleaning their rifles and kits for inspection during the height of WWI.

muzzle...so to speak. It was at this point that he realized his musket was still cocked, primed and loaded with a blank charge. His mind filled with horrific visions of what might have happened and what portion of his anatomy had been so precariously positioned in the line of fire, he quickly brought the musket to his shoulder and fired.

Men who were standing alongside him can recall to this day the fifteen-foot eruption of yellow vapor that shot out of his longarm, as well as the sudden gust of wind that sprang up out of nowhere and blew the foul discharge back into his own ranks. If you didn't think that it was possible for a sergeant to be "busted" to private in a reenactment group, believe me, you would be wrong because it happened that day.

Precisely what this little story is supposed to be a warning against, I am not sure. The mind simply reels with possibilities. But it certainly does beg the question of how you *should* clean the bore of a Civil War era musket — a topic we will cover in the next entry.

What About Black Powder?

Cleaning up after shooting black powder ammunition can be downright nasty, but not nearly as nasty as *not* cleaning up after shooting blackpowder ammunition. Do not, under any circumstances, delay cleaning for a day or even an afternoon, because you will be sorry...really sorry. For the purpose of this discussion, we will presume that the gun being cleaned is a percussion musket, but flintlocks, revolvers and other black powder firearms can be cleaned in similar ways with obvious adaptations.

For almost all black powder guns, the best cleaning solution is hot, soapy water. If this doesn't appeal to you, there are commercially available black powder cleaners as well. Either way, the procedure is usually the same. First, after making sure that the gun isn't loaded (obviously) just pour some of the hot, soapy water down the barrel until it is almost full. Let it sit for a minute or so. This will loosen up most of the filth. Then pour the dirty solution out and start again.

Some folks put their finger over the vent while doing this, or even block both the vent and the muzzle and slosh the solution around, but I don't like burning my fingers so I just turn the gun upside down so my stock won't get wet and just let it drain out of the nipple. This can cause extra clogging in the nipple, but for me it's worth it.

On the third batch of water, scrub with a synthetic bore brush to remove any stubborn spots. By now, the water should be coming out clean. If it isn't, then do it again.

Once the water does come out clean, run a number of patches soaked with the soapy solution down the bore. This should be repeated until the patches start to come out clean. And, of course, remove the nipple and clean it with a little brush wet from the solution; the hole from which it came should also be cleaned, as well as the general exterior area that might have been exposed to discharge from the primer during firing. Older primers and percussion caps give off very corrosive chemicals, so pay special attention to this step if you have not used non-corrosive primers. Lastly, lubricate and protect all the surfaces you just cleaned with oily patches.

These directions should make it clear why there is rarely an excuse for high-end black powder guns to be shot. All that hot water and soap can easily damage precious guns, especially the finishes on wooden stocks that do not react well to hot water.

A Better Black Powder Way

An even better method, that is much more protective of the wood, is to remove the barrel entirely. Once the barrel is off, you plunge the breech end in a bucket full of your soapy water or other cleaning solution. Use of a cleaning rod with a brush or tight patch in the bore will actually work like a syphon and pull the cleaning solution up through the vent until it fills the barrel, making cleaning much easier. The dirty solution can then be pushed out of the breech, plunger style, and fresh solution drawn in.

In order to avoid unnecessary wear on tang screws, this method is perhaps best reserved for guns with false breeches.

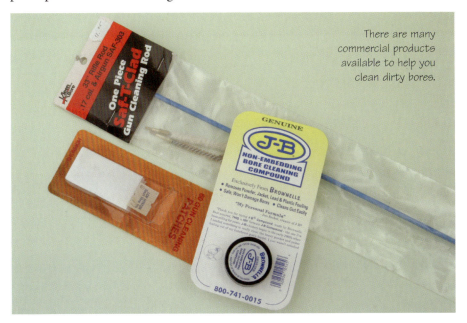

There are many commercial products available to help you clean dirty bores.

246 Cleaning Old Dingy Bores

How many times has a collector looked down the barrel of a perfectly wonderful firearm only to discover that the interior of the barrel is filthy and black? This isn't always the end of the world, but it is certainly worth going through the trouble of stopping further corrosion and removing what you can of the mess.

The first step is to repeatedly clean the bore as if you had just fired the gun. If this gives you the desired results, a nice application of oil should conclude the session. Some bore fouling, however, is so very deep that no amount of scrubbing seems to improve matters. While you might just decide to live with the problem at this point, be aware that there are a wide range of commercial bore cleaners for sale that might give you the results you are after. But, like all other chemical products, they need to be approached with caution. Some of these compounds are too abrasive for collectible firearms and can leave an unpleasant "frosted" appearance in evidence of their use. As always, experiment carefully before risking a valuable or precious piece.

247 Excavated Guns

Pistols, gun parts and other firearms items that have been dug up at battlefields, etc., can be an inexpensive and enjoyable addition to any collection. However, these items require special attention because they are almost always literally covered with active rust. You need to bring that rust under control and stabilize the artifact for display or storage. The biggest risk here is actually doing too much rather than doing too little. Overenthusiastic rust removal has damaged more artifacts than the rust itself, so show some restraint. Most rust works pretty slowly, so don't rush into things. If a musket part has waited for 100 years in the dirt, it can probably wait another week for you to research the proper approach to preserving it.

Dug relics like these 17th-century Indian lock parts from New York State require special attention.

Rust and Other Evils

202

After cleaning the artifact, treat it with a protective coating.

Since most dug-up guns have been removed from the earth and are made of iron, that is what we are going to address here. We will not give recommendations for items taken out of the water or any other special circumstance, because that truly requires professional help.

First, make sure it isn't loaded. I know that sounds silly, but never take any chances. Then, brush off the item with a nylon brush. Metal brushes are not a good idea for most situations. Next, get some fine, plain steel wool, and with gloves and goggles on, in a well-ventilated area (outdoors comes to mind), taking all other safety precautions and following product directions, scrub the item with kerosene. Some people find metal wire brushes useful here, but these can obviously cause damage to the underlying artifact and it will have to be your call on a case-by-case basis. Kerosene is flammable and volatile, and requires special handling and clean-up, so be careful.

This can be a tedious process and it should be. Remove the rust and get yourself down to the solid metal, any remaining finish on the metal, or a black stain over the metal itself. Do not polish the object smooth unless it was smooth in the first place. Black (or *extremely* dark brown) is the only color of rust that is your friend. Any other color of rust is bad and will have to go.

After you are done, clean the kerosene off with acetone. You can now either oil the item or coat it with an appropriate wax. There are lots of choices, including special varnishes...just don't use paint or anything silly.

If the artifact is such a hunk of rust that you can't make any headway with these directions, you might need to resort to electrolysis, but that is too advanced a technique to get into here and is probably best left to a professional artifact conservator.

And remember, anything that has been rusting for that long has a really serious case of rust, so you will need to monitor these items from time to time to ensure that active rust has not reappeared. Don't be surprised if you eventually have to strip off your protective coating and address the problem again.

Some Final Words

As you can see, there are many ways to approach the preservation of collectible guns and even the experts don't have all the answers. Remember that each gun is a unique object with its own special challenges. No one can give you an approach that will answer for every one of these unique objects, but hopefully this chapter has given you some ideas that will lead you to solutions that work for you.

Storage and Display

Air Conditioning and Climate Control

Think about some of the normally perishable things that have managed to last for centuries and centuries, only to be discovered in modern times by amazed archaeologists. The Dead Sea Scrolls and King Tut's Tomb come to mind for me. How did that stuff last for so long with all the natural fibers and colors intact? The answer, like in real estate, is "location, location, location." Tombs and caves in the desert. Places that are dry, have consistent temperatures and don't let in any sunlight. These conditions are what we want to recreate in our gunrooms.

For gun collectors, air conditioning or dehumidifiers are the first line of defense. Unless you live in the desert, get some! Humidity control is <u>the</u> most important aspect of preserving antiques of any kind. You will be amazed how much less work you have to do taking care of your guns when there is a consistent amount of moisture in the air.

Perhaps the worst possible situation would be rapidly increasing temperatures combined with elevated humidity. This is sort of like when a kid exhales on a car window to make it fog up. You don't want this kind of condensation happening on your guns!

Consistent Humidity Is Very Important

To some extent, the consistency of the humidity in the air is even more important than the amount of the humidity itself, or even the temperature. As a general guide, though, many museums recommend relative humidity levels of about 50% and temperatures of about 70 degrees for the storage of antique objects made of wood and metal, like guns. Also, while temperature can vary as long as the change is gradual, rapid and dramatic swings in temperature can cause quick shifts in relative humidity that expose your guns to unnecessary risk. While condensation is the obvious risk from overly humid air, another concern is that wood will expand and contract with changing humidity levels, which can lead to cracks.

The bottom line? Avoid sudden and significant changes in either temperature or humidity. And if you can control just one variable, let it be relative humidity.

Hygrometers

One of the most cost-efficient things you can do to protect your collection is to buy a hygrometer. This is a device that measures relative humidity and will tell you just what the status is in your gun room or display case.

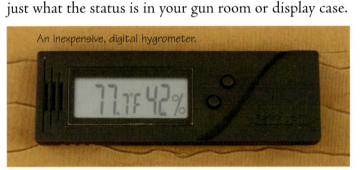

An inexpensive, digital hygrometer.

These devices used to be expensive, but today accurate digital devices smaller than a deck of cards can be purchased for about $30. Some of the most affordable models can be found for sale at cigar shops. Cigar enthusiasts need to measure the humidity in their humidors and the popularity of cigar smoking has made these units affordable and readily available.

Rather than just hoping that your guns are being stored in proper humidity conditions, spend a few bucks to be sure.

Identify "At-Risk" Pieces

When thinking about how to store your collection, it is worth setting some priorities. Which guns are most likely to rust or become damaged? For my money, blued guns have the most delicate finishes, and a single fingerprint can be all it takes to cause serious damage. At-risk guns of this type will require

This parlor rifle was stored in an attic near the ocean for about five years. This is the kind of damage that salty sea air can do to your guns. If you live near the water, take precautions.

special attention. Protect your most fragile examples first.

253 What If You Live Near The Ocean?

Wow — you're in trouble! I envy you the beautiful view, but not the storage challenges.

If high relative humidity is a problem, then what the heck, let's just add salt, which is about the most corrosive substance known to man. You get those wonderfully vaporous sea breezes that keep you cool on a summer night, but they can put rust on guns faster than it takes to tie your shoes.

Sea air is bad for guns...really bad. The easiest answer is to move. And no, I'm not kidding. I have experience with this, and wouldn't recommend it to anyone.

Short of moving, all you can do is try the ideas contained in these chapters and then monitor your collection on a monthly basis. Be extra careful to check the backs of things — the stuff that faces the wall, and you might not look at very often. Think very hard about acquiring airtight glass or Plexiglas display cases. And watch your collection like a hawk, because rust, my friend, is "blowin' in the wind."

254 Mildew, Mold and Other Biological Enemies

These bad guys are actually pretty rare on guns, and if you do see them, it will probably be in the form of white stuff on the wood. I have only seen mold on guns in the tropics or where guns are stored in enclosed spaces like strongrooms. Leather is a much more common victim in the average gun room, especially if you have used grease or oil as a leather treatment.

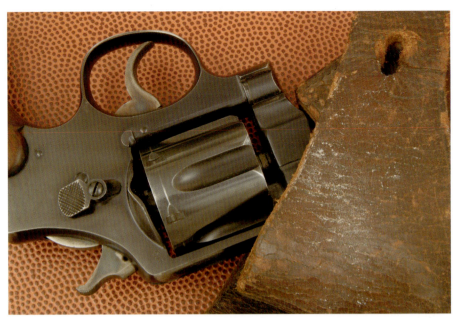
Mildew growing on the flap of a leather revolver holster.

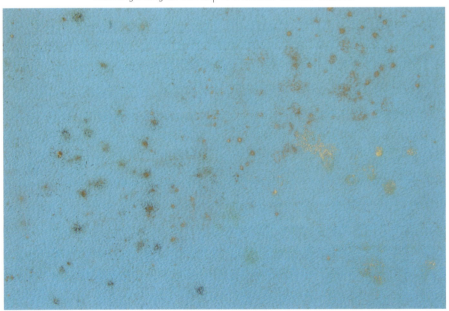
An extremely close-up photograph of mold on a vintage gun box.

    This isn't hard to prevent, however. Mold and mildew really like balmy high temperatures with lots of humidity and no air circulation. Fix these problems, and most mold will die off promptly. If you see mold or mildew on your guns, I can almost guarantee that you have rust, too, so it is a useful warning that something is very, very wrong with your climate situation.

255 The Dangers of Sunlight

Do you have paintings, vintage graphics or uniform items on display with your collection? How about leather holsters or gun belts? Put up some blinds that are rated to block ultra-violet rays. Sunlight can fade artwork, fabrics and other textiles faster than you might believe. With anything that has color, including gunstocks, sunlight should be avoided. Never put a gun with a wooden stock next to an unshaded window. It will bleach out in less than a year.

This piece of leather was left partially exposed to a sunny window. Notice how the top half is totally bleached-out by harmful ultraviolet rays.

If you are going to own antiques, then you are taking on the responsibility of preserving them for generations to come. Do the right thing and store them in conditions where they can survive undamaged. Back when we were camping in Boy Scouts, the troop leader always used to say, "Leave the campsite cleaner than it was when we got here." Let's give the same kind of attention to our legacy of collectible firearms.

256 Low-E Glass

"Low-e glass" is a term used to refer to glass that has low emissivity and blocks radiant heat transfer and ultra-violet rays. This is accomplished through a coating that consists of a very thin layer of metallic oxide or silver that is applied to the third surface of an insulating glass unit to block radiant heat

Blinds, used in combination with low-e glass windows, can do an excellent job of reducing the risk of light damage to your collection. Cloth is not enough to block u.v. rays; fiberglass or other light-resistant backings are a must.

transfer and ultra-violet rays.

Most homeowners choose low-e glass because it saves on heating/cooling costs over the long haul and is often required by code. If you are having the windows changed on your gunroom, however, you might be even more interested in the fact that these panes of glass are often quite good at protecting your collection from the sun. Ask your window dealer about what percentage of ultraviolet rays will be blocked. The extra cost for low-e glass, per window, is usually about $30.

Dust — The Silent Enemy

Protecting metal from moisture is, indeed, the first step in any preservation plan. But whether your approach is to use sealed cases, intense dehumidification, oil or wax, you still need to address the problem of dust. Most collectors don't really recognize dust as an enemy, but it is. The problem with dust is that it soaks up moisture, sort of like a microscopic sponge, and if left sitting on a gun or sword for too long, will result in speckles of corrosion or the disintegration of a fine finish. Let's look at some of the solutions.

Cases, Bags and Other Covers

If a gun is in a case, drawer, box or bag, it is out of dust's way. There are some excellent gun storage prod-

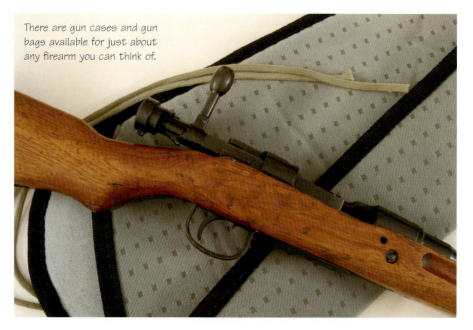

There are gun cases and gun bags available for just about any firearm you can think of.

Storage and Display

Dust equals rust. The tops of longarms on a gun rack will quickly attract dust like this.

ucts available. Check them out!

However, be aware that stuffing pistols in old socks (a classic collector's trick) might be a problem, because socks are fairly thin and can become damp over time, transmitting the moisture to the pistol inside. Anything that traps moisture is a problem and will require monitoring.

Also a problem are plastic bags (unless they are specially made for gun storage). Lots of people use supermarket type plastic bags to store their guns, thinking that they are keeping the moisture out, but in reality they are just creating a microclimate that is almost uniquely guaranteed to generate condensation.

259 Housekeeping

You should also look for ways to stop dust from entering the room where your collection is. For instance, are the windows properly sealed? Do you let pets in the room? Remember that pet dander is a major contributor of dust, not to mention the fur and hair factor. Vacuuming also can be a contributor. Most

Pet dander can be a major source of dust in the gunroom.

household vacuums spit out almost as much dust as they suck in because their filters are not very fine. Be sure to use a good HEPA (high efficiency particulate air) vacuum and change the bag regularly. If this is too costly, then consider a floor surface that can be washed rather than vacuumed.

An effective HEPA vacuum.

What If You Use Oil?

If you do use oil, either because of choice or because the nature of the surface being treated requires it, understand that it is even more important to keep the gun dust free. Be aware that traditional dusting methods, like feather dusters, are pretty ineffective on oiled surfaces, because the dust usually just sticks to the oil and won't come off. Dusting with rags can be more effective, but will also remove your oil in the process and doesn't always get all the dust. Oily rags are perhaps a better solution, if changed often.

Suck It Up

For waxed or unoiled exterior surfaces, traditional dusting can be pretty effective, but tends to push as much dust around as it actually removes. Vacuuming — delicately and with fine vacuum attachments — can be effective, but the danger of sucking down a loose part of a rare collectible might make this a pretty scary activity. Expensive, specialized low-suc-

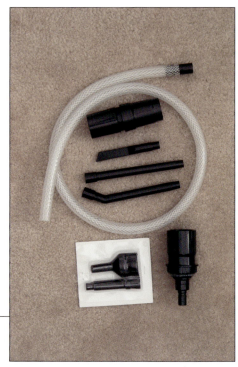

A micro-tool adapter kit that will work with most household HEPA vacuums.

tion vacuums for museum use are available through the Internet if this option appeals to you. There are also micro-tool adapter kits that can be purchased to make small tools fit on a standard-size vacuum's hose. But remember, if your vacuum isn't HEPA, you might be doing more harm than good. Hint: a small paint brush to get at nooks and crannies will help a lot with vacuuming.

The Risk of Residue

If you are skipping out on vacuuming, then you are left with traditional dusting. The biggest concern here is residue. Because feather dusters don't trap much dust, serious house cleaners generally dust with cloth rags dampened in ammonia or other liquid cleaning products. Some of these cleaning formulas are not things you want on your guns, particularly the organic parts like wood and leather. So if wet rags and dusters aren't any good, then what do we do?

A Simple, Inexpensive Answer to Dust

The answer is microfiber dust cloths. These have been tested by the National Park Service and appear to be safe. The fibers of these cloths (Tyvek and nylon) make an electrostatic charge that pulls in dust, pollen, hair and other undesirables. There are two kinds: the type you use once and throw away and the type you can wash and use again. If you use the single-use type, don't get the kind with a mineral oil coating which might leave behind an unwanted residue.

These dusting cloths are widely available and are also sold by Proctor and Gamble under the popular brand name Swiffer.® I have been unable to discover whether the Swiffer® cloths have mineral oil, although the product's packaging claims that it leaves no residue.

Swiffer® brand duster.

Storage and Display

White gloves aren't just for jewelry, coins and other shiny baubles, like this 1835 medal for excellence in arms making. More and more gun collectors are beginning to use cotton gloves when handling collectible firearms, especially those that are valuable or have delicate finishes. People who have acidic or damp hands should be particularly careful.

The White Glove Treatment

Back in the bad old days of gun collecting, we used to laugh at museum curators when they would put on their cotton gloves before handling a firearm. And I'll admit it...sometimes we still do. It all seemed so prissy and unnecessary. Slowly, however, this attitude has changed. At least a little.

I still think it's pretty silly to put on gloves before handling a rusty piece of junk with no original finish, but for truly fine firearms, it definitely is a good idea. The oil in our skin is highly corrosive to metal, and rust spots in the shape of fingerprints can be seen in almost any collection. My own hands are extremely acidic, so I always try to be very careful when touching someone else's guns. I often use cotton rags or clean cloth diapers, which do the same job, because taking gloves on and off repeatedly can become tiresome. If you don't handle a gun properly, do the right thing and wipe it down with a clean rag afterwards — especially if the gun is blued. Blued guns and fingerprints just don't mix.

Where can you get white cotton gloves? Museum supply companies sell them, but they are also used by jewelers. I got mine for free just by asking at the repair department of a high-end jewelry shop. And remember, they aren't really doing their job unless you keep them clean.

Gunroom Displays

Displaying our guns where we can see them every day is an important part of collecting for many firearms enthusiasts. The nature of our collections and local laws may affect how we choose to do this, but even in a large vault or strong room, attractive arrangements can make gun collecting more fun.

While there are plenty of gun racks and stands available commer-

Creating attractive displays is one of the true joys of collecting.

cially, many of these items can be made easily with just minimal carpentry skills. This isn't a shop manual, so we won't be going into blow by blow directions for these projects, but we will include some photographs of popular designs here to give you an idea of the possibilities.

Many gun racks can be made with very little woodworking knowledge.

Storage and Display

Simple padded wooden gun stands like this can be purchased inexpensively or made up from scratch with minimal woodworking skills.

Display Stands? Heavy Bases!

If you are making a display stand, one thing that you really don't want is for it to tip over, sending a pile of expensive guns crashing to the floor. Unless the guns themselves are so heavy that they provide stability on their own, it is recommended that the base of the stand be pretty darned heavy. Extra base width also goes a long way toward preventing unfortunate accidents.

Many styles of gun stands will require very heavy bases in order to prevent tip-overs.

Storage and Display

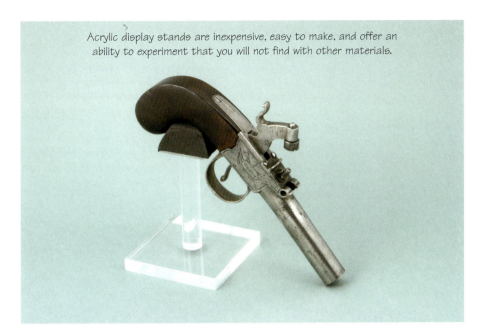

Acrylic display stands are inexpensive, easy to make, and offer an ability to experiment that you will not find with other materials.

Acrylic

Acrylic, also called by the brand name Plexiglas®, is a great see-through display material. It's easy to cut and it glues seamlessly, eliminating much of the countersinking and other finish work required of wood.

Acrylic comes in sheets and rods, and it can be bent quite easily using a plastic strip heater, which can be purchased for less than $30. Acrylic used to be extremely popular with hobbyists and could be purchased in just about any hardware store. Today, you might have to visit a plastics supply house or order from one of the many dealers on e-Bay.

Glass Display Cases

One of the best ways to protect a valuable gun from handling and moisture is to use an airtight glass display case with some form of climate control inside. These are pretty easy to build if you are handy, but unless you want to make a project out of it, you might prefer ordering one from a dealer. While most suppliers offer cases in standard sizes, one of which might suit your needs, I have had better luck ordering cases custom made to my own measurements. It usually doesn't cost much more and you can get exactly what you want.

Remember to leave some extra space around the gun…it can look awkward if the barrel is almost touching the glass. Also, if the case is against a wall, you might prefer having the back side of the case be a mirror so you can see both sides of your gun. Don't use a mirror, however, if you will be able to walk around the case and view it from the back.

Glass or Plexiglas®

Museum-style, airtight cases as described above can be made from either glass or acrylic. In general, I prefer real glass because it is heavier and less likely to tip over when bumped. Also, glass is harder to scratch and will usually look new for a longer period of time.

On the other side of the coin, acrylic is cheaper, usually has better looking seams, and if you are doing the project yourself, you might find it quite a bit easier to work with.

In case you were wondering, museums often use both. Glass is more common for permanent displays, whereas acrylic, because it is much lighter, is often chosen for exhibits that will need to be moved. Museums, however, usually use special kinds of acrylic that are amazingly expensive (thousands of dollars per large sheet) and have a durability above and beyond what you might experience with the normal variety.

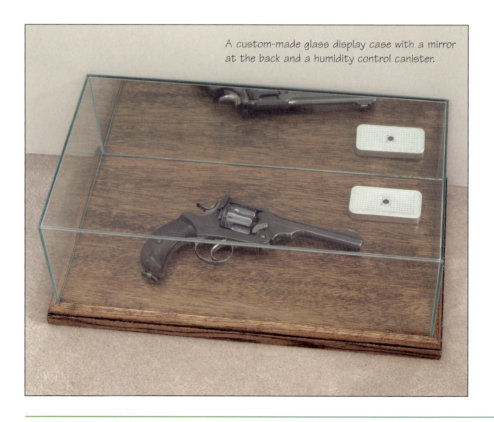

A custom-made glass display case with a mirror at the back and a humidity control canister.

Storage and Display

270 Hanging Guns on Walls

Lots of gun collectors like to hang their guns on the walls so they can see them and enjoy them every day.

This is great, except that plenty of folks use metal hooks, which slowly, bit by bit over the years, grind marks into your valuable weapons.

Unfinished wooden or plastic hooks/pegs are an option, but if you still want to use metal, there is a workaround. Buy some of that clear, chemically inert rubber tubing at a medical supply house or a home improvement center. Slip that soft tubing over your metal hooks and you are good to go. Closed-cell foam (like Volara®) can also be used for

Storage and Display

Wall hooks, whether they are wood or metal, need to be padded with a material that is soft. The material shouldn't stick to the gun, discolor it or promote corrosion. Many collectors try to get away with using metal hooks without padding, but slight movements and vibrations in your house will mark the gun over time.

this job of padding hooks. Since some collectors find the white color of the foam distracting, be aware that it can also be purchased in black.

And remember...any hardware that you use to suspend your guns should be fairly thick. Thin hardware absorbs the force of the gun's weight over a more narrow area of wood, and is therefore more likely to leave indentations or dents.

271 Gun Bags

You like those nice gun bags made out of patterned material that you see dealers using, but you can't find them...especially in longer sizes for flintlock muskets and other early longarms. No problem. Just contact Ace Case on the Internet at http://www.acecase.com/antique.htm or call them at 1-800-544-0008. They have all the soft cases you need for pistols on up.

Storage and Display

272 How to Line Storage Drawers, Boxes, Shelves, etc.

Many collectors wonder what they should use to line drawers, shelves, trays and boxes that hold antique ammunition packets with colors that can be damaged if improperly handled. The same goes for fabric items (like uniforms), delicate leather goods and other related collectibles that might be subject to chemical change.

The basic answer (once you have gotten them out of the damaging sunlight, of course) is that you want something that is chemically inert

Steel drawers are popular with both collectors and museums for pistol and accessory storage. In this photo, curator Erik Goldstein demonstrates the Volara®-lined drawer system at Colonial Williamsburg.

and won't retain moisture. For example, while plywood might be fairly inert, from a chemical point of view, if it is finished with a stain or paint, this covering might react with the object or simply become dangerously sticky in the heat of summer. And if you line a storage drawer with wall paper or contact paper, you might soon find the pattern embedded in your precious collectibles.

Another risk is a process called "out-gassing," which is when display materials such as paint, adhesives or upholstery give off gasses that might damage, discolor or encourage corrosion in the item being stored. Many synthetic materials, like foams and plastic wrap, can be made up of compounds that are at least partially manufactured from oil, coal and natural gas. Some of these products degrade in a harmful way, slowly giving off acidic vapors (usually chlorine) that might, in theory or reality, harm collections through either corrosion or discoloration.

The museum world, of course, has put a lot of thought into these issues, and the Internet is full of suggestions and resources. While there is really no need to repeat all of that information here, it is worth noting that one of the most popular storage substances is a dense polyethylene foam called Ethafoam®. Ethafoam® comes in various thicknesses and can be used for all kinds of applications from lining drawers and display boxes to wrapping around coat hangers to protect the fabrics in uniforms. Personally, I prefer a competing product called Volara®, which

Proper drawer lining is especially important for items with delicate colors or that might stick to other linings.

is more flexible and smoother. Other related products that might be useful when more stiffness is required are Coroplast® and Fome-Cor®, which are also made primarily from chemically inert polyethylene.

273 **Plastics, Foams and Carpets, Oh My!**
For the budget conscious, be aware that near-exact equivalents of some of these expensive museum storage materials are sold in office supply stores for wrapping packages for shipment, often at significant savings. However, it is often difficult to tell which synthetic display materials are safe.

For your reference, some of the materials that are "baddies" include: PVC, PVDC, PVA, acidic polyesters, polyurethane foams and chloroprene. The safer "goodies" include: polyethylene, polypropylene, polystyrene, acrylic and inert polyester. Most of the bad synthetics won't cause damage in a week or two, but would not be a great choice for permanent display or storage of a delicate item. Printed paper, like cartridge packets, old gun ads or original packaging, can be particular susceptible to out-gassing, as was described earlier.

274 **The Beilstein Test**
If you are wondering if the flexible plastic tubing that covers your gun hooks, or the bubble wrap you are using to protect your favorite pistol, is one of the "baddies" that gives off chlorine gas, the folks at Colonial Williamsburg's conservation lab tell me that there is a simple test. It's called the Beilstein Test, and they were kind enough to demonstrate it for us. It works for all kinds of plastics like foam, tubing, clear protective sheets, etc.

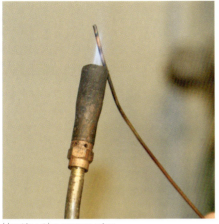
Heating the copper wire.

Touching the hot wire to the sample.

Negative for chlorine.

Positive for chlorine.

Basically, you get some copper wire that is 12- or 14-gauge and strip off the insulation. Then, using gloves and insulated pliers, you heat the end to glowing red in the flame of a Bunsen burner or propane torch. Keep heating the wire until it isn't giving off any color except the color of the flame, itself. If there is a green color, that means it could be dirty, so wash the wire (or just cut the dirty section off) and start again until it burns clean.

In dim light, briefly touch the red hot wire to a fragment of the material you are testing and then move the wire immediately back into the flame. If the flame gives off a green color, then the material has tested positive for chlorine and should not be used for the storage of your collection. If the flame does not change color, then the sample is probably free of chlorine, which is a good sign.

Naturally, given that the Beilstein Test involves a flame, a red hot copper wire and synthetic materials that could burst into flames, this test needs to be carried out with caution. For further directions, refer to this Internet article:

http://www.cci-icc.gc.ca/about-cci/cci-in-action/view-document_e.aspx?Document_ID=106

Rubber Bands

Since we are talking about inappropriate materials, it is worth mentioning rubber bands. Do not use rubber bands to attach items or tags to your guns.

The material in office-quality elastics will eventually degrade, decompose and fuse itself to your gun. This leaves a stripe in the metal that will be difficult to remove and permanently damages blued and browned gun finishes.

Numbering Your Collection

It can be quite helpful to number your collection. Some folks use numbering systems based on the date they purchased the gun. (4.1987.3 might mean that the gun was bought in April of 1987 and was the third gun purchased that day.) Other people just go with a purely sequential system starting with #1 and proceeding on up. Still other folks create number and letter

If you use numbering tags, choose ones made from a nonabrasive material.

systems based on what type of gun it is, but these codes usually get so complex that no one else can figure them out.

The basic rule for putting the numbers on the guns is to do no harm and make sure it is something that you can change without much trouble if you need to.

Traditionally, many museums and collectors have numbered their guns in discrete places with India ink, which is then coated with clear nail polish for durability. By the way, if you buy a gun that was once in a museum or famous private collection and it is marked or labeled in any way, don't remove it because it is part of the gun's provenance and adds to its value.

While the India ink method is pretty good for unfinished guns, I would not want to subject my blued and browned firearms to this kind of treatment. Because of this, I prefer plastic tags held on with fishing line or automotive zip ties. Pre-numbered plastic tags of this type can be purchased at many well-stocked hardware stores. There are also metal versions available, which look better than the plastic, but because they are metal they can scratch away at the gun over time and I don't usually recommend them.

Dummy Cartridges

Want to display your bolt action rifle with cartridges, but you want to do it the safe way? Use "dummy cartridges." These are inert cartridges and they can be purchased from gunsmithing catalogs for many of the more popular rifle systems.

Watch out, though. These dummy cartridges often look like the real thing and can easily be confused with genuine ammunition. They are great, however, for testing bolt action mechanisms and demonstrating how antique rifles operate.

Long-Term Storage

Dummy cartridges.

For truly long-term cold storage, what you need is an intimate and durable barrier against moisture, and there are a number of products on the market aimed at meeting this need.

One of the most common products is the VCI bag. VCI stands for "Vapor Corrosion Inhibiting." These bags are generally weatherproof, have tight seals and include a vapor inside the bag that is supposed to keep out corrosive elements. Be aware that these bags generally come in "short term" and "long term" varieties and that if you open the bag for any reason, you may have compromised its protective qualities and might have to purchase a replacement. Some systems actually allow you to custom make bags from a roll of material that is cut to size and sealed using an impulse sealer. The equipment demonstrated on the facing page is sold by Hansen & Hansen, 1-800-571-7337.

Supica on Gun Safes

Jim Supica, publisher of *Old Town Station Dispatch*, which has to be the most entertaining gun collecting catalog out there, has spent some time studying the question of gun safes and offers these opinions:

A large chunk of the cost of most gun safes lies in the glossy paint job, the brand name decal on the door, plush interior and celebrity endorsement/marketing. Some of these units are quite handsome, and may well be worth the extra cost to you for aesthetic purposes or pride of ownership. However, be aware of what you are actually paying for.

Types of safes: There are, in general, three security levels of safes to consider –

1. Security boxes - thin sheet metal, usually with a keyed lock, usually sufficient to keep kids out and (if screwed to wall studs and floor) discourage smash-and-grab opportunistic thieves. Typical of the type is the Homak brand sometimes sold through Wal-Mart.

2. Gun safes - heavier metal, quality lock, with or without fireliner. Generally will take time and tools to defeat.

3. Jewelry/cash safes - much more secure and harder to break into; usually too small, heavy and expensive for gun safe applications.

Evaluating a gun safe — In evaluating the "gun safe" class of safe from a security perspective, the following are important factors to consider, in approximate descending order of importance:

1) Thickness of steel, not only the door, but on all sides including top

A bagging system used by well-known dealers Hansen & Hansen, who report very good results. You cut the bag material to the required length and then seal with heat using an impulse sealer. If you leave extra length, you can cut the bag open and reseal if needed.

and bottom. 1/4 inch or thicker is very good. Less than 1/8 inch is not so good.

2) Quality of lock. The Sargent & Greenleaf (S&G) dial type seems to be the industry standard and is a good one. You can set these to your own chosen combination fairly easily with instructions provided. Electronic push-button locks make me nervous, but not for any good reason, just technophobia.

3) Door locking mechanism (live or dead bolt on both sides, although after a certain point total number of bolts used is not so vital).

4) Construction, particularly hinge type and door resistant to peeling.

5) Overall weight. Generally this goes back to the thickness of the steel, but can also be affected by firelining.

Important factors, not security related —

1) Overall size - Odds are, you will eventually fill whatever size you buy, so the bigger the better.

2) Interior racks/shelves - convenience & protection, how many can you fit in?

3) Door opening style - some open 90 degrees, some 180.

4) Fire lining.

Fort Knox, Browning, Liberty and others all offer good heavy S&G lock safes with beautiful finishes. I also like Sportsman Steel Safes of Long Beach, California, who seem to offer attractive prices and will sell direct to the consumer. Be sure to look at the weight of the safe without firelining to get an idea of the relative security of similarly sized safes.

I personally like the fire-lining option offered on gun safes. Some folks report that layers of sheetrock added to the outside of the safe can add comparable fire resistance for the do-it-yourselfers who already have safes without the fire-lining option. However, be a bit careful about using standard "fire safes" for gun storage. My layman's understanding is that some "fireproofing," particularly the kind found in safes designed to protect documents, works in part by releasing moisture when heated. That doesn't sound to me like a good thing for gun storage, so you might think twice before using a document safe for guns.

While we're talking about moisture, most gun-owners put a "goldenrod" in their safes to fight humidity (simply a plug-in electric rod which heats up.) Some say a low-wattage light bulb will serve the same purpose. That makes sense to me and seems to keep elephants away too, at least in Kansas. Also, some of those ultra-plush carpet-style linings look a bit like moisture traps to me. I don't know for sure, but I like to have something to worry about.

No safe is 100% burglar proof, but you can try to slow them down or encourage them to look for a softer target. Bolting a safe down to the floor and/or wall is important, since any safe can be hauled or dragged off to be opened at leisure. Also, remember that a safe is just part of a security system. Consider alarm systems and overall home security in conjunction with your safe.

280 Moisture Control Inside a Safe or Enclosed Display Case

Even if your glass display case or safe is in an air conditioned room, it has a microclimate of its own and may require its own moisture control. As was mentioned above by Mr. Supica, gun supply catalogs sell products to burn off moisture inside gun safes, and for some collectors low-wattage light bulbs have also proven effective, although these can also generate unwanted heat.

Yet other collectors report good results with silica, which is a substance much loved by the museum community for its moisture absorbing properties. For glass cases and other small-to-medium sized boxes, silica is probably the most popular choice. It comes in gel and pellet form, and does a great job. Eventually, it does absorb so much moisture that it is no longer effective, but it can usually be restored to its original potency by being heated. Follow the product's directions.

Silica is available in commercial packaging, usually including an indicator that will turn color when saturation has rendered it ineffective. For really large-scale applications, like large safes, etc., collectors might want to experiment with silica in the form of kitty litter. Ultra Pearls® is one popular brand that employs beads of silica. With such products, monitoring effectiveness is up to you. That's where hygrometers, as mentioned earlier in this chapter, really come in handy.

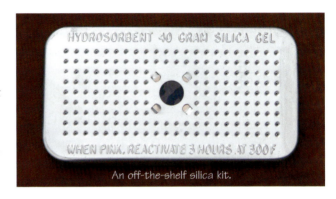
An off-the-shelf silica kit.

Look At What Museums Do

One of the places where I have gotten some of my best display ideas is from museums. Heck, they are in the business full time and probably know more about displaying collectibles than you or I ever will.

Museum display materials web sites and catalogs

Museum displays can give you some great ideas to use at home. Now all I need is my own stuffed buffalo!

Frazier Historical Arms Museum

Storage and Display

are an excellent resource, especially if you have accessories or parts that you want to show individually. While most top museums have workshops to make their own display mounts, you can purchase what are called "mount blanks" that are sort of spider-shaped metal structures that can be used to hold up all sorts of three-dimensional objects, just as long as they aren't too heavy.

282 Bayonetting the Ceiling

Back when I was a kid, I read an article in the *American Rifleman* by famous arms authority Harold Peterson. There was a photo in the article that always gave me a chuckle, in which Mr. Peterson showed himself handling a musket with the bayonet fixed. The caption read, "Long arms, especially with bayonets, must be handled with care and one eye always on the muzzle or bayonet point. Otherwise there is real danger of broken lights, punctured ceilings, or injured companions."

I thought this was pretty funny because who in the world could be stupid enough to stab the ceiling or a light fixture with a fixed bayonet. Hmmm. Well, it turns out that the answer is "me." I've stabbed the ceiling two times at my own house and once at a friend's. I've also smashed a light fixture and actually stabbed *myself* once (don't ask how!).

So you can laugh all you want, but watch it with those fixed bayonets!

283 Ammunition

Different types of ammunition need to be stored in different ways, both for safety and preservation. This book is not about ammunition collecting, so we aren't going to handle this huge topic here except to remind you to think about it. As with gun storage, humidity, temperature and light are big concerns. Also, keep all laws and regulations in mind and do not, under any circumstances, store ammunition where it can be put together with the gun that shoots it. Even if you don't have children in the house, this would be a huge liability that you just don't need.

German .22 ammunition made just before WWII. Poor storage has effected the exposed cartridge.

284 Wrapping Guns for Shipping

Now, we are going to talk about a touchy topic — how to protect guns from being damaged during shipment. We make no guarantees that the ideas described here will work for you (every situation is different and there is always risk). All we can do is describe what has worked for us.

A wrist crack caused by impact and twisting.

First of all, buy insurance. It sounds simple, but you would be surprised how many collectors choose to go without it. It is a common fault that we all probably suffer from — we are often willing to spend large amounts of cash on the gun itself, but tend to get cheap about the little stuff. Don't get cheap about insurance. The best kind is probably your own coverage added on as part of a collectibles insurance policy, but either way, be sure you are protected. Don't assume nothing will go wrong because the person selling you the item is a professional and should know how to wrap things effectively. The damaged weapons shown in this section are from the collection of the author and were damaged during transit from prestigious organizations.

In general, a custom-made wooden box, commonly called a "casket," is probably the most effective wrapping method. But because of construction costs and weight, it isn't cost efficient except for very valuable items. So we are often left making compromises. We balance cost against the risk of any potential damage. There are many choices available for shipping guns. First of all, for longarms there are cardboard gun shipping boxes. These are familiar commercial products and are widely used by gun dealers. Some are cheaply made and should be avoided; others are more sturdy. With proper padding, they do a surpris-

Ouch!
A nearly mint rifle takes a hit.

Storage and Display

A 17th-century musket literally torn in two during shipment by air freight.

ingly good job of protecting most sturdy longarms...especially on the ends. They do a less-than-perfect job of protecting packages from impact to the sides, as is shown by the Persian Mauser's broken wood illustrated in the photograph above.

For all but the cheapest longarms, I prefer using actual plastic gun cases. They are much more rigid, and their expense is often worth the extra protection that they afford. They are made to protect guns, the padding usually holds the weapon still in the center of the case, and they exist in many levels of quality, allowing you to choose a cost/risk equation with which you are comfortable. Pistols work the same way...yes, you can ship them in cardboard boxes, but a commercial pistol case will usually do a much better job (especially when double boxed with lots of peanuts), and many choices are available.

If you are looking for another option, I really like PVC pipe. You can buy it in widths to suit just about any gun, and it is very difficult to break. There are also heavy cardboard tubes that do a similar job. The best tubes are thick, of course, and that means more shipping weight, but better safe than sorry. As with cardboard gun boxes, you want to have a good deal of padding on either end, so that the container will absorb a lot of impact if it is dropped or struck.

When a gun box or tube is dropped from a height, it causes bone-jarring vibrations that can do a surprising amount of damage to gun stocks in particular. If you doubt this, just check out the illustration above. That musket wasn't struck by anything during transit; it was simply dropped. The tube was not well padded on the butt end, which was what hit the floor, and the 350-year-old stock, already weakened by worm holes, shat-

You can't see my tears in this photo, but they are there. If you do suffer a disaster, take your time while opening the package. Contact your insurance carrier immediately for instructions, and document everything that you do with photographs. Lastly, even extreme damage can often be repaired. Don't throw anything away! Save all the little pieces in zip lock bags.

tered in half at the wrist.

Like gun boxes, tubes tend to protect the ends better than the sides, so keep that in mind. It is also probably a good idea to wrap it in a plastic bag in case the package gets wet. Also, if there are multiple items (like a bayonet that goes on a rifle, for instance), be aware that a likely source of damage is that they will rub or bump against each other during transit.

Lastly, be sure to obey all laws, licensing requirements and shipping rules. That's a whole other topic that we can't handle here because the requirements change too often, but keep it in mind. And remember, you are shipping a gun (regardless of its age) and it is safer to send these items as deactivated as possible, with the bolts, cylinders, etc., removed — as well as being carefully padded. And for gosh sakes, don't ship ammo in the same box. That should go without saying.

We hope that you will find some of these suggestions useful. However, remember that shipping a collectible firearm always involves risks. The final question you should ask yourself is, "Do I really need to send this weapon at all?" Maybe the answer is that it just isn't worth taking a chance.

The Megapixel Challenge!

7 megapixels.

4 megapixels.

A comparison between two cameras, one with 7 megapixels and the other with 4 megapixels. Both cameras are made by the same company and are excellent pieces of equipment. Notice how the difference in megapixels does not matter very much for the small pictures (see left), but is really noticeable at full size (see below). There are also slight color differences between the two cameras, but this is not part of the test.

7 megapixels. Note the natural tone of the metal and rich detail. The engraving really looks three-dimensional here. While the view at right looks a bit brighter, this view looks more like the real gun.

4 megapixels. Notice the slightly jagged edges and cartoon-like tone. The background metal, in particular, lacks detail. In the fully-enlarged inset, this can be seen quite clearly.

Shooting Guns With A Camera

Shooting Guns With a Camera

285 Why You Should Buy a Digital Camera

One of the best tools for the gun collector is a good digital camera. Whether you are taking pictures of your collection for insurance records, for a scrapbook, to share on the Internet, for advertising or publication, there is a digital camera in your future. Unless you don't use a computer, film cameras are probably not worth looking at. I love film, but for speed and convenience of use, nothing can match the digital format.

While the cost of digital cameras has come down over the years, they are still significantly more expensive than film cameras. However, if you use the camera frequently, this extra cost will soon be overtaken by savings on processing film and making prints. Also, the digital cameras produce better, brighter, more pleasing results in the hands of novices than film cameras. The greatest advantages, however, are the ability to see the quality of results immediately (rather than having to wait for film processing) and the ability to send the photo files to fellow collectors over the Internet without having to own a scanner.

286 Megapixels and What You Need

Choosing a digital camera can be a confusing matter, indeed. However, it certainly does help to decide what you want to use the camera for before buying it. The most important specification of digital cameras is their megapixel count. To simply keep records and to send pictures over the internet, two megapixels is fine. In order to make quality prints of a normal size, three to four megapixels is required. If you want to take photographs for book illustrations or magazine articles, then five megapixels is good for 5x6 inch pictures. For larger pictures, six or eight megapixels is recommended. As we get into the higher numbers, the difference in quality seen with each increase is less and less significant. For instance, a three megapixel camera is much better than a two megapixel unit, but an eight megapixel camera is only slightly better than a six megapixel model.

What Brand Should I Buy?

This is a difficult question because models change so very quickly, and the state-of-the-art camera today will probably be obsolete by the time you read this. In general, Sony makes some excellent cameras with Zeiss lenses, but have the disadvantage of using proprietary memory strips that don't work with other kinds of cameras. Nikon makes excellent cameras in the $800 and higher price range, but their lower-end products don't seem to be as carefully designed. Canon makes excellent products in all price categories and generally has the easiest to use operating systems. For in-depth, unbiased reviews of the latest offerings, try www.dpreview.com or www.steves-digicams.com.

Whatever you do, make sure that your camera can focus up close and has a macro mode. You will want to take close-up photographs of markings and other features of your guns, and while most digital cameras are just great at this, it is worth checking.

Lastly, think about size. If you are just taking snapshots, simply buy what is comfortable for you to carry. But if you want impressive results, you should be using a serious-sized camera (sometimes called a "prosumer" model). This is one purchase where size matters. Don't use a pocket camera — no matter how many megapixels it has. There is just no substitute for lens size and a big camera with a large (diameter) lens will have the sharpness and light capture that you need to take better pictures. A lens the size of your thumbnail just won't cut it.

Built-in Lens or Interchangeable Lenses

If you decide to get a top-notch camera, one of the choices you are going to have to make is between an "all in one box" type with a built-in zoom lens and a 35mm digital SLR that can accept a variety of interchangeable lenses.

The very best built-in lens cameras have resolution and photo quality that rivals the more professional-looking 35mm digital SLRs. In general, they take excellent close-ups and can do just about everything that you need. The downside? Right now, the current models are relatively slow, have shorter battery life and capture slightly less light. They also tend to focus slower and sometimes misfocus in low light situations. None of these weaknesses will get in the way of your taking excellent photographs under normal lighting conditions. They can, however, be a real pain under less than ideal situations, like a gun show.

The 35mm digital SLRs by respected makers like Nikon and Canon have come down in price substantially in recent years, and can look like an affordable option. Be aware, however, that you will have to buy your own lenses, and the quality of the glass is everything. Don't get cheap on lens quality...it is your single most important piece of camera equipment.

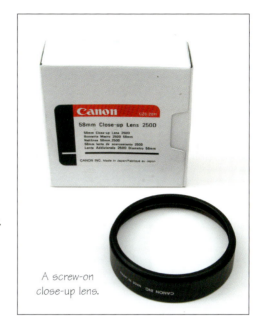

A screw-on close-up lens.

For gun photographs, you want to be able to take overalls and extreme close-ups for markings. The best lens for markings is a 90mm or 100mm macro lens. If you choose one of these, you might just find that this is all you need, because they are often great for overall shots, too. You just have to move the tripod back, because they don't have a zoom feature. For those who want a zoom lens (for convenience or because they want to take pictures of things other than guns), a good choice would be a medium zoom lens for the overalls. For close-ups, either add a macro or (for less cost and more portability) get a magnifying diopter that screws onto the end of your regular zoom lens. These don't work as well as a dedicated macro lens, but they are OK just as long as you get the more expensive type (usually by Canon or Nikon) that have two elements rather than one.

Camera Settings for Taking Serious Photographs

While it isn't too important to make your snapshots perfect, what do you do if you have a friend who is writing an article or a book and you need to give him publishable photo files? Unless you are a serious hobbyist, you might want to hire a professional to do this work (see below for suggestions about how to do this). But if you want to try it yourself, there are some basic guidelines that you need to follow.

First of all, make sure that your camera has enough megapixels and has a serious-sized lens, as explained earlier. Now for the settings. Every camera operates a little differently, but common themes apply. First of all, the "film speed" or ISO number is an important setting. Use the lowest number available, which is usually 100 or lower. The higher numbers are meant for sports or action shots and will look grainy.

Aperture is also very important because it controls the depth of field. Unless we want a particular artistic effect, which is rarely the case, good gun photography requires that everything be in focus. That means that the aperture should be small, which (ironically) means that the aperture number (or f stop) of your camera should be high. Start your setting at f22 and then experiment with higher numbers. If you are in a poor lighting situation (like a museum gallery) then you might have to go with lower numbers and sacrifice some depth of field, but photos taken at settings less than f16 are rarely satisfactory except for close-ups of markings.

Because aperature is so very important to photo quality, many photographers choose to work in "aperture priority mode," which is an option on most better cameras allowing you to have everything be automatic except the aperture. This is almost always the best way to shoot if you are using a tripod.

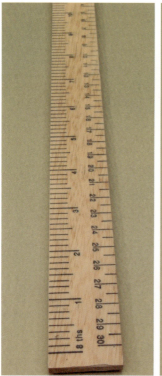

These two photos were taken with identical set-ups, except for different apertures. The left-hand picture was taken at f22. The right-hand picture was taken at f5.5. The picture at the left has much better overall crispness.

Shooting Guns With A Camera

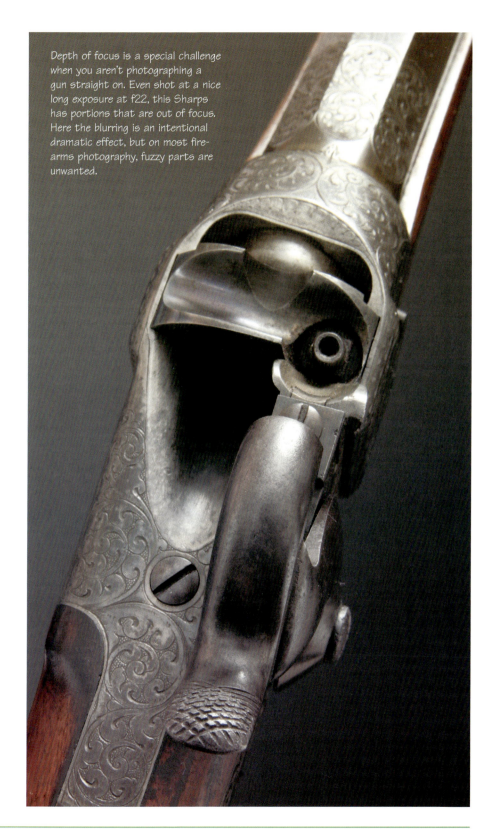

Depth of focus is a special challenge when you aren't photographing a gun straight on. Even shot at a nice long exposure at f22, this Sharps has portions that are out of focus. Here the blurring is an intentional dramatic effect, but on most firearms photography, fuzzy parts are unwanted.

There are two other settings that are of utmost importance: the size of the photo file created and the amount of compression applied. The first setting is usually called Image Size and is generally a numerical setting. You want the very highest setting available with the largest pixel dimensions possible. The second setting is often called Quality or Compression or JPEG Setting. We want this set to "Fine" or "Highest Quality" or "TIFF." Large file sizes are what we want. If your camera has a "RAW" setting, this will not normally improve your images over the "Fine" setting unless you are operating under challenging light conditions and are a real expert at manipulating photo files on a computer.

Color temperature is our last important setting. Experiment with this in order to get the most neutral, natural color. There are usually a variety of settings (cloudy, incandescent, etc.) that can be chosen manually, as well as an "Automatic White Balance" or "AWB" setting. "Automatic" usually works quite well out of doors but often does a poor job inside. If you are in doubt, take a photo including white or black items and then view the results to see if these areas include any undesired color tones.

Most better cameras have a custom white balance feature that allows you to take a picture of a white or gray card and apply the resulting measurement to all subsequent photos for the most accurate color reproduction...it is a great feature if your camera has it. But remember, you have to create a new custom white balance measurement every time the lighting conditions change.

What Makes A Good Gun Picture?

A good gun picture is one that shows the features that you want it to show. If it does that job for you, then it is a good picture.

In general, however, there are two approaches to gun photography. You can try to be artistic or you can try to be illustrative. Artistic photographs with dramatic lighting and sometimes dark, moody shadows can be quite beautiful, but don't usually please gun collectors because photos of this type can make it hard to see the details of a gun. Illustrative photos, sometimes called catalog-style photos, tend to be more popular with collectors. These pictures usually have few or no shadows and no "hot spots" or reflections on the metal. All of the gun will be well lit and all of the gun will be in focus. The background is simple and does not distract from the weapon. Everything from the grain of the wood to machining marks in the metal are crisp, clear and easy to see. This is the kind of photography that we recommend, and this is the kind of photography that we will try to help you achieve.

Avoid Disorienting Backgrounds

I don't know why, but everyone photographing a Scottish pistol wants to put it on the loudest tartan available, and everyone shooting a Western lever action wants to put it on a fur rug or an Indian blanket. Unless you really know what you are doing, please don't do this. These backgrounds will almost always overwhelm the subject. When you look at your photo, you don't want to see the plaid first and the gun second. Make sure that the background contrasts with the gun but doesn't distract your eye from what really matters. Light grey, beige, green and blue are all good choices. Bright red and bright yellow are usually too vibrant and should be avoided. As a general rule, with a dark gun use a light background and vice versa. If in doubt, use white. It's boring, but it is the safe choice.

If you do use white, however, remember that your camera's exposure meter will probably

Two photographs with distracting backgrounds.

give you inaccurate results on the automatic settings. The light meter will see all of that white background and assume that the overall photo is way too bright and has to be made darker. Your gun will often end up looking like a black blob. To compensate for this, either use manual exposure controls or an automatic meter setting that is center weighted.

Two photographs of a tiny toy gun from the 1500s excavated in London, England. Both shots were taken on a white background. The picture on the left was taken with the camera's automatic settings, showing how a white background can mislead even the very best light meters. The image on the right was taken with a longer exposure to give a more natural appearance.

Either way, with a white background you will probably want a longer exposure than what your camera initially suggests.

Get the Right Angle

It is often difficult to get the camera at an angle so that it shows the parts of the gun that you want to feature. For instance, if there is an important inscription, you will want it to read easily.

This is especially difficult if the gun is lying on the background material. If you are having trouble getting the right angle, try propping the gun up by putting an eraser or other soft wedge under the background or under the gun itself.

In this view, a flexible rubber eraser is being used to prop up an attractive advertising wood cut.　　　　　　　　　　(woodcut from the Herbert G. Houze collection)

Shooting Guns With A Camera

Erasers are good for posing firearms because they are soft, flexible and unlikely to cause damage.

Focus Tips

No matter how good your eyes are, your camera's automatic focus will probably do a better job than manual focus if you have good lighting conditions. However, be aware of what the camera is focusing on and don't be shy about refocusing if needed. For most gun pictures, you want the closest important feature to be what you are focusing on. Because of how depth of focus works, the area behind the focus point will be sharper than the area in front. So don't expect a crisp appearance on things that are much closer to you than your focus point.

Bracketing

Make it a habit to take three exposures of each shot. One just where the camera's automatic features suggest, one lighter and one darker. That way, even if you aren't

dead on, you will usually have a useful alternate to fall back upon. Some cameras even offer the option of bracketing automatically.

Buy a Tripod

There is just no way to get around the need for a tripod for most better gun photography. For depth of focus, we need long exposures (usually a second or much more) and you cannot reliably hand-hold a camera for exposures longer than 1/60th of a second. If you plan to do a lot of serious photography, then buy a lower-end professional model by Manfrotto or Gitzo. One feature that I really do recommend is a quick-release system, which allows you to take the camera off of the tripod for downloading to the computer without disturbing your set-up.

If you don't take many pictures, just buy the sturdiest one that they have on sale at your local department store. You don't want a tripod that wobbles...test it in the store. And remember,

Quick release is a nice feature for a tripod.

a tripod won't help very much if you are touching the camera when it goes off. The fanciest option is to use a remote control, but most digital cameras have self-timers that count down ten seconds before going off, which is really quite convenient and a great way to get around the expense of purchasing a remote.

On-Camera Flash is For Losers

OK, maybe that's a little harsh...but it isn't far from the truth. It is extremely difficult to get really good gun photographs with the built-in flash that comes with your camera, no matter how expensive it is. The results almost always show bright spots or reflections, harsh shadows and a blue color cast. Of course, if you are at a gun show and need to take a quick snapshot, on-camera flash is a great fall-back system, but it shouldn't be your first choice if you want pleasant-looking pictures.

Photographic Lighting Introduced

Lighting is the most difficult part of gun photography. And it's also almost entirely about convenience. Don't fool yourself into thinking that you need to spend thousands of dollars on professional lighting equipment. You don't. The ideal form of light can be found outdoors on an overcast day...look for the times when the sun is bright, but evenly diffused with cloud cover so that nothing casts a shadow.

It's entirely free, but it isn't reliable. In fact, some of my friends from southern California insist that overcast days never happen at all. Here in New England, perfect photography days usually happen one after the other all through Autumn. But unfortunately, we can't all carry around a perfect Fall day in our pockets. This is where artificial lighting comes in.

The Color of Light

One of the problems with artificial light is that it usually isn't white. Standard incandescent light bulbs give off yellow light. Standard fluorescent bulbs give off blue light. Your eyes and your brain adjust for this, making the light seem white — but it isn't. It's just an illusion.

Your camera, which sees much more accurately than we do, duplicates this yellow or blue light and there will be an unwanted tint, called a "color cast," on your pictures. Often, if there are two kinds of lamps in the room, you will see both unwanted colors at once. This effect is especially obvious on white objects and on metal.

Color casts are bad news and we want to prevent them. Your camera has white balancing features that were discussed earlier. Take full advantage of them. Aside from this, be aware

Two photos of a rifle's grenade launcher. The photo at top was taken with a fluorescent lamp on in the room, creating a blue color cast. The photo at bottom is without the color cast.

Sometimes a background can cause a color cast, too. Notice how the light is bouncing off of this bright yellow background, giving the gun an unintended yellow glow. On top, it almost looks like the wood is yellow.

of the sources of light where you are taking pictures. If you are outdoors, maybe the light will be green because it is passing through leaves. If you are indoors, maybe light from outside is passing through a red curtain in the window, filling the room with red light. Your eyes probably won't notice it, but your camera will! Perhaps you have a reading lamp in the corner with a stained glass shade, putting off all kinds of colors that you don't want. And, of course, there are all those incandescent and fluorescent lamps generating streams of yellow and blue.

The bottom line is that your camera's white balance controls can only deal with one light source at a time. If all the lights are incandescent...great. All fluorescent...great. All sunlight...great. Combinations, however, are

The pink color on this steel lockplate was caused by light coming through red blinds in a neighboring room. If you don't shoot after dark, it can be difficult to detect and eliminate color pollution problems of this sort.

a problem we need to avoid. If you are using artificial lighting indoors, the easiest approach is to wait until after dark, turn off all the lights in that section of the house, and have your photographic lights be the only source of light in the room. It's a pain, but it makes a huge difference in the quality of color photographs.

Flash Photography

The challenge of photographic lighting is to be able to reproduce perfect lighting conditions (remember that overcast day?) over and over again. For many professional photographers who shoot fashion or portraits, fancy flash set-ups are the answer. There are many excellent products out there that are either designed for a studio or for travel. On the whole, the dependable products are quite expensive and perform best with a fast exposure — which limits the depth of focus. They are not ideal lighting systems for still life photography.

If you need to travel a lot to take your pictures, then you might want to purchase one of these systems, but prepare to pay for it. Calling a camera dealer with a large professional clientele and telling them that you need a flash set-up for product photography would be a good way to get started. But for most collectors, this type of rig is unnecessary and will not give you better pictures.

The Almost-Free Option

If we don't want flash photography, then what do we do? Well, one answer might be to photograph outdoors, even though the day might not be quite as overcast as we want. One possible solution to the lack of clouds could be to use the shadow of a tree, but you will quickly find that shadows cast by natural objects almost always have patterns or uneven parts...and we don't want splotchy light or the shapes of leaves on our gun photos.

A better solution is a diffusion panel. Since the shadows cast by nature aren't perfect enough, we simply make shadows of our own. Go to an art supply store and buy the parts necessary to make an inexpensive

HOW TO MAKE A DIFFUSION PANEL

1. Fit the frame together. The pieces are preformed.

2. Lay out your sheet of Mylar on the frame.

(Continued on the next page)

HOW TO MAKE A DIFFUSION PANEL

(Continued from the previous page)

3. Staple or tape the Mylar in place.

2. You are ready to take some pictures!

frame...the kind that painting canvases are stretched over. Then, also at the art supply store, purchase a large sheet of Mylar, which is a translucent, but not transparent, plastic. Any white or transluscent wrinkle-free fabric or sheeting should work, but Mylar is easy to get and quite inexpensive. Next, staple or tape it to your cheap frame, and you are good to go. Just have someone hold your homemade diffusion panel between the sun and the gun and you are well on your way to some great gun photos without having spent more than about fifteen dollars.

One hint, though. Since the sun is rarely directly overhead, you might have to tilt the diffusion panel so that one side of the picture will not be darker than the other.

301 The Cheap Option

Of course, during the winter and on rainy days, shooting gun photos outdoors is impossible. If we are photographing indoors, we will need lights, and the best kind for gun photography are the continuous light types often called floodlights. These are much less expensive than flash units, but take up more room and generate a lot more heat.

You can purchase a professional set-up, in which case you should pay a lot of attention to the tripods and to overall durability, which are important selling points. If you want to spend less money, you might find yourself quite happy with workshop flood lights that you can buy at hardware stores, and which often come with clamps to hold them to supports or tripods of your own choosing. Many people prefer to equip these lamps with daylight-balanced compact florescent bulbs of fairly high wattage, which are nearly flicker free and do not get as hot as incandescent or other traditional bulbs.

Workshop floodlight equipped with a 100-watt daylight balanced compact fluorescent light bulb.

Pointing the lights directly at your gun will usually produce the reflections and shadows that we are trying to avoid. You will probably be happier with diffused or indirect lighting. Diffused lighting is the same kind of light we were looking for outdoors, so try diffusion panels of the kind we constructed in the previous section. Moving them closer or further away from the lamps will create different lighting effects for you to experiment with. For indirect lighting, you can bounce the light off of a large piece of white foam board (of the kind used by kids to mount school projects). This stuff also makes great photographic backgrounds, is available in a number of colors other than white and can be purchased everywhere from art supply stores to Wal-Mart.

Direct light has its uses. It can make a dull gun look bright and shiny, and is good for markings. But it is difficult to work with and usually creates unwanted shadows and reflections.

(right) There are many brands of foam board, one of the sturdiest being X-Acto. It comes in a variety of colors.

Shooting Guns With A Camera

Indirect light off of a white ceiling. In this set-up, a photographic "umbrella" is being used to bounce the light up, which doubles the effect. Ceiling height does make a difference. I get best results with 9 feet.

Perhaps the most simple and inexpensive method of creating indirect light is to point your floodlights at a white ceiling. This does not tend to work very well with drop ceilings made of insulated panels. A plain, white, painted ceiling is what you should look for. The light hits the ceiling, bounces down in a thousand subtly different directions and creates bright, shadowless illumination below. This is currently my favorite type of lighting for firearms. However, I would point out that the more you diffuse your light, the more lamps you are going to need. About 1,000 watts or more are required to light a scene brightly when bouncing off of the ceiling.

302 Special Equipment for Highly Reflective Subjects

The problems with highly reflective surfaces like silver and nickel plating are twofold. First, you will get bright, flashed spots where the light bounces off the metal. These look ugly. Second, you will probably be able to see yourself and your camera reflected on the metal, just as if it were a mirror. That looks silly.

The answer might be a light tent. Photographers have created light tents for ages, making them out of everything from plastic sheets to white trash containers. Basically, they are a three-dimensional cousin to the

A light tent being used to photograph a pistol with a reflective finish.

Shooting Guns With A Camera

Note the reflection of the photographer in the polished bolt of this military rifle. Eliminating these reflections is a challenge and is one of the key benefits of using a light tent.

diffusion panel. You surround the gun with white material that diffuses light, and you really kill the reflections. Light tents sometimes produce "milky" results that look too soft, but by changing the distances and angles of the lights themselves, outside of the tent, you should be able to diminish these problems.

Many of the product photographs that you see in catalogs and on eBay were shot with light tents. They are a very easy way to get shadowless photography. While it is a relatively simple project to make one, they are also made commercially in forms that can be folded down for easy travel and are relatively inexpensive. In general, most of the commercially made light tents work best with small items like pistols and accessories, but if you are shooting larger items like rifles you should be able to construct something out of PVC pipe and plastic sheeting in a few hours. Note that the sheeting does not have to be white...many clear types work quite well too if they aren't textured or overly reflective.

303 Cute Lighting Tricks I
Light Tables

Photographers and other graphic artists have long used light tables for viewing film. Some of these, intended specifically for viewing slides and negatives, can be quite useful for shooting small guns on a white, shadowless background.

The light table's surface is translucent frosted glass with a lamp underneath it. The quality of light is quite gentle and removes shadows

Note: Please be aware that if you use this method you will also need regular photographic lighting. The light table does not light the scene; it only eliminates shadows. Also, be sure that the background is coming out pure white and that you are not able to see the glass surface.

(left) A light table in action.

well without wrapping around the gun unnecessarily. The one big downside to light tables is that they get scratched up, and the scratches often show up in the backgrounds of the pictures.

Another way of creating the same effect is to place the gun being photographed on a glass coffee table covered by a piece of white paper. A light source shining upwards under the table completes the set-up.

Cute Lighting Tricks II
Milk Jugs

Do you need to take shadowless photographs of small items on a budget? In short, do you want the benefits of a light tent without having to purchase one? There is a way.

Fun with a milk jug.

You can get excellent results by taking a white, one-gallon milk jug and cutting off both ends. You stick the jug over your derringer or rare cartridge, put a floodlight or two outside, and stick the lens of your camera down the enlarged area where the spout used to be. There you go. A free light tent for small objects.

Cute Lighting Tricks III
Glowing Backgrounds

Vertical cloth backgrounds, like muslin, can be very useful in gun photography. Sometimes, photos using these backgrounds look like the cloth is positively glowing. That's because it is.

Photographers regularly put flashes or photo floodlights behind the cloth to give it that special appearance. This kind of special effect is inexpensive and can be quite effective.

306 Cute Lighting Tricks IV
The Dowel Trick

One nice trick for posing guns is to suspend them on dowels that are made of wood or soft metal. After securing the dowel with clamps to a chair or other sturdy platform, slide the gun, barrel first, onto the rod, pointing down. Then put the background well behind the gun and take the photograph straight ahead as if it were a portrait.

With this method, the shadows fall on the ground rather than the background, and the edges are given what seem to be extra sharpness. You can also light your background separately to make it either darker or lighter to your preference.

(above and right) The dowel trick.

Shooting Guns With A Camera

Of course, after you are through, you will have to rotate the photograph and use computer retouching tools to paint the dowel out, replacing it with the same color as the background.

This set-up is easiest for pistols but works great for longarms, too. If you want the "wet" look of direct lighting without the shadows, then this method is for you!

307 B&W For Those Markings

Do you need to read some faint or hard-to-see markings on your gun, and you aren't getting anywhere with a light and your magnifying glass? Try taking a close-up picture of them in black and white. Sometimes, eliminating the color from the situation makes changes in darkness and depth easier to see, revealing the shapes of markings that would otherwise remain unreadable.

This faint marking is invisible in a color photograph.

More than once, I have looked at black and white photographs of my guns only to discover markings that I didn't even know were there in the first place. Pretty neat!

There is also a trick with acid that some collectors use to reveal hidden markings, but you are going to have to learn that one on your own! It literally eats away at your gun and I'm not sure I want the responsibility.

308 Hiring a Photographer

For great results, nothing matches hiring a professional. But you don't want someone who only knows how to shoot brides and babies. The best choice, of course, is to hire a full-time gun photographer. There are some great craftsmen out there who can make even the most mundane gun look special.

If this isn't possible, then look for someone skilled at product photography, especially highly reflective items like jewelry and watches. Ask to see samples of their work, and examine the pictures for sharpness, clarity, lack of heavy shadows and reflections. Artistic presentation isn't nearly as important as whether the checkering will be in focus on your grips and the markings readable on your barrel top. Make sure your instructions are clear. You want the whole gun in focus, as much sharpness as possible, no shadows, no reflections and a bright overall appearance.

Tools, Gadgets and Tricks

Bore Lights

Simply put, I wouldn't be without one. You should never buy a gun, especially a vintage military rifle or sporting arm, without inspecting the bore. There are some great miniature units available out there, and they are cheap, so there's no excuse for not owning one.

Bore Scopes

Bore scopes are sort of like the ultimate bore light. Invented for medical examinations, they use fiber optics to give you detailed views of the inside of a firearm's barrel. They have great magnification (almost too much) and give you bright, clear looks at the inside of rifling and other hard-to-see spots. An eyepiece is attached to a long, thin metal tube that you slide down the barrel. An attachment at the end of the tube lets you look either down or to the side.

Most collectors don't own bore scopes because they are extremely expensive. However, some

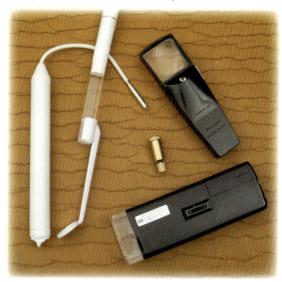

(right) There is an endless variety of lighting tools that can be used to inspect collectible firearms. Some favorites are a cartridge-sized bore light that can be dropped down muzzles, and a 30x pocket microscope.

One of the newer lighting tools on the market is the fiber optic wand. These flexible units can get light into the most remote corners of your gun and are a great addition to your tool kit.

Tools, Gadgets and Tricks

collectors of flintlocks have found them indispensable for discovering reconversions — a form of fakery where guns that were converted from flintlock to percussion in the historical period are returned to flintlock ignition in modern times in order to increase a gun's value. Bore scopes can be used to detect many of these reconversions because the fakers usually spend much more time on the outside of the gun than the inside. For instance, reconversion often involves the filling of the old touch hole (vent) and drilling a fresh one in a new location. You can often see the old, filled-in hole with a bore light.

Similarly, fakers sometimes use acid to create the appearance of wear on the outside of a reconverted flintlock's touch hole, but rarely go to such trouble on the inside of the barrel where no one can see it easily. If the outside of the touch hole shows corrosion but the inside is a freshly drilled hole, then that is a clear sign that skullduggery is afoot.

Where can you buy bore scopes? Medical supply houses…if you know exactly what you are looking for. The best route here would probably be to get a recommendation from a fellow collector who is already using one. One of the brands that I have tried and used successfully is the Hawkeye®, which is currently being offered in well-known gunsmithing catalogs. If you collect expensive flintlock guns that were often converted to percussion, like military flintlock pistols, a bore scope would be a very reasonable investment. Unfortunately, most of these units are not long enough to reach all the way down the barrel of a longarm, so length is something to consider if you decide to purchase one.

Don't Screw Up Your Guns

Nothing makes an experienced collector cringe quicker than seeing some knucklehead whip out an "el cheapo" no-name screwdriver and force it into the slots of gun screws where it just plain doesn't fit. We've all bought otherwise wonderful guns where all the screws are downright ruined, or where the metal and finish around the screws themselves are defaced by scratches, gouges and other evidence of screwdriver malpractice.

Laziness! That's the only reason for this to ever happen. There is no excuse, except perhaps not knowing the right way to do it. So let's fix that right here and right now with a little lesson in

A mangled screw.

A poorly fitting screwdriver blade will quickly damage the slot. Use the entire cavity.

screwdriver mechanics.

The Fit Is Everything

312 The only way to remove a screw without causing damage is by using a screwdriver that fits perfectly. What you need to do is fill the whole slot of the screw head. The dimensions of the screwdriver's blade need to match the width of the slot, the length of the slot, depth of the slot and the angle of the slot. There shouldn't be any empty space. The worst kind of damage is done when the screwdriver's blade does not fill the whole length of the slot, or if it doesn't reach down to the bottom. You need to use every little bit of those walls inside the screw slot, so that the maximum amount of surface area is being used when force is applied.

Spend Some Money On The Right Equipment

313 Most collectible guns use slotted screws. Slotted screwdrivers can come with parallel heads/blades (these are the common ones found in most garage tool boxes), tapering blades (these come to a fine, thin end) and hollow-ground blades (where the sides are hollowed out near the end). For most firearm applications, hollow ground should be your only choice. There are some exceptions to this rule. For instance, some old flintlocks actually have tapering slots. For these I like the original antique turnscrews that come in cased sets of dueling pistols.

In most instances, hollow ground is the way to go, but take your time

Tools, Gadgets and Tricks

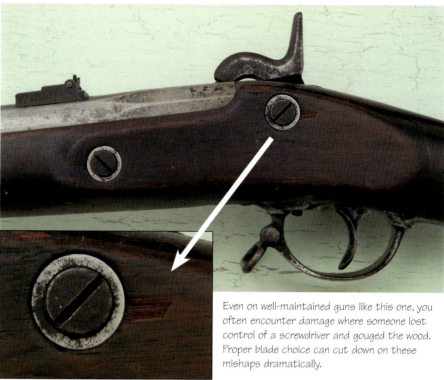

Even on well-maintained guns like this one, you often encounter damage where someone lost control of a screwdriver and gouged the wood. Proper blade choice can cut down on these mishaps dramatically.

Gunsmithing screwdrivers like the model shown here are a great investment. Make sure that you also purchase a wide variety of heads to get the ultimate fit.

to determine the shape of those screw slots. In some cases, you might actually have to custom-grind a screwdriver tip in order to get the right fit.

The Right Head For The Right Job

Since gun screws come in all shapes and sizes, you would, presumably, need a huge set of screwdrivers in

Tools, Gadgets and Tricks

The best screwdriver in the world won't do you much good unless you get a wide selection of heads that are appropriate for the types of guns that you collect. These heads often connect to the screwdriver's shaft with a magnetic lock, and are inexpensive if purchased as part of a set.

order to fit them all properly. Rather than trying to assemble such a set, most collectors will prefer to get a special package of hollow-ground gunsmith's screwdrivers where there is one handle/shaft that fits a large selection of interchangeable heads. Brownells, the gunsmith supply company, offers these in many configurations and they are an excellent choice. Just make sure that you are getting a large enough choice of heads in the shapes that you are going to need. Some of the heads offered are in shapes that only appear on very modern guns; if you don't need these, don't waste money on them.

Get a copy of the Brownells® catalog (1-800-741-0015) or go to their website (www.brownells.com) to check out the selection. Their "house set" is inexpensive and quite good.

315 Get That Slot Clean

Now that you have chosen the right blade from your gunsmith's screwdriver set — one that really fills the slot in every dimension — make sure that the slot itself is clean and free of obstructions and debris. Screw slots collect all kinds of lint, oil, dirt — you name it. And that junk in there is standing between you and the perfect fit you need. So take some time and clean it out, especially those bottom corners. Often, a wooden matchstick or a thin piece of cardboard can do the job just fine. If there is an obstruction that is fighting back, you might want to use something more precise, like dental tools. I love to have dental tools around the gun room because they let you work in tight spaces with precision. Buy a set — they're cheap.

Penetrating Oil

If a screw hasn't been used in a long time or just seems tight, try a drop of penetrating oil. Let it sit and then come back to try it again later. But for gosh sake, don't force things. Also, be aware that penetrating oil is not the best thing for delicate plated finishes, and there might be a risk of flaking.

What To Do With Totally Ruined Screws

If a screw is totally messed up, or if it won't come out with the above methods, the first thing you might consider is whether you actually need to remove it. If not, perhaps you should let sleeping dogs lie.

If you do need to get it out, then you might want to consult with a competent gunsmith. Sure, there are rigs you can build to press down and forcefully draw out stuck screws, and totally ruined ones can be drilled out and replaced, but if you aren't nifty with tools, I don't recommend it. If you do happen to be clever with your hands, then there are plenty of gunsmithing manuals out there to help you find your way.

Transmission Syringes

Transmission syringes are the kind that can't be used for intravenous injections and, therefore, are legal to buy at most pharmacies. They are great for getting glue, solvents and other liquids into really tiny spaces — which can be

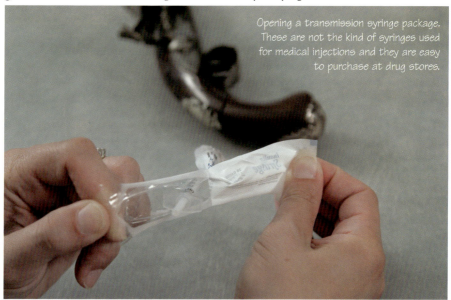

Opening a transmission syringe package. These are not the kind of syringes used for medical injections and they are easy to purchase at drug stores.

Transmission syringes are great for getting into tight spots. They can cut down on the mess of applying glue, solvents and other liquids.

really useful in repair work. I always keep a couple around in case I find myself in a tight spot. Many people use them for almost all glue applications just because they offer so much accuracy and control.

319 Surplus Cleaning Kits

Looking for a cleaning kit for a military caliber rifle? Don't overlook some of the really nifty military surplus kits that are available out there. The nicest kits are probably the Swiss ones, but there are other options, like German H&K rifle kits, too. These kits are generally very inexpensive and much better made than most products that you will find for sale at a gun show. They will usually be slightly used, however.

Surplus cleaning kits are a great bargain, but can be worn and dirty from their military use. Shop carefully.

The zenon beam, high power and even light of this flashlight make it a real winner.

SureFire Flashlights

320 It used to be that all flashlights were more or less created the same. Not any more. There's a new sheriff in town, and its name is SureFire®. These flashlights have set the standard for military and law enforcement use, and they are standard issue for the F.B.I.

I have to thank renowned dealer Herb Glass, Jr. for introducing me to this excellent evaluation tool. What he said while demonstrating it for me is that you will have to establish a whole new standard of condition when using this light. He couldn't have been more correct. In fact, when you use a SureFire® you need to be very, very forgiving of your guns, because you are going to see every little thing that is wrong with them...and more. I'm not kidding. It is like having the "Eye of God" in your hand. The zenon beam is even, powerful and penetrating — about three times what you get with a normal high-quality flashlight. And the quality and whiteness of the light, itself, is exceptional. When guns are illuminated with a SureFire®, you not only see graduations in the finish that would otherwise be invisible, you also see the precise, exact colors. Sometimes it almost seems like you can see straight through the metal and out the other side of the gun.

The down side of all this is that they are expensive. SureFires® start out at about $35, and most models cost well over $100. For our purposes, however, the least expensive models like the G2 are perfectly fine.

Just stay away from the LED models, which are excellent products but do not have the same powerful beam as their regular "personal flashlight" line. And be warned that the lithium batteries that they use are pretty expensive. You might be tempted to get the rechargeable battery unit, but the price (more than the cost of the flashlight itself) will probably make you hesitate.

321 The Gun Show Kit

Do you go to gun shows hoping to make a great buy? Great, but don't go unprepared. Be sure to bring the stuff that you might need in a pinch. Did you buy a bore light as recommended earlier? Great...bring it. Other ideas might include a magnifying glass, a small but powerful flashlight (lighting at shows is often horrible), a bore gauge, a set of screwdrivers, a tape measure, a small photo album of your collection and a selection of your favorite reference books and price guides.

I wouldn't go carrying the reference books around, but they are great to have in the car in case the need arises...which it usually does. I also suggest bringing along a couple of gun bags or hard cases. You might buy something precious, and getting it home safely is an important concern.

322 Removing Pins Properly

Most guns are at least partly assembled using pins. Removing these pins correctly is not easy. Just look at the barrel pins on any old military musket, and you are almost sure to see gouged-out wood around these pins where they were repeatedly driven out incorrectly, permanently defacing the wood.

When you need to take a pin out of a collectible gun, the first step is to observe what kind of pin it is. Does it have a taper? In other words, is one end thicker than the other end. On some guns, like the Martini-Henry, certain pins only go out in one direction, and trying to remove them backwards will quickly distort the pin and ruin it. On the Winchester Single-Shot, all the pins have to be driven out from left to right, except the

Gouged-out wood is a common sight around barrel pins.

If you are going to remove pins from your guns, get the right tools for the job.

main lever pin, which goes out from right to left. Always remove such pins by pushing them towards the thick end or they will get stuck and you will be in a real jam...so to speak.

The tool that you use to remove pins is called a Pin Punch or Drift Punch. Gunsmithing catalogs sell these punches as sets, and there are even some sets that are specific for individual manufacturers, so shop carefully and ask the dealer plenty of questions. The punch sets sold at hardware stores rarely meet the needs of gun collectors, so it is recommended that you make your purchase from a gunsmith supplier.

Punches, because they are thin but take a lot of punishment, are pretty easy to break, and when this happens, you not only lose the tool but can damage your gun in the process. In order to address this problem, you should also purchase a set of Starting Punches, which are tapered punches that only work for the first fraction of an inch, but won't actually penetrate the hole much. These punches do the brute work of getting the pin loose, and save the more delicate punches from the biggest risk of breakage.

Domed pins on a S&W.

Before you start hammering away, check whether the pin you are trying to remove has a flat head or a rounded head. If the head is rounded or domed, as is found on many higher-quality guns, you will need to use a special type of punch called a Cup Tip Punch. This variety has a hollowed-out tip so that the dome of your pin will not be flattened down.

Driving pins correctly is a challenge and will require some practice, but remember, always work slowly and, if in doubt, consult with a competent gunsmith.

Dental Tools

Dental tools aren't just for hygienists anymore! Every gun collector should own a set. They are just great for cleaning out tight spots that you can't reach with brushes. For more delicate jobs, just wrap a cleaning patch around the dental tool and get at all the nooks and crannies. They also make perfect probes for inspecting intricate lock mechanisms. Need to clear out a filthy maker's mark or proof mark in a hurry? Dental tools do the trick. And, by the way, those inspection mirrors that dentists use can come in handy, too.

Where do you get them? Well, they are so popular with firearms enthusiasts that they are often sold in gun supply catalogs. But you can also get them on the Internet or ask your dentist if he has any used sets available. They aren't very expensive at all and are well worth the investment. Just be careful when using them, because they are made of pretty hard metal and you can scratch guns with them if you aren't careful.

Steaming out Dents

A number of collectors have reported good results removing dents from gun stocks by steaming them out. They take wet cotton rags, lay them over the dent, and then press down on the exact spot of the dent with a very hot metal object. The steam is supposed to pull the wood up to fill the dented area, and it is assumed that a certain amount of sanding, oiling, etc., will be required to make the spot look "right" again. The hot metal object used to do this steaming is usually either a household flat iron or a heated screwdriver blade.

Personally, I have never had much luck with this technique. The end result almost always looks a little unnatural and, to my eye, worse than what I started with. You, however, might make out better, especially on gun stocks that no longer have any original finish.

325 The Old Candle Smoke Trick for Marks in Metal

Need to record a maker's mark or other stamping but don't have a camera handy? Some people put tracing paper over the mark and rub gently with a pencil to get an impression. That doesn't work very well, though. On guns with no finish, another method is to light a candle, tip it a bit so that it makes black smoke, then direct the smoke onto the marking. This will leave behind a greasy film. Next, you take scotch tape and press it over the mark, using a pencil eraser to push it into all the depressions. The black residue will stick to the tape. Now, stick the tape to an index card. You should get a decent impression of the mark, and a better one than you would have gotten with tracing paper. But don't burn your gun!

326 The Wooden Match Trick

Have a wood screw that has stripped its hole and keeps falling out? Old timers used to break off a section of wooden match stick and put it in the hole, then turn the screw back in. The soft wood of the match would give the threads something to bite into and hold the screw in place.

327 Wooden Flints

If you want your guns to have the proper flintlock profile, but don't feel like buying flints, wrapping them in red leather, etc., then you might consider just using a

A wooden wedge is an attractive alternative to using real flints.

properly shaped wedge of wood. It's cheap, it's easy, it won't scratch the gun and it looks kind of classy.

The Penny Trick

An old-time trick for removing pockets of rust on a blued surface was to scrape it with a copper penny, which is softer than the surface you are trying to save but harder than the rust you are trying to take off.

This works pretty well, but supposedly there is a risk of bimetallic corrosion, which is a special kind of rusting reaction that can happen when two different metals are put into close contact with each other. While bimetallic corrosion is a real and serious concern for many kinds of antique items, I haven't seen it be much of a problem on guns. What I do sometimes see, however, is the steel surface getting discolored by the penny, which can leave behind rubbed-off copper on all of the places that you have been scraping. Washing with mineral spirits as you go would probably help prevent this and would also clear away the loosened rust so it doesn't become an abrasive.

So the penny trick is a cool idea, but it has its liabilities.

Cracked Wood?

AcraGlas® barrel bedding material is an excellent glue for fixing cracks in wooden stocks. Many people also report top notch results with the liquid form of Superglue®. As always, if you plan to shoot a gun or if it is a valuable piece, you really should consult a gunsmith.

Some people would disagree with using AcraGlas® and similar synthetic products, however, because once the repair is done, it is fairly difficult to undo the work, if necessary. In other words, it works well but isn't easily reversible. If you are looking for a more reversible option, then you might want to experiment with Hide Glue or Fish Glue, which are old-fashioned glues made from organic components. They are inexpensive and available from woodworking supply companies.

Surgical Tubing

Many folks who are gluing cracked or broken gunstocks are confused about how to secure the two pieces of wood while

If clamps don't work, try tubing.

Tools, Gadgets and Tricks

Clamp marks on a gun barrel. While the marks on this Brown Bolt Action Rifle come from the factory, most others are from sloppy repairs.

the glue sets. We often see patterned indentations in guns where unpadded vices were used, so obviously that isn't the best method.

In general, rubber clamps are a safer options but you will need a good selection to get the proper fit. One tool that has worked well for us in gluing gun stocks is the tan surgical tubing that medical technicians use for tourniquets while drawing blood. It is elastic and can be wrapped around the wood to make a very secure fit. However, make sure that you aren't sloppy in the application of your glue, because some glues do adhere to the rubber tubing, which can cause a bit of a mess.

Superglue® Rules!

Superglue® is great. Some purists might argue otherwise, but over the years I've used this stuff a lot for little repairs and patches. It comes in a gel for when you need something a bit thicker, and the normal, thin type can be applied to tight spots using a transmission syringe.

331

It's a Hobby: It's OK to Have

332

Enjoy Yourself

Okay, maybe you shouldn't enjoy yourself quite as much as the naked guy on the facing page, but I honestly believe that if you aren't having a good time in gun collecting, then you are doing something wrong. This is a hobby full of amazing objects and wonderful people. I just can't understand collectors who grumble all the time and don't even seem to get excited by their purchases. If that's how you feel, then why bother?

A couple of months ago, my college-age nephew wanted to know why I love old guns so much. "What's the attraction?", he asked. My answer was that collecting guns is a little bit like falling in love. Every gun you buy brings you some of the passion and excitement of a first date.

In fact, the more I think about it, buying a new gun for your collection has more in common with flirting in Junior High School than adult courtship. When you are a teenager, you fall in love body and soul. It might not last forever, but it sure is intense. And that's just what it feels like to make an important purchase at a gun show. You see what you want from across the room. You are struck speechless. Your heart beats out of control. You are willing to do totally irrational things to make the acquisition. Common sense sometimes flies out the window.

Long before you make a direct approach, you send your friends by the object of your desire to take a discrete look and give you their opinions. You don't want to seem "too interested," but you can't help it. After some dancing around and negotiations, an agreement is reached and the gun is yours. You immediately send photographs of your newfound love to all your pals so they can be appropriately envious. They all tell you how lucky you are and you feel like a million bucks.

Fun

Sometimes, your enthusiasm is unrealistic and you learn to regret your decision — a sensation that feels like you've been kicked in the stomach. This is part of the process, though, and (if you are smart) you aren't discouraged by the occasional disappointment and learn the lessons of experience.

Most adults don't get to feel like teenagers very often. "Real life" has a way of tempering such extreme desires. I guess that's why so many of us learn to love "the hunt" of gun collecting. It makes us feel like kids again. And that's not such a bad thing.

suppliers and contacts

Man at Arms for the Gun Collector
The must-have magazine for gun and sword collectors. Highly recommended. By the way, I'm the editor and we are the NRA's official gun collector publication. 1-800-999-4697, 401-726-8011, www.manatarmsbooks.com

Surplus Military Gun and Cleaning Equipment
Cheaper Than Dirt! 1-800-421-8047, www.cheaperthandirt.com

Fabric Gun Bags and Sleeves
The Ace Case Company, 1-800-566-1775, www.acecase.com

Gun Collection Insurance
Jack Richardson, 1-888-7OLD-GUN, www.historicfirearms.com

Renaissance Wax
The U.S. distributor for Renaissance Wax is Cutlery Specialties, 6819 S.E. Sleepy Hollow Lane, Stuart, FL 34997-4757. (772) 219-0436. www.restorationproduct.com

National Park Service Display and Preservation Notes
http://www.cr.nps.gov/museum/publications/conserveogram/cons_toc.html

Civil War Regimental Rosters and Soldier Records
www.civilwardata.com

NRA Gun Collector Club List
http://www.nationalfirearmsmuseum.org/collector/gun_club.asp

C&R Rifle Disassembly
www.surplusrifle.com is a great site with disassembly and other practical instructions for the most common military surplus rifles.

SureFire Flashlights
www.surefire.com

Northern States Conservation Center
All sorts of display and preservation supplies.
www.collectioncare.org

Potomac Display
Riker boxes, shadow boxes, custom-made acrylic display cases and shelves. 410-875-3340, www.potomacdisplay.com

Benchmark Catalog
Museum mount blanks and exhibit supplies. 609-397-1131, www.benchmarkcatalog.com

EZcube
The light tent illustrated in this book was purchased from TableTop Studio, 805-566-0315 http://store.tabletopstudio-store.com/ezlite.html

U.S. Martial Firearm Serial Number Info.
Springfield Research Service, P.O. Box 6322, Falls Church, VA 22040.

Colt Factory Letters
Colt's Manufacturing Co. Inc., Historical Dept., P.O. Box 1868, Hartford, CT 06144. 860-236-6311. http://www.coltsmfg.com/cmci/historical.asp

Winchester, Marlin and L.C. Smith Serial Number Data
Cody Firearms Museum, Cody, Wyoming 82414. 307-587-4771.

Smith & Wesson Letters of Authenticity
Mr. Roy Jinks, Historian, Smith & Wesson, P.O. Box 2208, Springfield, MA 01102.

Civil War Regimental Rosters and Soldier Records
www.civilwardata.com

Gunsmithing Supplies
Brownells, 200 S. Front St., Montezuma, Iowa 50171. 1-800-741-0015. www.brownells.com

Camera Equipment
B&H Photo, 1-800-336-7408, 212-502-6234, www.bhphotovideo.com

Blackpowder Supplies and Gun Parts
Dixie Gun Works, Inc., Box 130, Gunpowder Lane, Union City, TN 38281. 731-885-0700. www.dixiegunworks.com

Gun Laws, State and Federal
http://www.nraila.org/GunLaws/Default.aspx#

National Gun Show Calendar
http://manatarmsbooks.com/showcal.html

Bayonet Information
The Society of American Bayonet Collectors is a great organization. http://bayonetcollectors.org

Custom and Precision Bullet Molds
NEI Handtools is a recognized source. www.neihandtools.com

Cornell University Making of America Web Site
A great resource for research. http://cdl.library.cornell.edu/moa

U.S. Patent Office Images of Patent Records
A wonderful resource...especially if you have the patent number. http://www.uspto.gov/patft

American Memory Collection
The Library of Congress has a wonderful collection of images and videos on-line, many of which relate to weapons or military history. It is called the American Memory Collection. http://memory.loc.gov/ammem

New York Times Archives
It is now possible to search the article archive or the *New York Times* for the years 1851-1980, including advertisements. There is a small fee to download images of pages in which you are interested. This is a treasure trove of information about gun manufacturing and use. http://pqasb.pqarchiver.com/nytimes/advancedsearch.html

Glass Display Cases
Fine Home Displays will make them to your specifications. (866) 381-2FHD. www.finehomedisplays.com